LIFE IN THE
Victorian & Edwardian WORKHOUSE

LIFE IN THE
Victorian & Edwardian WORKHOUSE

MICHELLE HIGGS

The
History
Press

First published in 2007 by Tempus Publishing

Reprinted in 2009 by
The History Press
The Mill, Brimscombe Port,
Stroud, Gloucestershire, GL5 2QG
www.thehistorypress.co.uk

British Library Cataloguing in Publication Data.
A catalogue record for this book is available from the British Library.

ISBN   978 0 7524 4214 3

Typesetting and origination by
Tempus Publishing Limited
Printed in Malta

CONTENTS

ACKNOWLEDGEMENTS

While writing this book, I received help and encouragement in locating information and illustrations from a number of different sources and institutions. I would like to express my gratitude to the following:

The staff of Dudley Archives, Durham County Record Office and Ceredigion Record Office; the Northern General Hospital History Project, Sheffield; the Sheffield Teaching Hospitals NHS Foundation Trust; Mike Spick at the Sheffield Local Studies Library; Frances Collinson at the Gressenhall Farm and Workhouse – The Museum of Norfolk Life; Philip Bye of the East Sussex Record Office; Elaine Fisher at the Slough Museum; Paul Johnson and Tim Padfield at the National Archives; Elizabeth Green of Hackney Archives; Dr Paul Davies; Margaret Towler; Ian Beach; Lisa Robinson; Ann Gray; Derek George and Judith Hawkins.

Thanks are also due to Kevin Towers of the West London Mental Health NHS Trust for granting permission to publish information from the records of Alfred Woodhurst; Lyn Howsam of the Northern General History Project for being so generous with her time and research; Chris Sanham for sharing information from the Maria Rye Children Database 1868–1896 and John Sayers for his research on specific home children in Canada.

I would also like to express my thanks to the following people, who generously shared their research about their ancestors and without whose help this book would be the poorer:

Mari Ambrose; Jill Barrett; Phil Bristow; Benjamin Caine; Harry E. Clarke; Wilfred William Ellesmore; Roger Harpin; Carl Higgs; Christopher J. Hogger; Judith Holmes; Bruce Isted; Maud Jarvis; Derek Jenkins, Barbara Towle, Richard Robinson and Joy Bedson; Sheila Kirk; Colin Leathley; Pat McGrath; Yvonne Moore; Sandy Norman; Lynn Nugent and Norma Robinson; Edwin Pickett; Ruth Piggott; Ken Ripper; Alan Tweedale and Janette Woodhead.

Thanks are also due to the late Margaret Twelvetree for sharing her memories of Pontefract and Stratford-on-Avon Union Workhouses; and to the late Maurice Cuerton for his research about his ancestor Charles Cuerton, and to his widow Marie for granting permission to publish the information.

Finally, I would like to thank my husband Carl for his unfailing love and support, and my family and friends for their encouragement during the writing of this book.

ILLUSTRATIONS

INTRODUCTION

In the nineteenth and early twentieth centuries, generations of working-class families lived in fear of the workhouse, variously called 'the union', 'the bastille', 'the spike' or simply 'the house'. This fear has become such an integral part of workhouse mythology that it is sometimes difficult to separate fact from fiction. Which is the more accurate representation of the average Victorian workhouse? The horrific conditions of the workhouse in which poor Oliver Twist stayed, or the well-run example at Wapping which Dickens visited in 1860?[1] The answer is paradoxically neither and both. There is no such thing as a typical workhouse because the conditions within it depended on the calibre of its staff, 'the size of the union' and 'the wealth of the ratepayers.'[2]

What was life really like in a workhouse, either as an inmate or a member of staff? This book aims to identify the types of people who entered the workhouse and their reasons for doing so, their living conditions and diet, the work they had to undertake and to look into their monotonous day-to-day routine. It will also describe the roles of the different members of staff, the conditions they worked and lived in, and their reasons for becoming workhouse officers.

By piecing together the available evidence from workhouse records and regulations, censuses, dietary tables, workhouse plans and local studies, it is possible to build up a picture of workhouse life. This will always be slightly out of focus as records are missing or incomplete and direct evidence from inmates and staff, in the form of letters and testimony, is rare.

While undertaking research for this book, a small, at first seemingly insignificant, detail was found. Although the inmates and staff of all workhouses were recorded in the national censuses, anyone trying to locate their ancestors in Dudley Union Workhouse on the 1861 census is faced with an immediate problem. The enumerator carefully named all the members of staff in the workhouse but recorded the inmates simply with initials.[3] No first or last names are given.

It is not known if this method of recording was at the instigation of the workhouse master or whether the decision was taken by the enumerator himself. However, it could be interpreted in two ways. There was a real stigma attached to being a workhouse inmate. Recording the inmates with initials could be evidence of a compassionate workhouse master or enumerator, trying to preserve the anonymity of the inmates. Alternatively, it might also be evidence that the inmates were viewed as simply initials in a register, not worthy of a full identity.

Whichever interpretation is correct, in other censuses researched, the names of inmates are given in full. This is just one example which illustrates that the running of workhouses varied throughout the country because they were run at a local level. No two workhouses were ever 'exactly alike'.[4] As a result, the experience of workhouse life for both inmates and staff differed widely across England and Wales.

I

THE NEW POOR LAW

In November 1836, a 'most daring' attempt was made to murder Richard Ellis, the master of Abingdon Union Workhouse. Shots were fired from the workhouse garden through the sitting-room window, narrowly missing the master's sister and an elderly pauper. Abingdon was the first of a new breed of workhouse built as a result of the Poor Law Amendment Act of 1834. The workhouse had been open for inmates for about a month and it was believed that the violent attack against the master was a protest against the new Poor Law legislation.[1]

Before 1834, each parish was responsible for its own poor. The able-bodied who had fallen on hard times or were unemployed, for whatever reason, could expect to be granted outdoor relief from the parish overseer of the poor in his or her own home. The sick and elderly might also be looked after in a small parish workhouse which was 'seen as a relatively unthreatening and even friendly institution'.[2]

THE NEW POOR LAW IN ACTION

After 1834, there were four main changes to the Poor Law system. Firstly, a central authority, called the Poor Law Commission, was to regulate the new Poor Law. The Poor Law Commission, based in London, was made up of three commissioners who had the power to issue rules and regulations for the new Poor Law. They were supported in their role by assistant commissioners. (From 1847, responsibility for the Poor Law passed to the Poor Law Board. After 1871, the Poor Law was administered by the Local Government Board.)

Secondly, parishes were to group together into 'unions' to benefit from economies of scale. It was proposed that approximately thirty parishes join together to create each new union. Each union was to be run by a board of guardians which would meet weekly and report regularly to the Commission. It was the responsibility of the assistant commissioners to oversee the setting up of the new unions. However, it was no easy matter to obtain agreement from each parish, and those parishes which had joined together under earlier legislation known as the Gilbert Act often refused to be brought into the new system.

Thirdly, accommodation was to be provided for paupers in workhouses under 'less eligible' or worse conditions than those of the poorest independent labourer. The intention was that only the truly destitute would seek relief in the workhouse and that it would be a last resort. Any applicant who refused to enter the workhouse was said to have 'failed the workhouse test'.[3]

In the 1830s and 1840s, these new workhouses, the 'unions', like the one at Abingdon, sprang up across England and Wales approximately twenty miles apart. The buildings were austere and prison-like and were deliberately designed to be starkly different from the more domestic parish workhouses of the eighteenth century. The design and appearance of the new union workhouses created a real visual deterrent and was 'meant to represent the new approach to relief provision.'[4]

The old parish workhouse at Framlingham, Suffolk.

Finally, and most contentiously, 'outdoor' relief for the able-bodied was to be minimal so that those applying for poor relief had to enter the workhouse. The Commission's Report of 1834 concluded that 'the great source of abuse is outdoor relief afforded to the able-bodied'.[5] One of the main objections to building new workhouses for both paupers and guardians was the stipulation that outdoor relief be reduced or abolished to the able-bodied poor. To withdraw such a basic, traditional right, and force paupers to enter the workhouse was thought to be inhumane and implied that poverty was a crime.

In addition, outdoor relief was considerably cheaper than indoor relief. It was argued that the building of new workhouses would be a heavy burden on the ratepayers. The small Lampeter Union delayed building a new workhouse until 1876 because the guardians calculated that 'if a man went into the workhouse he would cost the Union 1s 9d a week, but if he was given relief outside the workhouse it would cost only 9d, a saving of 1 shilling per week.'[6]

Many unions chose to adapt existing parish workhouses rather than bear the expense of building new ones. This decision was not popular with the Poor Law Commission, as adapted parish workhouses were rarely able to provide sufficient accommodation to classify the inmates separately.

By 1840, 14,000 parishes had been incorporated into unions with only 800 parishes remaining outside the system. However, most of the 350 new workhouses built by 1839 were in the south of the country.[7]

PROTESTS AGAINST THE NEW WORKHOUSES

A major flaw in the legislation of 1834 was that the Commission had no power to order the building of new workhouses, although they could order alterations to existing buildings. In practice, unions could repeatedly delay implementing the new Poor Law, and many chose to do so.

The authors of the Report failed to recognise the differences between the industrial north and the more agricultural south and thus their contrasting experiences of poverty and

The slums of Tower Street, Dudley, where the old parish workhouse was situated.

treatment of the poor. The attack at the Abingdon Union Workhouse was by no means the only form of protest against the Poor Law Amendment Act, dubbed by critics the 'Whig Starvation and Infanticide Act'. With resistance strongest in the north, there were riots against the new Poor Law in 1837 and 1838 in Oldham, Rochdale, Todmorden, Huddersfield and Bradford.[8]

As a result, there were very few workhouses built in the West Riding of Yorkshire or in Lancashire until the 1850s and 1860s.[9] However, protests against the new Poor Law were not confined to the north. There was staunch opposition in Wales while few new workhouses were built in Cornwall, and in Dudley, Worcestershire, the new union workhouse was not opened until 1859.[10]

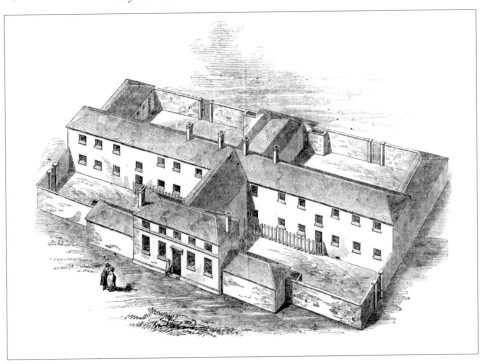

The Andover Union Workhouse built to a standard cruciform design. (*Illustrated London News*, 7 November 1846.)

DESIGNS OF NEW WORKHOUSES

The Poor Law Commission issued model plans for the building of the new union workhouses, some of which were produced by the architect Sampson Kempthorne. Although the unions could, in theory, invite designs from other architects and builders, in practice, most of the new workhouses were based on one of Kempthorne's designs. There were two main designs for a three-storey mixed workhouse – one cruciform and the other Y-shaped with a hexagonal boundary wall.[11]

The first new union workhouse at Abingdon was a variation on Kempthorne's first Y-shaped design with an extra fourth storey. The British Almanac noted how it provided 'with great facility, the division into six yards, for the better classification of the inmates. In the centre [of the] building are the governor's rooms, for the inspection of the whole establishment.'[12]

Whichever design was chosen, the layout of every union workhouse was similar. In each design, there were six exercise yards for the infirm, the able-bodied, and children aged seven to fifteen, with the sexes segregated. These areas were separated by high walls. There were day rooms for the infirm and able-bodied, a schoolroom and a master's parlour which was usually placed at a central position so that he could observe the day-to-day routine in all parts of the workhouse.

The walls which formed the boundaries around the exercise yards to the outside world contained the workrooms, washrooms, bakehouses, the 'dead house', the refractory ward and the receiving ward. On the first floor were the dormitories, the master's bedrooms, the dining hall and the Board Room where the guardians would hold their weekly meetings. The lying-in ward for expectant mothers and the nursery was on the third floor separating the boys' and girls' bedrooms.[13]

The design of the new union workhouses allowed for the most contentious of systems to be put into place: the classification and segregation of the sexes and families.

2

THE WORKHOUSE SYSTEM

Throughout the nineteenth and early twentieth centuries, the threat of the workhouse cast a long shadow over the lives of many who lived just above the breadline. Before the advent of the welfare state, all life could be found in the workhouse because it had to 'combine the functions of schools, asylums, hospitals and old people's homes, as well as being the last refuge for the homeless and unemployed.'[1]

The workhouse inmates were therefore a mixture of the elderly, the sick and the destitute, abandoned mothers and children, lunatics and those without employment, either seasonal or in times of economic depression. These were people who were forced into the workhouse as a last resort.

The number of inmates typically decreased during the summer, particularly in rural areas, because seasonal, labour-intensive agricultural work could easily be obtained by men, women and children. Numbers increased dramatically in winter, particularly if the weather was harsh, and in times of severely depressed trade and high unemployment.

ADMISSION TO THE WORKHOUSE

There were three ways in which a pauper could be admitted to the workhouse. Firstly, he or she could present an order from the relieving officer. Secondly, an order could be issued by the board of guardians. Finally, 'in any case of sudden or urgent necessity', the master could authorise admission to the workhouse.[2]

On arrival, the pauper would be taken to the receiving ward by the porter. It was the porter's responsibility to search male paupers for prohibited articles, which included alcohol, cards and dice, matches and 'letters or printed papers, as books, pamphlets, etc., being of an improper tendency.'[3] Female paupers were searched by the matron.

The medical officer would then examine the pauper to determine if he or she was able-bodied or sick, and therefore which class the pauper would fall into. The classification system was a strict form of segregation and consisted of seven classes as follows:

Class 1   Men infirm through age or any other cause.
Class 2   Able-bodied men and youths above the age of fifteen years.
Class 3   Boys above the age of seven years, and under that of fifteen.
Class 4   Women infirm through age or any other cause.
Class 5   Able-bodied women and girls above the age of fifteen years.
Class 6   Girls above the age of seven years and under that of fifteen.
Class 7   Children under seven years of age.

The bell at the Stourbridge Union Workhouse. (Courtesy of Carl Higgs.)

If the pauper was deemed to be sick, he or she would be sent to the sick ward. If the pauper was able-bodied and free from disease, he or she would be sent to 'the part of the Workhouse, assigned to the class to which he [or she] may belong.'[4]

Before leaving the receiving ward, the pauper was bathed and disinfected. In most unions, his or her hair would be crudely cropped. Finally, the pauper was given an ill-fitting workhouse uniform and a pair of heavy hob-nailed boots, while his or her personal clothes were taken away, to be returned only on leaving the workhouse.

Uniforms varied around the country but most were dull brown, grey or blue and all were shapeless. At the Ecclesall Bierlow Union, the male inmates wore uniform suits made of 'fustian or drab moleskin with calico shirts and strong shoes' while the women wore 'gingham gowns or black or blue worsted skirts with blouses and blue linen aprons… [and] Shambery petticoats and coarse cambric caps…'[5]

In 1843, the guardians of the Warrington Union 'selected a dress for the men consisting of a coat and waistcoat made from grey cloth with trowsers [sic] of brown fustian-striped cotton for womens bed gowns – blue cotton for petticoats – black and white straw bonnets and mob caps…' The guardians added that the men's clothing 'should be made from dark olive velveteen with metal buttons on which the words "Warrington Union" would be stamped.'[6]

The workhouse uniform immediately marked out the pauper as an inmate if it was worn in the street. While the mandatory wearing of a workhouse uniform could be seen as a show of discipline and an attempt to de-humanise the pauper, there was another more practical reason. In an institution where large numbers of people lived closely together, the spread of disease was an ever present risk. Bathing the pauper, taking away his or her often filthy clothes and replacing them with a clean uniform could help to minimise this risk.

In 1838, after a visit to Dudley Union Workhouse, the Assistant Poor Law Commissioner drew the attention of the board of guardians to the fact that 'the inmates of the Workhouse were not clothed in dresses belonging to the Union', at the same time he states that it was 'not his wish

Entrance to the Birmingham Union Workhouse, Western Road. (Courtesy of Lisa Robinson.)

that the Inmates should be dressed in any way as a mark of degradation, but for the purpose of preventing the introduction of disease and securing cleanliness – and further in order that the Paupers may on their leaving the Workhouse be furnished with their own clothing in the same state (with the exception of it being cleansed) as it was on their entering the Workhouse.'[7]

SEPARATION OF THE FAMILY

The next stage was feared the most: the separation of the family and the sexes, husbands from wives, parents from children, boys from girls. There was no way to avoid this rule. An able-bodied man with a family could not enter the workhouse by himself. The whole family had to apply for relief and enter the workhouse together. It is very unlikely that the decision to enter a union workhouse would ever have been taken lightly.

The separation of the family, including husbands from wives, and the forced ending of normal sexual relations within marriage was intended to improve the moral fibre of paupers and prevent 'breeding' or procreation of new paupers. This was the inhumane face of the workhouse: the break-up of the natural family unit and the relationship between parent and child. It was felt that it was particularly important to separate children from the other paupers, especially the vagrants and able-bodied women, many of whom were considered immoral.

This splitting-up of families led to considerable misery and distress and was unacceptable to many paupers. Apart from staying in a large, bleak, prison-like building which, in itself was intimidating, especially for children and the elderly, the fact that every pauper had to cope on their own could be intensely distressing. Even young children were separated from their families, and only children under the age of four were allowed to sleep with their mothers.[8]

Charles Chaplin, who spent some time in the Lambeth Union Workhouse as a child in the 1890s, recalled the moment when he and his sibling were first admitted with their mother:

> Then the forlorn bewilderment of it struck me: for there we were made to separate. Mother going in one direction to the women's ward and we in another to the children's. How well I remember the poignant sadness of that first visiting day: the shock of seeing Mother enter the visiting-room garbed in workhouse clothes. How forlorn and embarrassed she looked! In one week she had aged and grown thin…[9]

Despite the fact that legislation was passed in 1847 to allow old married couples to stay together, in the majority of cases elderly couples who had lived together for a lifetime continued to be separated on entry to the workhouse.[10]

There were countless examples of misery caused by the segregation policy. One man who was deeply affected by it was James Lilley, a thirty-three-year-old collier who was an asthma sufferer. He was admitted to Dudley Union Workhouse on 20 October 1862 with his wife Sarah and three young daughters, but was discharged the same day by his 'own wish because he was afraid to be in the receiving ward without his wife.'[11]

It seems that James Lilley would rather have starved in the streets than be separated from his wife and family. Just over a month later, on 29 November 1862, Sarah Lilley was re-admitted to the Dudley Union with her three daughters. She was described as a widow. She left the following day of her own accord.[12]

Once admitted, paupers were free to leave at any time after giving notice to the master, but it would have been a difficult decision if there were no family or friends to turn to outside of the workhouse. A small minority of inmates were regular 'ins and outs', who came and went at their own desire, and according to their need at the time.

WORKHOUSE DAILY ROUTINE

Life inside the workhouse was deliberately disciplined and monotonous. When the 1834 Poor Law Amendment Act was passed, the Commissioners drew up a model timetable which all unions were to follow. This was amended only slightly some years later.

Punctuated by the ringing of the workhouse bell, every minute of the paupers' daily lives was accounted for. The inmates rose at 5 a.m. from March to September and at 7 a.m. during the rest of the year. Half an hour after rising, there was a daily roll-call in the various wards. There were prayers before breakfast from 6 to 7 a.m. (or 7.30 to 8 a.m. in winter). This was followed by work tasks until 12 p.m. After the hour for dinner, there was more work until 6 p.m. when supper was served, after which there were more prayers. Paupers had to be in bed by 8 p.m. at the latest.[13] At mealtimes 'order and decorum'[14] was to be maintained. Most unions interpreted this to mean that meals were to be eaten in silence. Smoking, alcohol, cards and games of chance were all forbidden.

ACCOMMODATION

Although the union workhouses were administered centrally by the Poor Law Commission in London, the conditions within each individual workhouse depended upon the calibre of the staff and the generosity of the board of guardians and ratepayers. Many unions provided the bare minimum of essentials for the inmates and others were dubbed 'pauper palaces' for their alleged extravagance.[15]

An entry in the Dudley Union Visiting Committee records in December 1861 explains the financial situation more fully:

> The Committee are anxious to promote the comfort and happiness [of the inmates] in every possible way and to have the House made as complete as is desirable – consistent with the duties which the Guardians owe the ratepayers.[16]

Inside the workhouse, furnishings were deliberately kept to a minimum. Beds were usually wooden and few inmates had 'the luxury of a single bed.'[17] This was despite the order that 'More than two paupers, any one of whom is above the age of seven years, shall not be allowed to occupy the same bed, unless in the case of a mother and infant children.'[18]

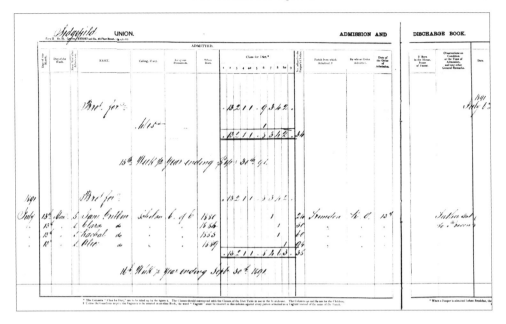

Admission and discharge register from 1891 recording the admission of the Gribbon sisters to the Sedgefield Union Workhouse (see p.43). (U/Se 122. Reproduced by permission of the Durham County Record Office.)

When the Lampeter Union Workhouse was opened in 1877, the guardians ordered bedding for the new wards. They included fifty palliasses (straw mattresses) and fifty tuck mattresses, fifty pairs of sheets and fifty pairs of blankets plus forty-four quilts.[19] Pillows were considered an unnecessary luxury in most union workhouses.

Until late in the nineteenth century, the walls of most workhouse day and sleeping wards were bare, while in the dining room there were only 'the roughest wooden tables and backless benches.'[20] Apart from a Bible, 'adults had nothing to read and children nothing to play with.'[21]

DIET

The diet inside the union workhouse matched the conditions – sufficient but extremely monotonous. Starvation was unlikely as three meals a day were guaranteed. Most unions chose one of the six model diets set out by the Poor Law Commission which supplied each inmate with between 137 and 182oz of solid food per week including meat, bread, gruel, milk and cheese.

The rations were strictly recorded by the workhouse master and were considerably less than the 292oz of solid food provided for prison inmates, but still more than the 122oz the average independent labourer received.[22]

The house diet at the Dudley Union Workhouse in July 1874 consisted of 5oz of solid meat on two days, bacon on one day (4oz for men and 3oz for women), suet pudding on two days and broth and pea soup on the remaining two days. For breakfast, the inmates were given porridge, and for supper, bread and cheese.[23]

It has been argued that the quantities of bread allowed in the workhouse 'were higher than the poor could afford.'[24] Research has revealed that meat was a rarity for the poorer Lancashire workers in the 1860s,[25] yet it was usually offered two days a week in the workhouse.

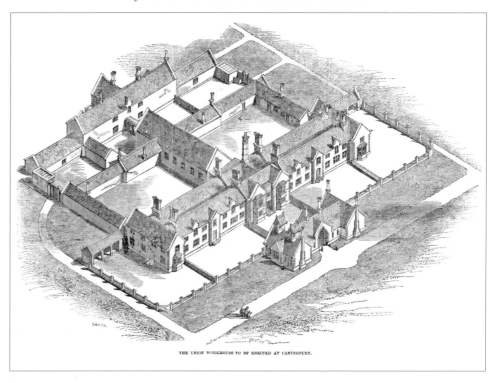

THE UNION WORKHOUSE TO BE ERECTED AT CANTERBURY.

The proposed design for the Canterbury Union Workhouse. (*Illustrated London News*, 7 November 1846.)

In fact, it was the quality rather than the quantity of food which inmates and observers criticised. Gruel was particularly unpalatable as it was 'a thin oatmeal porridge made with water and unflavoured with milk or sugar...'[26] The coarse, often stale, workhouse bread was 'served with such small quantities of fat that it was difficult to eat.'[27]

The workhouse medical officer could make suggestions to alter the diet, which then had to be sanctioned by the guardians and the central authorities. In 1883, the guardians of the Dudley Union wrote to the Local Government Board with their plans for 'substituting Fish for Dinner one Day in every week instead of meat.' This was considered 'more beneficial in promoting the health of the Inmates as well as reducing the cost of maintenance...' The fish was to include 'Cod Fish, Codlings and Haddock.'[28]

Menus were only varied on special occasions such as the traditional Christmas dinner of roast beef and plum pudding plus fruit, tobacco and ale, usually paid for by benefactors, or at Easter when buns were often provided.

WORK TASKS

Every able-bodied pauper had to complete work tasks as part of their daily routine. The partially disabled paupers were also to be 'occupied to the extent of their ability.'[29] A variety of tasks were demanded of the inmates across England and Wales including oakum-picking, stone-breaking, pumping water, working the 'crank' of a corn mill and cleaning. The work tasks are described more fully in the chapters on the able-bodied men, the able-bodied women, the elderly and the vagrants.

PUNISHMENTS

As order and discipline in the workhouse had to be maintained at all times, there was a long list of punishable misdemeanours. Offences which would deem a pauper disorderly included using obscene or profane language, threatening to strike or assault anyone, refusing or neglecting to work and playing at cards or other games of chance. The master could punish a disorderly pauper:

> …by substituting, during a time not greater than forty-eight hours, for his dinner, as prescribed by the Dietary, a meal consisting of eight ounces of bread, or one pound of cooked potatoes or boiled rice, and also by withholding from him, during the same period, all butter, cheese, tea, sugar, or broth, which such pauper would otherwise receive…[30]

A pauper would be deemed refractory if he or she repeated or committed more than one of the disorderly offences. Other refractory offences included drunkenness, disobeying or insulting any workhouse officer or guardian, striking any person and damaging workhouse property. The guardians could order a refractory pauper 'to be punished by confinement in a separate room, with or without an alteration in diet…' for up to twenty-four hours.[31]

The master had to keep a meticulous record of any punishments meted out in the workhouse. At the Foleshill Union Workhouse in November 1865, Hannah Smith was punished for 'Swearing and causing a great disturbance in the washhouse and ward, and being insolent to the Master of the workhouse after being cautioned three days before.' Her punishment was 'Alteration of diet for two days as per Article 29.'[32]

SETTLEMENT AND REMOVAL

The laws of settlement, which were relics of the old Poor Law, were still strictly enforced. In the 1860s, a Poor Law Inspector reported the case of a:

> …tradesman who had lost his job just before he had lived long enough in the same place to become irremovable. He was ordered back to his native county, and even though, before he could be moved, he had recovered his old job and ceased to draw relief, he was still carried off forcibly from the place where he had both a home and work to a place where he had neither…[33]

Later in the nineteenth century, by mutual agreement unions might give out-relief to 'non-settled' paupers whose legal settlement was in another union, instead of removing them.

3
THE ABLE-BODIED MEN

Able-bodied male inmates were a rarity in workhouses across England and Wales, except in periods of economic depression or harsh weather. It was this class of inmate, more than any other, that the workhouse and the Poor Law Amendment Act of 1834 was designed to deter.

WHO WAS CLASSED AS ABLE-BODIED?

A man was classed as able-bodied if his health or age did not prevent him from working, and if he was merely destitute because of a lack of work. Able-bodied men fell into Class 2 of the workhouse classification scheme which also included youths above fifteen years of age. When they did appear in the workhouse, able-bodied men were more likely to be unmarried or widowed than men with families.

Underpinning the new Poor Law was the 'workhouse test' whereby outdoor relief to the able-bodied was to be abolished and the workhouse offered in its place. It was believed that only the truly destitute would be prepared to enter the workhouse. Early feedback from unions in the south was encouraging with a large drop in the number of able-bodied men seeking relief reported.

For example, in December 1836 at the Cuckfield Union, 149 men applied for relief. 118 men were offered the workhouse but only six men accepted. This was at a time of harsh, snowy weather when there was no outdoor work available. Sixty more men applied for relief and five entered the workhouse, although three of these men left within a few hours.[1] While these statistics were trumpeted as proof of the success of the new Poor Law, it is not known what happened to the men who refused to enter the workhouse. The authorities believed these men to be self-supporting, but if they were unable to find work during the winter both they and their families would have experienced abject poverty until the weather turned for the better.

The Bosham Workhouse was one of the workhouses in the Westbourne Union which, under the old system, was well-known for the laxity of its discipline. When the able-bodied labourers were told that they would receive no relief except in the new Westbourne Workhouse, 'they all refused to enter it and all found work for themselves and have supported themselves ever since.'[2]

Daniel Smart, the clerk for the Westbourne Union reported that: 'The labourers are now much more diligent and willing to please… Masters are therefore more willing to employ them. Many for the same reason give higher wages…the greater part have been absorbed.'[3]

THE PRESENT AND THE FUTURE.

JOHN BULL. "I'LL DO MY BEST TO HELP YOU OVER THE CHRISTMAS—YOU MUST THEN LOOK TO MY FRIEND YONDER."

The Present and the Future. Many working-class families chose to pay subscriptions to a sick club or friendly society, as a kind of insurance policy in the event of illness. (*Punch*, 15 November 1862.)

CONTINUATION OF OUTDOOR-RELIEF FOR THE ABLE-BODIED

The absence of able-bodied men in the workhouse did not necessarily mean that the Act was a successful deterrent. As with so many other aspects of workhouse administration, the fact that unions were governed locally by a board of guardians meant that they responded to problems in their own local area in the way they thought best. Where there were localised issues such as depression in a particular industry or an extremely harsh winter, the guardians chose to ignore the Poor Law Commission's order that no able-bodied man was to receive outdoor relief. Boards of guardians which were known to be particularly benevolent towards the local poor also defied the order and continued to give outdoor relief.

For example, at the Bromsgrove Union in January 1841, the guardians recorded that:

> Thomas Hawkins aged fifty, an able-bodied man residing in and belonging to Tardebigge, a widower having applied to this Board for outdoor relief until the weather breaks; he being unable to follow his usual employment of brickmaking in consequence of the frost and to procure other work, and he having eleven children at home only one of whom is able to maintain himself at the present time, four partially and six being wholly dependent on their father for support. The Board considering this a case of emergency and one sufficiently urgent to justify them in departing from the Rule of the Poor Law Commission prohibiting outdoor relief from being given to any able bodied person. Order that relief be given to Thomas Hawkins to the amount of twenty shillings by eight weekly instalments by way of a loan.[4]

The weather also caused problems in February 1855, when the guardians of the Dudley Union reported that the able-bodied men were 'in a state of fearful destitution through not

SEASONABLE ADVICE—"PUT BY FOR A FROSTY DAY."

*Seasonable Advice – Put By For A Frosty Day. (*Punch*, 23 February 1861.)*

being able to obtain work on account of the present intense frost (who will all be able to get employment when the frost shall break up).' It was decided to 'administer relief from day-to-day in kind.'[5]

From the early days of the Poor Law Amendment Act, rural Norfolk unions had adhered strictly to the regulations prohibiting outdoor relief to able-bodied men. However, the difficult farming conditions of the 1840s meant that 'the trend in poor relief was thereafter reversed in Norfolk.'[6]

The scarcity of employment in key industries also caused problems in industrial unions. At one such union in December 1847, there were 'numerous applications for relief from able-bodied labourers, Miners and Workmen from Ironworks' and there was a 'certainty of a very great increase owing to the stopage [sic] of many Ironworks in which men of the above descriptions are employed…'[7]

However, despite fears about a nationwide economic depression, in the 1860s just over 5 per cent of indoor paupers were able-bodied men and they usually made up just under 5 per cent of outdoor paupers.[8] Even during times of severe hardship such as the Lancashire cotton famine, the proportion of able-bodied men on outdoor relief 'was only about 6 per cent of the national total.'[9]

While the motives of some unions for granting outdoor relief to able-bodied men with families were humanitarian, it was widely acknowledged that the burden on the ratepayer was higher if families had to be maintained as indoor paupers in the workhouse. This was because a grant of outdoor relief was insufficient and had to be 'augmented by small earnings and receipts from private charity.'[10] In 1860, it cost nearly 3s 6d a week to maintain a pauper in an Eastern Counties workhouse but the average for outdoor relief was significantly less at 1s 9d a week.[11]

In December 1871, the Local Government Board sent out a circular to the unions across England and Wales 'calling for greater strictness, including the total refusal of relief, except in the workhouse, to able-bodied single men and women, as well as to unmarried mothers, deserted wives and widows with only one child.'[12] In 1877, after a query from the guardians of one union, the Local Government Board stated that 'so long as there is room in the Workhouse, they do not think it expedient that outdoor relief should be given to single able-bodied men.'[13]

The Outdoor Relief Regulation Order of 1852 had recommended that 'at least half of any assistance given to the able-bodied was to be in the form of food, fuel or other necessary articles.'[14] However, many unions preferred to give relief to the able-bodied wholly in money. The Poor Law Board objected strongly to this and in 1879 wrote to one union explaining that 'the Board attach much importance to the principle of giving relief to able-bodied men half in kind, as a long and wide experience has shown that the administering of relief in this form is beneficial, both as tending to diminish the chance of imposition and to secure that a portion of the relief is applied to the wants of the family.'[15]

The commissioners had found that 'adequate outdoor relief would work if partly given in kind (bread and potatoes) and in return for work on parish roads.'[16] However, they 'failed to realise that the poor preferred a 9s or 10s wage to relief payments of 3s, food enough to get through the week, and work on the roads.'[17]

ABLE-BODIED MEN WITH FAMILIES

It was the married man with a large family who was hit hardest when unions enforced the new Poor Law regulations to the letter. Previously, he might have expected to receive outdoor relief from a benevolent relieving officer without too much persuasion. Now, when he applied for relief, he was offered the workhouse for himself and his family, with no other alternative.

Jeremiah Dunn was one such married man with six small children. In July 1847, he was a weaver living in Little Pearl Street, Spitalfields in London. He wrote to the Poor Law Commissioners, complaining bitterly of his treatment by the guardians of the Whitechapel Union. He explained that 'through the depression of the silk line he is reduced to the greatest distress and has been compelled to apply to the White-chapel Union for relief'. He and his family were admitted to the workhouse for three weeks and were 'turned out without a farthing in the world to assist him.' He was forced to apply for relief again, and was re-admitted for another week, then discharged. Jeremiah applied to the magistrate, compelled by 'starvation.' Although the magistrate forwarded his request for admittance to the relieving officer, he refused to admit Jeremiah and his family to the workhouse. Jeremiah added that 'had not the Magistrate humanely relieved your Petitioner from the Poor box his family and himself must have Perished.' It is not known what the reaction of the Whitechapel Union's guardians was to this complaint or what happened to Jeremiah and his family.[18]

Twenty-two-year-old William Ripper and his pregnant wife Sarah were admitted to the Mint Street Workhouse in London in December 1849. It is not clear whether William, a journeyman sweep, was ill or simply unemployed at the time. The couple's eighteenth-month-old daughter Harriet did not go to the workhouse with them so it is likely she was being looked after by other family members. Sarah gave birth to a second daughter, Mary Ann, on 23 December. The family left the workhouse on 10 January 1850 but, unusually, they returned the following day for Mary Ann's baptism. This may have been because the baptism was urgent as Mary Ann was dangerously ill. She died three days after being baptised.[19]

The Stourbridge Union Workhouse, taken when it was the 1st Southern General Hospital, 1915. When the building was a workhouse, the extensive gardens would have been tended by inmates.

WORK TASKS FOR THE ABLE-BODIED IN THE WORKHOUSE

There were a wide variety of work tasks which the guardians of unions across England and Wales could give their able-bodied inmates to complete. Many were similar to those given to vagrants, a fact which aroused much indignation. From stone-breaking and oakum-picking through to wood-chopping, pumping water and working the 'crank' of a corn mill, the tasks were to be undertaken 'in return for the food and lodging' at the workhouse.[20]

At the Great Yarmouth Union in 1884, able-bodied men were put to work instead of 'loafing about and making the workhouse a club house.' As a result, all the able-bodied men, except two, left the workhouse. These two men and the tramps:

> …were put to work in a shed divided in to fourteen cubicles, five and a half feet square (one man to each cubicle, which was locked) shifting shingle with a shovel through a hole ten inches square. They had to move a ton an hour. They worked a nine-hour-day with one hour allowed for lunch. The shingle was then carted back to its place of origin.[21]

One of these able-bodied men was William Shipley, a sixty-eight-year-old sawyer. He had worked for a shipbuilder in Great Yarmouth and the Haven Commissioners and finished work in 1879 'as he was no longer fit for this occupation'. Four years earlier, his wife had died and he went to live at his daughter's house 'except for a few weeks, when he went turnip hoeing in the country.' When his daughter was no longer able to keep him, he was admitted to the workhouse. Shipley performed the work task of shifting shingle for nine weeks before refusing to do it any more. The case prompted complaints about the nature of the work task because the men who 'are unfortunately compelled to seek refuge in the workhouse are treated like criminals and given solitary confinement.'[22]

Charles Harvey (or Henry) Atkins, a shoemaker or cordwainer, became one of the regular able-bodied 'ins and outs' at the Christchurch Union, being admitted 'no less than twenty-nine times between November 1885 and October 1887, sometimes reappearing on the same day as his discharge.'[23] Times must have been hard in shoemaking as Charles was listed as an able-bodied inmate at the Christchurch Union at the time of the 1891 census. It is believed that Charles was the man referred to as 'Atkins' in 1896 who 'was forcibly ejected from the boardroom, having on many occasions wearied the Guardians with his petty grievances.' On this occasion, he had demanded of the board whether they were 'Guardians of the poor or guardians of the Poor Law.'[24]

In London, the authorities experimented with turning one workhouse at Poplar into an 'Able-Bodied Test Workhouse'. From 1871, all the children, sick and aged at Poplar were removed to neighbouring workhouses. All able-bodied applicants for relief from the twenty-five London unions were given an 'Order for Poplar'. On admittance, inmates were expected to break granite or pick oakum. This deterrent workhouse was a temporary success because 'the average stay was under three weeks and 600 of the 800 beds were never occupied.'[25] By 1882, Poplar had become an 'ordinary mixed workhouse in all but name' simply because it was uneconomical to run such a large workhouse which was mostly empty.[26]

WORK FOR THE ABLE-BODIED RECEIVING OUTDOOR RELIEF

From the 1860s onwards, many unions, especially those in urban areas 'made use of a device tried earlier on a smaller scale, the opening of Labour Yards or Stone-yards, either in the workhouse or on separate premises.'[27] Applicants for relief received a weekly allowance in return for attending at the workhouse every day to carry out a work task. They became 'semi-inmates of the workhouse, living in their own homes but subject during the day to workhouse labour and workhouse discipline.'[28]

Unions' criteria for qualification to work in a labour yard varied across the country. At the Dudley Union in January 1858, it was resolved that 'the able-bodied Applicants for parochial relief be employed at levelling the ground at the new Workhouse at a uniform rate of two shillings per day and upon the following scale of time:

For a single man – three days a week
For a married man with one child – four days a week
For a married man with two or three children – five days a week
For a married man with four or more children – six days a week'[29]

Throughout the 1860s and 1870s, labour or stone yards were used in unions across England and Wales as a means of providing work for the able-bodied unemployed. Preference was invariably given to married men with families as it was believed that unmarried men could move out of the area to find work if necessary.

The labour yards were opened and closed according to need. In May 1868 at the Wolverhampton Union, the guardians gave notice for the 'discharge of all the single men, and those with Wives without families.' At Walsall, the number of able-bodied men at the stone yard averaged about fifty and they had also been given notice. The Stourbridge Union had employed sixty men to break stones in the cold weather but 'none were now employed.'[30]

The Dudley Union continued to give outdoor relief to their destitute able-bodied. In February 1879, they decided that:

...every Adult person not suffering under any temporary or permanent infirmity of body to whom, or to whose Wife if he be liable to maintain such Wife or Child, whether legitimate or illegitimate, under the Age of Sixteen, Relief shall be lawfully granted out of the workhouse.

Such able-bodied paupers were to undertake work tasks in exchange for relief. Males were to 'Break One Ton Weight or by admeasurement one yard of Rag Stone or to Pick 4lbs of Oakum per day' while females were to 'clean, wash or perform such other duties as may be required to be done in the Workhouse.'[31]

In 1887 at the Great Yarmouth Union, approximately 150 unemployed men 'had been out of work for some weeks and all of them had large families'. The chairman of the board informed them that the guardians could not provide work and could only give them an order for the workhouse 'which of course no respectable man would accept.' Finally, the guardians agreed to give work to the 'deserving cases amongst the unemployed.' A variety of work was offered including levelling sand hills, extending roads and breaking stones. The men were also 'employed in stacking concrete blocks for use in underpinning the Town Hall which had subsided on the west side.'[32] Five years later, when offering work to relieve unemployment, the guardians of the Great Yarmouth Union gave preference to 'those men who had more than three children who were less than fourteen years of age. Their maximum wage was two shillings and sixpence a day.'[33]

In the 1880s at the Christchurch Union, able-bodied men were put to work breaking up seven hundredweight of Mendip stone between 7 a.m. and 3 p.m. The guardians also set the able-bodied men to pick four pounds of oakum per day. When complaints were made about the 'painful fingertips' caused by this work, the guardians 'refused to believe it was true'. One guardian commented that 'to some people any work produced a disagreeable sensation.'[34] Oakum-picking was a common work task in most union workhouses. At the Samford Union in Suffolk in 1842, the master 'purchased at Harwich 8 cwts of old rope for the purpose of the employment of the able-bodied in the House in picking the same into oakum.'[35] The task of oakum-picking is described in greater detail in the chapter on the vagrants.

Some unions were more humane in their treatment of their able-bodied poor. In 1873 at the Mitford and Launditch Union, the guardians decided that:

> ...the Paupers in the workhouse who are employed in washing, cooking, grave digging, funerals, emptying privies and drains, and in other laborious work...should be allowed extra diet of Beer, in no case exceeding two pints per head, per day, when so employed...[36]

MIGRATION

One way of finding work for the able-bodied was to send whole families to the industrial north, an option which many southern unions were keen to explore. In 1837, the clerk of the Westbourne Union wrote to R.M. Muggeridge Esq. of the Migration Office in Manchester. He made an enquiry as to whether employment could be found in Manchester for George Hawkins, an agricultural labourer, with a wife and six children aged between one and thirteen. George had been transported for seven years for the crime of stealing wheat. The clerk informed Mr Muggeridge that George had been on board the hulks until six months earlier. George was recommended as a candidate for migration by the clergyman of Stoughton and other officials. Unfortunately for George, the Migration Office was seeking families with three or four children over the age of twelve who could be found immediate work. George's application was rejected and subsequently, in the same year, he deserted his family.[37]

DESERTIONS

Unions across England and Wales found the large number of deserted pregnancies and families a heavy financial burden on the ratepayers. With dogged determination, they sought to trace

Crowds of dock labourers and their families outside Whitechapel Workhouse. The freezing of the Thames had prevented them working and outdoor relief had to be issued. (*Illustrated London News*, 3 March 1855.)

those men who had deserted their families, in order to both extract financial contributions and, in some cases, to prepare a prosecution.

In November 1879, the guardians of the Dudley Union ordered 'That all Cases of Desertion be advertised in the *Poor Law Unions Gazette* at a reward of one pound in each case.' The board did not have to wait long for a response. Just two weeks later, they authorised 'that a Reward of £1 be and the same is hereby granted to James Winfield for the Apprehension of William Ward at Nottingham and Samuel Dudley at Warrington for Desertion.'[38]

DISRUPTIVE ABLE-BODIED MEN

Where large numbers of able-bodied men were inmates of the workhouse, they could cause severe disciplinary problems for the staff, especially in smaller workhouses. In 1851 at the Great Yarmouth Union, the workhouse contained 'a large number of idle and dissolute characters'. It was requested that police officers lodge at the workhouse to keep order after a serious riot caused damage to the property to the value of five pounds.[39]

Later in the year, there was another riot and the ringleader, Charles Girdlestone, was arrested after seriously injuring one of the policemen's hands. This man, a twenty-two-year-old labourer, was the 'terror of the workhouse' and his behaviour was so violent that he had to be transported to the court handcuffed and 'strapped down on a barrow' accompanied by seven policemen. It was reported that 'he used the most violent and disgusting language and resembled a maniac rather than a human being.' Girdlestone was sentenced to forty-two days' hard labour while three other guilty paupers had to work the treadmill for twenty-one days. While in prison, Charles Girdlestone's violent behaviour led to him being flogged and a soldier from Norwich was sent for, 'whose vigorous application of the cat reduced Girdlestone to obedience.'[40]

Despite his criminal and violent record, the Great Yarmouth Union could not refuse to re-admit Girdlestone to the workhouse. After being re-admitted, he was sent back to jail 'after threatening to cut the throat of an official at the workhouse.' It appeared that 'the conduct of this ruffian was consistent with the formidable reputation that he had acquired' and he had to be handcuffed. However, 'with his immense strength he was able to slip free of his restraints. He was subsequently put in irons but he was still able to demolish part of the wall of the cell in which he was confined.'[41] By the time of the 1861 census, Charles Girdlestone appears to have become a reformed character as by then he was employed as an able seaman in the Royal Navy.

In February 1850 at the Bethnal Green Workhouse, eight of the able-bodied paupers wrote to the Poor Law Commissioners alleging that they were:

> …kept locked in the cell yard to break stones and kept on Bread and Water every other twenty-four hours because we cannot break five bushels of stone per Day being Mechanics and never broke any before….we have been this last three weeks kept on Bread and Water not having any meat but on Sundays have become very weak and most of us having large families and are not allowed a days liberty to look for employment – so that we have the very least chance of taking our familys [sic] out…[42]

The fact that unions like Bethnal Green did not allow inmates to leave the workhouse temporarily to look for work made it doubly difficult for them to break the cycle and become self-supporting again. They would always have to take a chance that work would be available on leaving the workhouse. Other unions were more enlightened and recognised the problem. At the Sheffield Union, 'the able-bodied paupers were released every Wednesday afternoon to look for work.'[43]

INTO THE TWENTIETH CENTURY

Able-bodied male inmates in the workhouse continued to be a rarity at the beginning of the twentieth century. The 1905 Royal Commission found that 'only a small proportion of the able-bodied inmates were fit for employment' with a quarter being over fifty-five years old.[44] This was an age when their chances of finding employment were greatly reduced. By 1911, the classification of the able-bodied was abandoned by the central authorities in recognition that the scheme was distinctly flawed.

When able-bodied men did apply for relief, they were more likely than ever to be offered the workhouse than outdoor relief. Moral grounds were used to determine whether an able-bodied man was entitled to outdoor relief. This applied to 'any able-bodied man who could not convince the Relieving Officer that he had always been sober and provident…'[45]

Attitudes to the able-bodied by the Poor Law authorities remained negative and derogatory. In the late nineteenth century at the Salford Union, able-bodied men who were admitted to the workhouse were sent out to work in the streets 'with a large 'P' for 'Pauper' emblazoned across the seat of their trousers – a sight which would not have seemed out of place a hundred years earlier.'[46]

4
THE ABLE-BODIED WOMEN

One of the largest classes of inmate in workhouses across England and Wales was that of Class 5: able-bodied women and girls over the age of fifteen. This was a direct result of the policy adopted with the passing of the 1834 Poor Law Amendment Act which refused outdoor relief to 'unsupported women'. Such women formed the second largest group of inmates 'outnumbered only by the old, in nearly every workhouse.'[1]

A woman was classed as able-bodied if she was not sick and was capable of work if it was available. She could appear in Class 5 as a result of her husband becoming ill and being unable to work. More common reasons were becoming pregnant, being deserted by a husband or lover or becoming widowed. Able-bodied women might also enter the workhouse if they were unable to find work themselves or they had been returned from service.

UNMARRIED MOTHERS

One of the main reasons for an able-bodied woman to enter the workhouse was pregnancy. If a woman became pregnant and was abandoned by a husband or lover, or her family turned her out, the workhouse was the only available option.

Mary Bryan was an unmarried able-bodied woman who entered the Dudley Union Workhouse in October 1866 'age thirty-one' and pregnant.[2] She was described as a 'hawker', a pedlar of wares. According to the censuses, she was from County Cork in Ireland. Nothing is known of her family. Despite her pregnancy, it is highly likely that Mary would have been set to work in the workhouse and would not have been transferred to the lying-in ward until she went into labour.

This was a common practice in workhouses across England and Wales. At the Manchester Union Workhouse in 1894, Emmeline Pankhurst, in her role as a newly appointed female guardian, recalled seeing pregnant women 'scrubbing floors, doing the hardest kind of work, almost until their babies came into the world.'[3]

As an unmarried pregnant woman, Mary Bryan would have been considered less respectable than a married or widowed expectant mother. Critics of the new Poor Law felt that the classification scheme which separated the paupers into distinct classes was flawed because it 'had no separation on moral grounds'.[4] The classification scheme made no distinction between 'the unfortunate deserving character and the hardened "fallen" woman', and, from the very beginnings of the union workhouse, the Victorians were concerned about the effect of this contact 'between the respectable and the feckless poor'.[5]

Louisa Twining, founder of the Workhouse Visiting Society, believed that the 'separation of such persons from the more hardened offenders should be carefully attended to, as well as a distinction between married women and all others.'[6]

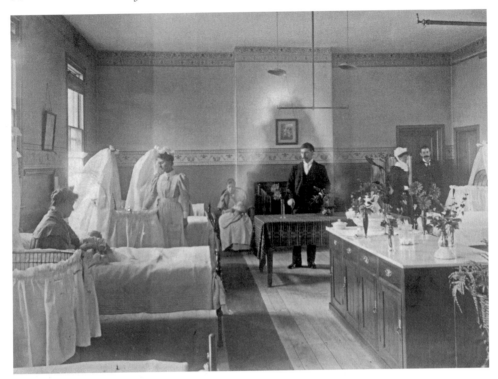

The lying-in ward at the Fir Vale Workhouse, Sheffield. (Courtesy of the Sheffield Teaching Hospitals NHS Foundation Trust.)

Many unmarried pregnant women or young girls found themselves in the workhouse because they had been disowned by their family. Others were sent to the workhouse simply because their family was unable to support them. This could happen if the family was already receiving outdoor relief from the union or there were other dependent children in the family. It is believed that eighteen-year-old Margaret Grundy was forced to enter the Foundry Street Union Workhouse in Horncastle, Lincolnshire when she became pregnant in 1863. Her mother, Elizabeth, was a widow and was recorded as a 'pauper' on the 1861 census, although she was not a resident of the workhouse. This indicates that Elizabeth was receiving outdoor relief and it would have been impossible for her to support Margaret and her new daughter, Sarah Jane.[7]

If a pregnant woman was entitled to outdoor relief and there was a problem with the delivery of her baby, it is probable that she would have been attended to in her home by the parish medical officer. In such cases, it is unlikely she would have given birth in the workhouse. The exception might be if the pregnancy was not straightforward or labour was problematic and there was time to move the woman to the workhouse infirmary.

It is believed that twenty-two-year-old Emily Dolby was expecting twins when she was admitted to the Dudley Union Workhouse in December 1895, and that they were born prematurely. This would probably have been considered a difficult birth and so it proved to be. Emily's chain-maker father was a widower who was looking after three children under the age of five after the death of his wife three years earlier. It is highly unlikely that he could have supported Emily, even if she had had a straightforward pregnancy.

Emily's child, Thomas, was born on 20 December after a long and difficult labour. There is no evidence to prove or disprove the theory that there was another twin born to Emily. Tragically, Emily died two days later on 22 December 1895. The cause of death was recorded as 'Albuminuria, Purpeural Eclampsia, Exhaustion'. A poignant entry in the St James's Church parish registers records the burial of Thomas, who died aged eleven months at the Dudley Union Workhouse in December 1896.[8]

In November 1866, a month after her admission to Dudley Union Workhouse, a 'Male Infant' was born to Mary Bryan. She named him Thomas. Once her baby was born, Mary would have been allowed between a couple of weeks and a month with him in the nursery. By 1878, the guardians of the Dudley Union decreed that 'all Women admitted for Confinement should attend before the Board at the expiration of the month, or as soon as convalescent, for the direction of the guardians.'[9]

It was at this point that a decision had to be made. Emmeline Pankhurst described the stark choice of:

> …staying in the workhouse and earning their living by scrubbing and other work, in which case they were separated from their babies; or of taking their discharges. They could stay and be paupers, or they could leave — leave with a two-week-old baby in their arms, without hope, without home, without money, without anywhere to go.[10]

The unmarried mothers with illegitimate children were in a difficult situation when it came to leaving the workhouse. In 1857, Emma Sheppard, one of the first workhouse visitors, wrote to *The Times* stating that: 'I have seen dozens of them, softened and brought to their senses by long seclusion in that fearful ward and longing to lead a better life when they left. But who would employ them?'[11]

Jane Chetter was another unmarried mother who had to make the difficult decision to leave the workhouse. In the 1860s, she had three illegitimate children who were all born at the Shifnal Union. Two of these children died in infancy and the third was looked after by Jane's parents. This meant she was able to take up a position in service to a prominent farming family. In the 1870s, two more illegitimate children followed before Jane was able to break the cycle of pregnancy and the workhouse. Finally, in 1879, when Jane was thirty-five, she married Charles Powell, an agricultural labourer at Sheriffhales.[12]

Despite the potential hardships, Mary Bryan chose to leave the Dudley Union Workhouse with her baby Thomas in February 1867. More than four years passed before Mary was admitted again. She was either able to maintain herself and Thomas or it is possible she was in another workhouse. From 1871, the regular entries in the admission and discharge registers of Dudley Union show that Mary became one of the despised 'ins and outs', coming and going when the need arose. Mary had two more illegitimate children, Jane (born in 1869) and James (born in 1872). They were not born at the Dudley Union.

The reason for Mary Bryan's admittance was always 'destitution' and for discharge 'own desire'. Mary became a problem to the guardians of the Dudley Union as she was often violent and disruptive. Her offences were serious enough for her to be regularly sent to prison. On 9 June 1872, she was taken away by the police with her baby son, James, and on the following day, she was sent to prison for two months 'for violent conduct and breaking seventeen sqrs of Glass in Two Windows.'[13]

Four months later in October 1872, she was again convicted by magistrates and sent to jail for fourteen days, this time without her baby. In May 1874, Mary was sent to prison for seven days for 'Violent Conduct and beating another inmate'. The inmate is not named in the workhouse records.

It is not known why Mary was so violent. She would have been all too aware what the consequences of her offences would be. However, despite her violent and disruptive record, Mary could not be refused admission to the workhouse. She was not classed as a lunatic or idiot so she could not be sent elsewhere.

Sometimes violence was justified and was merely a means to an end. At the Bromsgrove Union in August 1862, the master reported to the guardians that 'Ann Brown had wilfully broken several panes of glass in the women's ward.'[14] However, there was no punishment for Ann because the guardians discovered that the master had 'refused to allow her to see her child'.[15] In fact, it was the master who was reprimanded and his attention was drawn to his contract and his duty to observe the eighth regulation of Article 99 of the Consolidated General Order. Under this regulation, the master was to 'allow the father or mother of any child in the same workhouse, who may be desirous of seeing such child, to have an interview with such child... in a room in the said Workhouse to be appointed for that purpose.' Ann Brown's behaviour had brought her to the attention of the board and helped her to achieve her goal of seeing her child.

Rose White, a nineteen-year-old inmate at the Lampeter Union entered the workhouse on 28 November 1890, 'she being with child'. Rose 'gave birth to twins (Bastards)' on 16 December but one of the babies died three days later. In January 1891, the master of Lampeter Union wrote 'Edgar the infant child (the last of the twins) of Rose White died on the 19th instant.'[16] Although this must have been a traumatic time for Rose, the sad irony is that without her twins to provide for, she was in a better position to find work and provide for herself. There would be no question of her being placed in service with two babies in tow, unless she had family who could look after them or she could afford to put them out to nurse.

Another Lampeter inmate was nineteen-year-old Alice Davies, who, along with her illegitimate child, was admitted to the workhouse in September 1895. The guardians of workhouses were always keen to make errant fathers face up to their responsibilities and pay for the maintenance of any children if forced into the workhouse. Alice Davies knew who the father of her child was. On 20 September, an affiliation order of 2s 6d per week was made upon the putative father. The master recorded that 'The child has since been put out to Nurse' and that Alice had been discharged to go to service.[17] It is not known if Alice was ever reunited with her child.

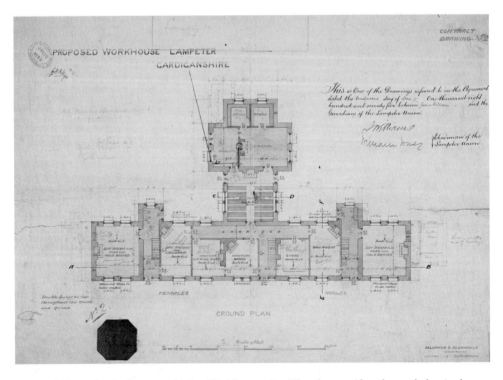

Proposed Plan 2 for the Lampeter Union Workhouse, 1875. The plan specifies obscured glass in the lower panes of the sash windows so that children and adults could not see each other. (Courtesy of Ceredigion Record Office.)

The inmates at Stratford-on-Avon Union Workhouse, *c*.1902. (Courtesy of Edwin Pickett.)

When girls reached the age of thirteen, they were found a situation and sent into service. In many cases, going into service was a dangerous path to follow. Thirteen-year-old Maria Conkerton left the Sedgefield Union in County Durham on 11 December 1876 to go into service for 'Jane Johnson, Gentlewoman of Sedgefield'.[18] However, on 8 February 1877, just two months later, Maria was re-admitted to the workhouse 'pregnant'.[19] Nothing is known of her child. This pattern continued as, in later years, Maria was regularly admitted to the workhouse with other illegitimate children.

As Maria had lived in the workhouse prior to her being returned pregnant, she cannot have felt the fear of the unknown that Dorothy Hatcher's pregnant mother felt in the early 1900s:

> Mother had to walk the long way from Shadoxhurst to the Union at Tenterden....cast off by everyone, scorned by those who could have shown sympathy. Mother said that she felt like looking for the nearest pond and ending it all. The nearer she got the worse she felt. She was terrified at what was going to happen to her.[20]

The Poor Law Commission was anxious to make sure that unmarried mothers were not singled out by workhouses. In 1839, they decreed that the workhouse 'ought not to be used for punishing the dissolute or rewarding the well-conducted pauper.'[21] However, in June 1839, the East Retford guardians punished an inmate called Selina Hill who had 'suffered the Barbers Boy to have connection with her'. Her hair was cut short and she was 'not allowed to wear a cap for three months'.[22] In 1838 at the Swaffham Union, the unmarried mothers were punished in another way. They were excluded from the Coronation dinner and from the annual Christmas dinner.[23]

Although it was a practice frowned upon by the central authorities, some unions nevertheless forced their unmarried mothers to wear a different coloured uniform from the other inmates.

Such distinguishing dress could take many forms. At the Gressenhall Workhouse in 1866, the single women were required 'to wear a distinguishing overdress or *Jacket*, of the same materials as the gown, coming down to the hips'. Hence the expression *used and felt as a term of reproach*, of 'Jacket women'.[24] In 1838 at the Westbourne Union, yellow dresses were to be worn by 'such Female Inmates who for any immorality or other misconduct appeared to the Guardians to deserve to be openly disgraced.'[25]

At the New Forest Union, the unmarried mothers and children formed a quarter of the inmates. Reverend Herbert Smith was the chaplain of this union in 1836 and he spent a lot of time ministering to the women with illegitimate children. He wrote in his diary that he had pointed out to them that 'their situation is the consequence of their own sin and that they ought to feel thankful that they have found such a refuge.'[26]

The large number of deserted pregnancies and families represented a huge financial burden for unions across England and Wales. Whilst all unions actively sought the men who had deserted their wives, and, in some cases, found them, another alternative was to assist in the emigration of large families. In one particular case, the guardians of the Dudley Union were prepared to pay for a wife and her family to join her husband in Fall River in North America. In November 1884 they actively assisted the emigration of thirty-five-year-old Mary Cooper and her six children ranging in age from one to eleven years of age. As Mary had received a 'free pass' from her husband to go to America, the guardians paid the sum of £3 'for the purpose of conveying her and her six children and their luggage from the District of Sedgley to Liverpool.'[27]

DESERTED WIVES

For many desperate women, the daily grind of life and struggling to provide for one's children alone was too much. Some women made the difficult decision to desert their children, consigning them to the workhouse. In November 1892 in Sedgefield, County Durham, Cath (also known as Kate) Jameson, a thirty-one-year-old woman, was deserted by her husband. She and her four children, Mary Ann, John Thomas, William and Selina Jane were admitted to the Sedgefield Union Workhouse, discharging themselves a week later. Over nine months passed before the family was re-admitted in August 1893 so Cath was either reconciled with her husband or was able to support herself and her family. Selina died in the workhouse and another child, Emily, was born to Cath. The family again left the Sedgefield Union.[28]

However, on 18 April 1895, Mary Ann, John Thomas and William were re-admitted to the workhouse because they were 'deserted by mother'. Cath kept her baby Emily with her but sent her other children to the workhouse.[29] Nothing else is known of Cath and Emily. Perhaps she remarried or set up home with another man. Either way, she does not reappear in the Sedgefield Union registers. There is no record of any action being taken against Cath Jameson for causing her children to become chargeable to the Union.

At the Lampeter Union, desertion of children by their mother was taken more seriously. Margaret Jenkins was another regular in the workhouse with her four children, Thomas, Margaret, Mary and David. On 6 August 1878, she sent her children to the workhouse 'apparently deserting them in a cowardless manner threatening them on their refusal to come in.'[30]

On 9 August a warrant was issued against Margaret, 'a woman living apart from her husband'. Two weeks later, Margaret Jenkins was 'committed to Jail for six weeks…for deserting her children.' At this time, she also had another child, Sarah, aged just seven months, who was 'obliged to be sent out to be nursed'.[31]

Deserted wives were not confined to the working classes. In 1837, Daniel Smart, the clerk of the Westbourne Union made repeated enquiries on behalf of a Mrs Oliver who had been deserted by her husband, Thomas Oliver Esq., a special magistrate in Jamaica. He wrote to her

The Southwell Union Workhouse, now owned by the National Trust and open to the public. (Courtesy of Carl Higgs.)

husband in Jamaica, stating that his wife and children were receiving 6s per week from the parish. Daniel Smart concluded his letter: 'I cannot refrain from adding as a friend that the destitution of your family is extreme and I need not say most disgraceful.'[32] When no reply arrived from Jamaica, Daniel Smart turned to Mrs Oliver's brother-in-law, William Orme, Esq. of Old Swinford, Stourbridge. He argued that:

> I am sure I need not say that if the unfortunate Lady should be driven by her loss of six shillings a week to choose between the Workhouse and any less honourable means of support and should unhappily choose unwisely, the reflection that something like £15 a year has been saved by forcing her to such an alternative will be but a poor consolation for the misery and disgrace.

William Orme was prepared to pay for support for six months if the guardians continued to press the Colonial Department which employed Thomas Oliver. Finally, money was received from Thomas Oliver.[33]

WIDOWS

Becoming widowed and therefore having no means to support herself and her children was another common reason for an able-bodied woman to enter the workhouse. Widows were considered more respectable than their unmarried counterparts, providing they had not had any illegitimate children.

The Lilley family has already been mentioned in chapter two. Sarah Lilley and her three daughters had to be re-admitted to the Dudley Union Workhouse in November 1862 after Sarah's husband James, an asthma sufferer, died. She discharged herself and her children the following day. It is not known how she supported herself and her daughters after this time.[34]

Being separated from their children was one of the main reasons for the reluctance of women to enter the workhouse. In the 1860s, Henry Mayhew reported meeting a widow who was 'on the game who acknowledged that she would rather support her children in this way than be separated from them in the house.'[35]

WIVES WITH HUSBANDS

Some married able-bodied women entered the workhouse with their husbands who were sick and unable to work, or who could not find work. At the Mitford and Launditch Union in Norfolk, in February 1841, Honor Dickerson 'the wife of James Dickerson' was punished 'for throwing some Bread over into the Able-bodied men's wards.' Honor had probably intended to give the bread to her husband. For this offence she was 'confined in the Dungeon…for eight hours.'[36]

DISRUPTIVE ABLE-BODIED WOMEN

Once they turned thirteen, girls were usually sent from the workhouse into service. However, those who were found unsuitable by their new employer were promptly sent back to the workhouse. Now in Class 5, these impressionable young girls mixed with the unmarried mothers and prostitutes. These women often caused disciplinary problems for the staff. In 1865, the guardians of the Dudley Union Workhouse reported:

> …great difficulty with a number of refractory and dissolute young women who have been repeatedly in situations as domestic servants, but have as repeatedly left their situations and returned to the house. They have…too much liberty though picking 3lb of Oakum each per day, and they are exercising a very contaminating influence upon the other inmates. We think that under 98 & 99 of the Consolidated Order of the Poor Law Commission, these disorderly females should be separated from the other inmates and kept to hard work.[37]

Disruptive able-bodied women were a problem in other workhouses too. In 1894, at the Foleshill Union Workhouse, two able-bodied women named Mary Bloxham and Florence Paddy were punished 'For assaulting and using bad language to Pheobe [sic] Morris, an imbecile inmate. For using bad language and continuing to annoy the Industrial Trainer.' Their punishment was that 'bread and water should be given to them for forty-eight hours…'[38]

PROSTITUTES

It was well known that it was often the workhouse itself which had converted 'poor sinful girls' into 'depraved and degraded women'.[39] A servant's life was one of endless toil and drudgery and, in many cases, girls sent into service quickly discovered that 'no life could be worse than that of maid-of-all-work in a single-servant family.'[40] For such girls 'a brothel', or back-street lodging with frequent 'gentlemen callers', was often a haven of luxury compared to the average servant's basement kitchen or cheerless attic…'[41] Infection with venereal disease was depressingly inevitable. However, only in the larger workhouses was there the luxury of a separate 'foul' ward for the sufferers of venereal disease.[42]

Oakum-picking at a London workhouse, early 1900s. (The National Archives, ref. PRO30/69/1663 f.38. Reproduced by permission of the grand-daughter of the late Malcolm MacDonald.)

WORK TASKS

Like the other inmates, able-bodied women were required to complete work tasks which could consist of cleaning and scrubbing, working in the laundry, preparing food or tending to the babies in the nursery. Cleaning was by no means a light work task. This could involve up to nine hours of scrubbing and cleaning floors on hands and knees. Another task often given to women was the picking of oakum, a tedious task involving the unpicking of old rope.

In smaller workhouses, with a staff consisting of only a master and matron, able-bodied women were vital to the smooth running of the workhouse since they could undertake many of the more arduous daily tasks. George Bowes, the master of the small Sedgefield Union, positively welcomed able-bodied women into the workhouse. In December 1888 he lamented the fact that 'we have no able-bodied women in the workhouse to do the necessary work, consequently part of the washing remains undone, a quantity of the Inmates clothing wants repairing and a number of pairs of Stockings refooting.'[43]

If able-bodied women were unable to find a way to support themselves, they were likely to become one of the regular 'ins and outs' to the workhouse. Many such women became institutionalised and found it difficult to leave. Both Maria Conkerton, the girl who became pregnant when she was sent out to service, and Mary Bryan, the violent, unmarried hawker, died in middle age in the workhouse.

INTO THE TWENTIETH CENTURY

In the 1890s and early 1900s, many unions across England and Wales reviewed their classification scheme. This re-classification by character was intended to benefit only the deserving poor. The Sheffield Union adopted a classification by character scheme, under which there were four classes: A, B, C and D. Deserted wives 'whose character is very good, and whose desertion is not through any fault of their own' were assigned to B class. Meals were taken in the day room and 'their sleeping and all other accommodation is separate from that of the inferior classes.'[44]

The guardians of the Christchurch Union also sub-divided their classification scheme in an attempt to differentiate between the 'deserving' and 'undeserving' poor. The most favoured group of 'A' inmates included widows with children and deserted wives with children 'with ten years' residence in Christchurch (Union) without having claimed poor relief previously, and unable through no fault of their own to maintain themselves...'[45]

Inmates in the 'A' group were allowed privileges 'such as permission to walk in the grounds, frequent leave of absence, a separate table in the dining hall and better clothing.' They no longer had to sleep in a dormitory with the other inmates as their 'sleeping arrangements were upgraded and divided into personal cubicles, over 7' by nearly 3' in size.'[46]

The inmates considered least 'deserving' such as the unmarried mothers, prostitutes and refractory women fell into the 'C' group who were not allowed any privileges, were supplied with a downgraded diet and had to wear a distinctive uniform 'of the oldest and worst description'. In addition, this class of inmate was to undertake 'all the most disagreeable work'.[47]

The workhouse continued to be a refuge for unmarried mothers well into the twentieth century. The fact that an unmarried woman had had an illegitimate child would place her amongst the 'undeserving' poor in the updated workhouse classification schemes. This would apply whether she was a respectable woman who had made one costly, regrettable mistake, or if she was a prostitute with a large number of illegitimate children.

5

THE CHILDREN

Workhouse children were deemed to be '...the only group of inmates to be held blameless for their predicament'.[1] As such, more effort was made on the part of the guardians of each union to help them escape the poverty trap than for any of the other workhouse inmates. This class of inmate also received the most benefits from charity. Once admitted to the workhouse, children under the age of seven were placed in Class 7 and boys and girls between the ages of seven and fifteen were placed in Class 3 and 6 respectively.

For many children, the workhouse could be a refuge if they had no home of their own or if there was no-one to look after them. This could happen if a child was orphaned, if one or both parents were sent to prison or if he or she was abandoned by his or her family. Some children were also regularly admitted to the workhouse with their siblings and parents.

ORPHANED CHILDREN

In the nineteenth century, the term 'orphaned' could refer to the death of one parent as well as both parents. In October 1880, two Roman Catholic orphans, Edward and William Lawlor, aged eleven and eight, became inmates of the Dudley Union Workhouse. Both their parents were dead. Shortly after, they were sent to the St Francis Home, Shefford, Bedfordshire, at a considerable cost – £10 per annum each.[2] In 1887, the guardians refused to contribute towards the cost of fifteen-year-old William's emigration to Canada. It went ahead nonetheless and William became a 'home child', departing from Liverpool in July 1887 in Cardinal Manning's party on the SS *Sarmatian*.[3] William fought in the First World War and was killed in action in April 1917 at the assault on Vimy Ridge in France.[4]

ABANDONED CHILDREN

Children might also be abandoned by their families. Sometimes, when there were a large number of children in a family, a few of the children might be sent to the workhouse to ease the burden on the parents.

Four sisters named Jane Elizabeth, Clara, Rachel and Alice Gribbon were first admitted to Sedgefield Union Workhouse in County Durham in July 1891 when their miner father, Arthur, was sent to prison. Their mother, Mary Ann, had died some time before this and there was no other family to look after them. In August, the master of the workhouse recorded that 'Arthur Gribbon, Pitman, Trimdon,...visited his children on Tuesday last, and wished them to stay in the workhouse a fortnight longer, so as he could make provision for them at home & would be glad to pay the Guardians for their maintenance.'[5] The children were discharged into their father's care on 1 October.

Left: John Bates who, as a child, spent several periods in the St Giles Workhouse. (Courtesy of Sandy Norman.)

Below: Mary (Bates) Boyd (far right) with her children and sister-in-law. With her brother John, she spent time in the St Giles Workhouse as a child. (Courtesy of Sandy Norman.)

Almost a year passed before the sisters were admitted again to the Sedgefield Union on 1 September 1892. The master recorded that the children were 'filthy with vermin' and were 'deserted by their father'.[6]

As the eldest of the sisters, Jane Elizabeth, born in 1880, was not destined to stay in the workhouse for long. In November 1893, she was sent into service at Ferryhill Station but was returned six days later as she was sick with 'a case of Quinsy'.[7] In April of the following year she was sent into service again, but returned to the workhouse six months later. She remained there until December 1895 when she was discharged at her own wish.

Clara, the second oldest of the Gribbon sisters, born in 1884, was sent into service several times from the workhouse between 1898 and 1899. She returned to the workhouse and remained there until October 1900. It appears that there was a problem with her health as the guardians had sent her to a specialist. However, she 'took a fit about six o'clock in the evening and died at 9.30 that evening. The Doctor was in immediate attendance but could do her no good.'[8]

Rachel, the third Gribbon sister, born in 1885, also found it difficult to settle when sent into service. In April 1900, Rachel was sent to her third situation with Mr and Mrs Wilding at Preston. She stayed there for two years until Mrs Wilding wrote to the master of Sedgefield Union to say that:

I have done my very best to give her a chance in life but this last six months she has been so cheeky and disobedient. I cannot keep her any longer, so it will be better for her to be near Lizzie [her oldest sister] she is old enough to look after her now.[9]

The youngest Gribbon sister was Alice who was just three years old when she was admitted to the Sedgefield Union in 1892. It was not long before Alice was 'adopted' by Mr and Mrs Peacock of Trimdon in March 1893. This arrangement did not work out and Alice was sent back to the workhouse three months later. She remained at the Sedgefield Union until April 1898 when she was taken by George Bowes, the master to Mrs Morris in Church Street, Sunderland. George Bowes reported: 'I think she will have a very comfortable home'.[10]

George Bowes made regular visits to the children who had been boarded-out, apprenticed or adopted from the Sedgefield Union. On 15 March 1900, he went to visit Alice Gribbon in Sunderland and:

…found that the Aunt who took her from here had left town (whereabouts not known). The person… to whom Alice was taken had had great trouble with her, owing to her dishonesty. Finally the officer for cruelty to children had taken her & she had been sent to one of Dr. Barnardo's Homes in London.[11]

Alice became a resident of the Dr Barnardo's Home in Ilford, Essex and two years later, in July 1902, she became one of the countless 'home children' sent to Canada. She was in a party of children on board the SS *New England* in Liverpool, bound for Boston, USA. Her final destination was Ontario. Nothing is known of her life in Canada.

Children could also become workhouse inmates when one or both of their parents were in prison and there was no-one else to look after them. In December 1899, five-year-old Fred Dent was forced to enter Huddersfield Union Workhouse with his two youngest siblings when his mother was sent to Wakefield Gaol, after pleading guilty to the charge of keeping a disorderly house. In August 1901, Fred and his siblings were moved to the newly built Children's Home at Outlane near Huddersfield. At the age of ten, Fred was apprenticed to Mr Elijah Swallow of Thongsbridge 'the hiring… having proved satisfactory was confirmed'.

Between 1909 and 1910, Fred emigrated to Australia. It is highly likely that this emigration was assisted by the guardians of the Huddersfield Union. When the First World War broke out, Fred enlisted with the Australian Imperial Force and fought at Gallipoli and later in France.

After the war, he settled in England, having married Annie in Huddersfield in 1917. However, at the end of 1919, the couple decided to settle in Australia.[12]

Whenever babies or infants were abandoned in the union, they were brought to the workhouse. Unless the parents could be found, such children would become chargeable to the union. It is not surprising then, that, in November 1896, the guardians of the Dudley Union ordered that an advertisement be placed in the *Poor Law Union Gazette* 'for the Apprehension and Conviction of the Parent or Parents who Deserted a Male Child in the General Waiting Room at the Dudley Station of the Great Western Railway Company.' They were prepared to offer '...a Reward of Two Guineas'.[13] It is not known if the parents were found but the publicity was successful as, a few weeks later, the guardians recorded that 'the application of Mr Job Tomkinson of 44 Bloxwich Road, Willenhall to adopt the Male Infant Child...found at the Dudley Railway Station be accepted.'[14]

CHILD INMATES WITH PARENTS

Many children arrived at the workhouse with their siblings and parents. If an able-bodied man could not find work, he and his whole family had to enter the workhouse. However, it was more likely for children to be admitted to the workhouse with their mother who had either been abandoned by her husband or was widowed or unmarried.

Mary Bates, born in 1884 and her older brother John, born around 1882, spent several periods in the St Giles Workhouse at Endell Street, London with their mother Ann, described as a hawker. Their father, Alfred, a boot and shoemaker was alive at the time and may have been a resident at another workhouse or infirmary. At one time, when Mary was just five years old, she admitted herself to the workhouse and was sent to the Central London sick asylum in Cleveland Street. At the age of six, Mary was sent from the workhouse to an Infant Poor establishment at Hampstead.

Despite such humble beginnings, both Mary and John worked their way out of the workhouse. In 1901, seventeen-year-old Mary was working as a servant. John became a soldier, joining the West Yorkshire Regiment in 1907. He served in India between 1907 and 1911 and was demobbed in February 1914. John was put on reserve in June of that year and, at the outbreak of the First World War, he was a Lance Corporal. Tragically, on 20 September 1914, John was killed in action.[15]

Mary Ann Mangan (Manggon), born in 1889, was a frequent inmate of St Marylebone Workhouse with her parents and siblings. The family appears to have used the workhouse when their need was greatest and discharged themselves when able to find work. Mary Ann was sent from the workhouse to St Edward's Roman Catholic School at Totteridge. Between 1898 and 1899, Mary Ann's mother, Johanna, regularly admitted and discharged her from St Edward's. After Johanna's death in November 1899, Mary Ann became a permanent resident of St Edward's. This was despite her father still being alive.

Like countless other children in schools or institutions run by religious organisations, Mary Ann was destined to become a 'home child', sent to Canada under the auspices of the Catholic Emigration Association. On 2 July 1903, she was one of a party of fourteen children aboard the SS *Bavarian* bound for Canada, arriving on 11 July 1903. Between 13 July of that year and 27 September 1904, Mary Ann was assigned to three different homes. Her first situation was with a family in Iberville, Quebec for a term of two years. She was to be paid $14 for the first year and $36 and clothes for the second year. Mary Ann wrote from one of her placements that 'I want to keep in this place...I am well feed [sic] clothed & well treated. I am nearly speaking French...' Learning French was another challenge faced by British children who emigrated to French-speaking parts of Canada.[16]

Servant's Agreement.

I, *John T Jamieson* do hereby agree to hire myself as Servant to *Mr J. Bradley* for the Term of ~~Half-~~ one Year to commence on the *23rd* day of *November* 1901, at the ~~Half-~~yearly Wages of £ *nine pound* payable Half-yearly and I the said *John Bradley* hereby agree to retain and hire the said *J. T. Jamison* for the above Term, and upon *his* being able duly to perform such Service, to pay to *him* the said Wages, at the times above-mentioned, and on the event of *his* not being able to fulfil such Service, through ill-health or other un-avoidable cause, then I agree to pay a proportionate amount of Wages up to the said *23rd Nov: 1902*, leaving my service, or becoming incapacitated and unable to perform this contract of hiring and service

Name of Servant, *J T Jamieson*

Name of Employer, *John Bradley*

Geo. H. Procter, Printer, Stationer, Bookbinder &c., 8, Market Place, **Durham**.

Above: Servant's agreement for fourteen-year-old John Thomas Jamieson of the Sedgefield Union Workhouse, 1901. John had been an inmate for six years after he and his siblings were abandoned by their mother. (U/Se 40. Reproduced by permission of the Durham County Record Office.)

Right: List of items for fourteen-year-old William Jamieson's outfit on leaving the Sedgefield Union Workhouse to work for a farmer in Thornton-le-Street, 1903. Like his brother, John Thomas, William had been in the workhouse since 1895. (U/Se 40. Reproduced by permission of the Durham County Record Office.)

SEDGEFIELD UNION.

Union Workhouse.

Sedgefield. 190

Dear Sir,

Kindly issue Orders upon the several Tradesmen for the supply of the undermentioned articles required for the use of the Workhouse, for the Week ending _____

Yours truly, _____ Master

Mr. ALFRED M. APPLETON,

Clerk to the Guardians of the Sedgefield Union.

TRADESMAN'S NAME	ARTICLES REQUIRED	TRADESMAN'S NAME	ARTICLES REQUIRED
	Wm Jamieson' Outfit		
3.	Day Shirts	2	V. Flannel
2	Night "	3	Prs Stockings
6	Pkt H'kfs	3	Scarves
1	Muffler	1	Gloves
3	Ties	2	Prs Boots
2	Caps	2	Linen Jackets
3	Collars	3	Fronts
1	Comb	1	Sofa
1	Brush	3	Suits
1	Pr Leggins	2	Prs Braces
1	Top Coat	1	Tin Box
1	Prayer Book	1	Hymn Book
	Sundries for Mending purposes		

Nov: 18th 1913.

Indenture for Charles Cuerton, who was to be apprenticed to John Forge, owner of the ship *Brilliant*, 1867. (Courtesy of the late Maurice Cuerton.)

LIFE IN THE WORKHOUSE

On arrival at the workhouse, children were immediately separated from their parents, and indeed from their siblings if they were not the same sex. They were then bathed and given workhouse uniforms, just like the adult pauper inmates. The children's uniforms varied around the country. In Norfolk, it consisted of 'striped and checked gowns with aprons for the girls, and jackets and trousers of a coarse cloth with a spotted neckerchief for the boys.'[17] At another workhouse, the boys' uniform was described as being made of a material which 'has the further demerit of an intolerable and unwholesome smell until it has several times been washed.'[18]

After bathing, the children's hair was cropped short for hygiene purposes. Lice were an ever present problem in the workhouse, especially when large numbers of children were living and sleeping in close proximity to each other. This closely cropped hair marked the children out as workhouse inmates wherever they went. In some unions, the girls were allowed to grow their hair back before going into service. However, this was not the case in other, less humane, unions.

According to the Consolidated General Order, children were to be allowed regular contact with parents and siblings if they were also inmates of the workhouse. At the Dudley Union in May 1862, after a complaint from the schoolmistress and schoolmaster regarding 'the evil attending the visits of the Parents to their Children in the schools at improper times,' it was resolved that 'an opportunity shall be allowed for Parents and Children to meet in the Dining Room every Evening for half an hour commencing at ½ past 6.'[19]

Children did not escape punishments, whether the offence was accidental or otherwise. In the punishment book for the Aston Union, it was recorded that on 7 September 1869, George

Briggs, a twelve-year-old boy, was given 'six stripes by the Schoolmaster with a Birch Rod for dirtying his bed.' George was punished a week later for the same offence with three stripes. Three months later, the same offence and punishment occurred.[20]

TREATS AND ENTERTAINMENTS

Throughout England and Wales, the plight of workhouse children struck a chord with the local community. Organisations and charities frequently offered them free admission to their entertainments. At the Dudley Union, the workhouse schoolchildren were regularly invited to the Castle Fete, free of charge, by the committee responsible for the event. Other treats included trips to the Lower Gornal Flower Show, Mr Culleen's Circus, and invitations to participate in songs of service at various non-conformist churches.[21] Here, the workhouse schoolchildren had the opportunity to mix with people who were not workhouse inmates.

Despite these outings, it is highly unlikely that they compensated for the fact that workhouse children were social outcasts. The closely cropped hair of workhouse children would have marked them out as inmates wherever they went. Such outings would surely have made the children realise how isolated and different the workhouse was in comparison with the outside world.

WORKHOUSE SCHOOLS

The nature of the education given to workhouse children was such that they might be able to escape the poverty trap on leaving the institution. Little was expected of them academically. Religious education figured prominently in the school timetable. At the Dudley Union, hymn and prayer books, Bibles, scripture prints and maps of Palestine were procured for the workhouse school with a grant from the Privy Council.[22]

The transitory life of a child whose family was also in the workhouse, and the often short-lived appointments of school staff, cannot have helped promote stability in the workhouse school. After all, the schoolmaster or schoolmistress would become a surrogate parent to the child whilst he or she was an inmate of the workhouse.

Most medium to large unions had their own workhouse schools. H. Bowyer, a schools inspector, described workhouse schools as generally opening:

> on to a yard enclosed by high walls, with a circular swing at its centre... The windows are mostly small and square; and if they should happen to look on an adult ward, they are darkened by whitewashing the glass. During the dark winter days the instruction of the children is much hindered by want of light...[23]

The comment about white-washing illustrates the Poor Law Commission's view that the adult paupers were a contaminating influence on the children.

From 1861, unions could send workhouse children to local schools.[24] There were both critics and advocates of this system. Andrew Doyle, a Poor Law Commissioner, believed sending workhouse children to local schools would upset workhouse discipline.[25] A school inspector in the 1860s who was in favour of workhouse schools pointed out that:

> ...because the schools are smaller, the children are more under the command of the teachers, and more disposed to study from the very dullness and monotony of their lives, which renders the drudgery of learning to read, write, and sum, so distasteful to the ordinary schoolboy, a relief and an amusement to the workhouse child.[26]

FORM A.

Form to be filled in by those applying to emigrate Children through the Catholic Emigrating Association.

The Catholic Emigrating Association.

President—
REV. E. BANS,
CRUSADE OF RESCUE, 337, HARROW ROAD,
LONDON, W.

Hon. Secretary—
ARTHUR CHILTON THOMAS,
FATHER BERRY'S HOMES, 105, SHAW STREET,
LIVERPOOL.

Form of Application for the Emigration of a Child

Which must be filled in, and sent to the Hon. Secretary before a Child can be accepted by the Association. No case can be considered unless the medical certificate on the back is filled in. A copy of baptismal certificate should also be sent.

Name of the Branch responsible for case .... Crusade of Rescue.

1.—Child's name ...... Mary Ann Manggon

2.—Age last birthday .... 14 .... Date of Birth .. Mar. 9. .... Year of Birth .. 1889

3.—Church of Baptism .... Town of Baptism .... Date of Baptism .... 18......

4.—Height .. 55 .... Chest Measurement .. 32

5.—Has the candidate expressed willingness to go to Canada ? ......

6.—Are the parents living or dead ? ......

7.—Name and address of parent, or nearest relative, if an orphan ...... Crusade of Rescue

8.—If not an orphan, do parents object to emigration ? ......

9.—In what Institution, Home, Orphanage or * Industrial School has the child been educated ? ......

.... St Edward's Totteridge ....
* If an Industrial School, state the reasons of committal. The greatest care should be taken in selecting Industrial School cases for Emigration.

10.—Length of time in the School .... 3 1/2 years

11.—Is it proposed to pay £12 to the Catholic Emigrating Association to include outfit ? ...... yes

Or is it proposed to pay £8, the present Guardians finding outfit* ? ......

Name and address of person responsible for payment ...... Crusade of Rescue

If this Association is to provide outfit, give size of following articles : hat .. 21 1/2 .. collar .. 12 .. boots .. 3

The Head of the Institution or Home in which the child is should be asked to answer the following questions most carefully :
Children of bad character are returned to England, thus involving useless expenses to those sending them out.

12.—Is the child honest ? yes .... Is it free from sulky temper ? .... yes .. Is it moral ? ......

13.—Is its disposition good, fair, or doubtful ? .... good .... Is it bright and intelligent ? .... yes

14.—Does it understand that it will have (a) to work on a farm ? .. yes .... (b) To allow its wages to be banked

till 18 ? .... (c) To abstain from smoking ? .... (d) To live in country away from theatres, etc.? ......

15.—Does the child suffer from nocturnal incontinence of urine or the like ? .. no

16.—Has the child made its First Confession ? ...... Has it made its First Communion ? .. yes

17.—Has the child been Confirmed ? .. no .... Will it go to Holy Communion within a week before starting ? ......

18.—On what date will the child be ready to start ? ...... July 2.03.
A month's notice should be given of intention to send any child by any party.

Give particulars of any illnesses ......

Remarks or Instructions ......

Emigration papers for Mary Ann Mangan (Manggon) who became a 'home child' to Canada, arriving under the auspices of The Catholic Emigrating Association. (Courtesy of Pat McGrath.)

Smaller workhouses did not employ their own schoolteacher but sent their children to the nearest school instead. These children had the opportunity to mix with children who were not workhouse inmates which would have been a break from the monotony of workhouse routine. At the turn of the twentieth century, the children from the Freebridge Lynn Union walked one and a half miles from the workhouse to Gayton village school. They carried their lunch with them in a covered basket 'as it was too far for them to return for lunch to the workhouse.' The other schoolchildren envied the workhouse children their delicious lunches 'especially the biscuits'.[27]

Some unions chose to set up so-called district schools away from the workhouse. The Wigmore schools, opened in 1872, were made up of children from the Walsall and West Bromwich Unions. Industrial training was a vital part of the children's schooling at Wigmore and the boys were taught 'the trades of the tailor, shoemaker, baker, and gardener…the girls are employed in the laundry and at other useful domestic avocations.'[28]

Later in the nineteenth century, all workhouses paid greater attention to the industrial training of the children in an attempt to prepare them for the world of work. In London, industrial training was provided much earlier. In 1850, Charles Dickens visited the Pauper School at Norwood where there were nine hundred children. The boys were 'kept four days a week at school, and two days at work' in tailoring, shoemaking or farrier workshops. The girls had 'three days' schooling and three days' training in household occupations – such as cleaning the house, washing, ironing, mangling and needlework.'[29] On a visit to another industrial school at Swinton near Manchester, Dickens dubbed it a 'pauper palace' because it was so well run.[30]

BOARDING-OUT

Towards the end of the nineteenth century, unions moved towards boarding-out their pauper children within the parish as a better, more humane alternative to housing them in the workhouse. Children were boarded-out with 'foster parents' who were vetted by the union and paid to look after them. In some cases the foster parents were relatives of the children they looked after. It was still the responsibility of the union to check on the welfare of the children who were boarded-out. In larger unions, this responsibility often fell to members of the Ladies' Visiting Committee, while in smaller unions it was the master's responsibility.

At the Lampeter Union in 1896, the master visited Maggie and Rosie Jenkins who were boarded-out from the workhouse. He recorded that:

> I visited these orphans aged eight & five respectively…[who] are residing with their Uncle & Aunt who receive from the Union for their care and maintenance 2/6 per each child. I am pleased to say that the children appear to be well taken care of. They are looking well, clean and happy…[31]

At the Bromsgrove Union in November 1892, a boy named James Monk was returned to the workhouse after being boarded-out because of 'his bad conduct and his stealing and cashing a postal order. It was resolved that the child remain in the workhouse pending inquiries being made with a view to getting him into an industrial school.' A month later, James Monk was sent to Hereford Industrial School. In July 1896, the guardians heard that James had completed his training. He was found employment with Messrs. Henderson & Spalding, Printers, London and was in receipt of a good wage. It was stated that 'he will be carefully looked after for at least the next three years.'[32]

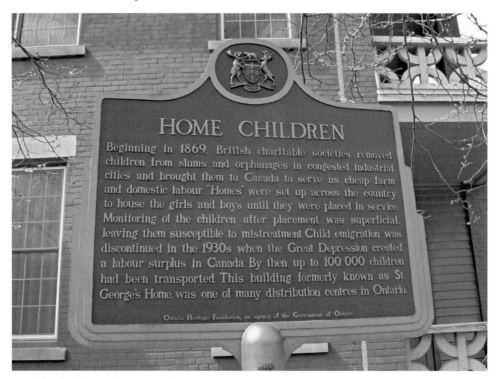

A plaque in Ottawa commemorating the 100,000 'home children' sent from Britain to Canada between 1869 and the 1930s. (Courtesy of Pat McGrath.)

'SCATTERED' OR COTTAGE HOMES

Other unions took the option of setting up 'scattered' or cottage homes for the children away from the main workhouse. At the Christchurch Union, the first cottage homes were opened in 1896, built on twenty-one acres opposite the workhouse.[33] There were four homes, two for boys and two for girls, which were each run by an assistant matron. However, a superintendent and matron had overall responsibility of the cottage homes as a whole.[34] A similar system was in operation from 1894 at the Sheffield Union.[35]

SPECIALIST INSTITUTIONS

Towards the end of the nineteenth century, specialist institutions sprang up to provide places for children from workhouses. They were certified by the Poor Law Board and included provision for children with special needs such as epileptics, idiots, cripples and the deaf and blind.

The guardians of the Dudley Union paid for several of their children to attend and live at specialist institutions. In September 1876, a blind seventeen-year-old, John Hobson, was sent to the Blind Institution, Edgbaston, 'to be taught a trade at a cost including Maintenance of Two Guineas per quarter.'[36] Economic foresight was at work here. If disabled paupers could not learn a trade, they would have no way of even attempting to escape poverty and would very likely be a lifelong burden. John was able to utilise the skills he had been taught at the Institution as by 1891 he was earning his keep as a basket-maker and hawker.

Mary Ann Mangan (Manggon) who was sent to
Canada as a 'home child' in July 1903. She later married,
had seven children and was Head of Housekeeping at
Ottawa Hospital. (Courtesy of Pat McGrath.)

Another Dudley Union inmate, Arthur Holloway, a sixteen-year-old idiot, was sent to the
Western Counties Starcross Idiot Asylum in October 1900 'for the purpose of being taught a
Trade'. This was to cost the union 12s per week and £4 8s 8d in clothing.[37]

Training ships were to become another option for workhouse boys towards the end of the
nineteenth century.

In 1912, ten-year-old Hector Bloomfield was sent to the Wellesley Training Ship from the
Chester-le-Street Union. At the workhouse, he was 'continually absconding and…recently
returned from a home where he was boarded-out, on account of stealing money.'[38] It was
hoped that he would settle on the training ship.

LEAVING THE WORKHOUSE

It is difficult to imagine the problems a child would face after being brought up in an
institution and then leaving it to face the even harsher realities of independence. The effects
of institutionalisation for a child who had spent his or her formative years in the workhouse
could be two-fold. It could instil a determination in the child to escape the workhouse
and stay out of it. However, this might be more prevalent in children who had entered the
workhouse later in their childhood and knew what the alternative of a real home was like.

On the other hand, there was a belief that:

> …those who were brought up in the workhouse were marked by a tendency to regard the
> workhouse as their natural home. They had been accustomed to the workhouse from early
> infancy…and when they were adults there was nothing to deter them from entering it.[39]

It was in the interests of all unions to take into careful consideration the future of the children in the workhouse. At eleven, twelve or thirteen years of age, children were boarded-out, apprenticed to learn a trade or sent into service. Apprenticeships and situations where girls could go into service had to be chosen carefully, as did possible homes where children could be boarded-out. If both children and employers were happy, there was less chance of the children being returned to the workhouse. This, in turn, ensured that the financial burden on the ratepayers was reduced.

IN SERVICE

Between the ages of eleven and thirteen, workhouse girls were sent into service. Some workhouses advertised in the local newspaper for placements whilst others were approached directly by employers looking for servants. At smaller unions such as Sedgefield in County Durham, the master himself used his local contacts to find placements for the workhouse children.

While boys were well catered for in terms of industrial training, it seems girls were less prepared for the world of work. In the 1880s, the Dudley Union attempted to solve this problem. A 'Training Home' for some of the girls was established under the auspices of the Dudley Girls Friendly Society 'for the purpose of training such girls for Domestic duties and obtaining for them suitable places of service.'[40]

APPRENTICESHIPS

Boys were apprenticed out to trades in the hope that they would be able to support themselves afterwards. However, it has been argued that the trades taught to workhouse children such as shoemaking and tailoring would earn them low wages and, therefore, the children were likely to return to the workhouse in later years.[41] A critic from the 1860s warned that instructors of shoemaking and tailoring were only easy to find because the trades were already saturated.[42]

In unions situated near the coast, the fishing industry was a useful source of apprenticeships. In February 1857, seventeen-year-old Charles Cuerton, an inmate of St Marylebone Workhouse, was indentured to John Forge, a fishing smack owner of the ship *Brilliant* from Barking, Essex, for a term of five years. The guardians of St Marylebone paid the sum of five pounds to John Forge, in return for which he was to teach 'the said Apprentice the business of a Seaman, and provide the said Apprentice with sufficient Meat, Drink, Lodging, Washing, Medicine, and Medical and Surgical Assistance…and so provide for the said Apprentice, that he be not a charge to the said Parish…'[43]

Apprenticeships were not always restricted to businesses within the union. In March 1897, Frederick Broadley of the Bromsgrove Union was apprenticed to the 'International Steam Trawling Company' at Grimsby. A few weeks later, the guardians received a letter from the company stating that 'Frederick was off on a fishing expedition to Iceland'. On 4 May, the board received a letter from Frederick 'stating that he liked the sea and would rather be on the sea than on land and that after another trip he should be bound.'[44]

EMIGRATION

For some workhouse children, especially orphans (although not exclusively), emigration to another country was an option. Once the cost of emigration was paid for, the emigrating child would no longer be chargeable to the union. Church organisations, both Anglican and Roman Catholic, were at the forefront of child emigration.

STRANGERS.

FATHER CHRISTMAS. " WHAT ! NOT KNOW *ME !*—OH, THIS MUST BE ALTERED ! "

Strangers. (Punch, 29 December 1883.)

From 1869, Maria Rye specifically recruited Anglican girls from workhouses to go to Canada, regularly sending circular letters to the unions. She 'preferred to take the children from the workhouses because then the education was undertaken and paid for by the workhouses and not by herself.' She bought 'with contributions from some influential men, the old court-house and gaol at Niagara-on-the-Lake, Ontario.' This was converted into a distribution home and named 'Our Western Home', officially opened on 1 December, 1869. Almost immediately upon arrival, the children were placed with families.

By 1872, thirty-six unions including London, Bromsgrove and Hereford were using Miss Rye's services. In the same year, with the support of *The Times*, Miss Rye raised money to buy Avenue House on the High Street in Peckham. Avenue House was under the authority of Miss Rye's sister, Elizabeth, the superintendent. It catered for about sixty to seventy girls who were given three month's training before being sent out to 'Our Western Home'.[45]

Sixteen-year-old Mary Ann Webb was sent to Avenue House in November 1886 by the guardians of the Dudley Union.[46] She had spent five years at the Dorset Home Industrial School in Poole as a punishment for 'stealing oranges'.[47] Her widowed mother was a blind inmate of the Dudley Union Workhouse and had granted consent for Mary Ann to go to Canada. Mary Ann arrived in Canada on the SS *Circassian* in April 1887 and was placed in service with a doctor's family in Ontario.[48]

While Maria Rye recruited girls for emigration, other church societies recruited boys and families of both sexes. In May 1885, eleven-year-old Steven Geoghan and his sisters Grace and Laura were sent from the Stoke-on-Trent Union Workhouse to Liverpool, where they joined the SS *Parisian* bound for Canada. The children travelled with the Catholic Protection Society of Liverpool and their names were changed to Gagan on the passenger list. It is not known why the children were sent to Canada. In ordinary circumstances, union workhouses had to obtain permission from parents before emigration could be sanctioned by the Poor Law Board. It would appear that the children's mother, Louisa, was abandoned by her husband and believed him to be dead. She re-married in the same year the children emigrated, giving her marital status as 'widow'. In fact, her husband was still alive. Louisa may simply have realised she could not provide for her children and believed that a new life in Canada was a better option for them. On arrival in Ottawa, the children were sent to a certified industrial school before the girls went into service and Stephen was sent to be a farm labourer.[49]

INTO THE TWENTIETH CENTURY

By the beginning of the twentieth century, most medium to large unions had moved their children out of the workhouse, either by boarding them out with foster parents, to cottage or 'scattered' homes or to specialist institutions.

The move towards more specialised institutions meant that living conditions for workhouse children would generally have improved. Yet the stigma of being a workhouse child still remained, something which was doubly difficult to escape if the workhouse was also a child's place of birth. From 1904, in order to prevent prejudice against children born in the workhouse, registrars of births could disguise the place of birth by substituting 'a fictitious name or non-committal street number for the workhouse address.'[50]

THE ELDERLY

The workhouse was feared the most by the elderly. Old men and women who became workhouse inmates suffered the indignity of knowing that their lives would end in the institution. This was sadly inevitable for the elderly if they became ill and could no longer support themselves. Such a fate was more likely if they also had no family to look after them, but old men and women with grown-up children also frequented the workhouse. Elderly inmates fell into Class 1 and 4 as they were 'men and women infirm through age or any other cause.'

LEAVING HOME

In the Victorian period, it was not uncommon for parents to have buried their children before they reached old age. One inmate at the St Pancras Union Workhouse was a feeble, elderly woman 'beyond threescore and ten' who had lost her husband and her children. She explained to a visitor: 'I have no-one to care for me now. I have buried my husband two years ago. He died in the men's ward. I have also lost nine children. Haven't a relative to wish me well, or when I die to close my eyes...'[1]

Reluctance on the part of the elderly to enter the workhouse was understandable. It meant a loss of independence and leaving the home in which he or she might have lived for years. In the 1870s, an old labourer became an inmate of a West Country workhouse. He:

> ...felt cut-off from all that was reassuring and familiar. Although the food was better than he had 'existed on for years'...it was not his dinner. He was not sitting in his own chair, at his own old table, round which his children had once gathered. He had not planted the cabbage, and tended it while it grew.

The dormitory in which he slept was:

> ...not his old bedroom up the worm-eaten steps, with the slanting ceiling, where, as he woke in the morning he could hear the sparrows chirping, the chaffinch calling, and the lark singing aloft.[2]

Going to the workhouse was a bitter pill to swallow for those who had been fiercely independent, and had always been able to get by and look after themselves. Flora Thompson recalled the day an elderly man known as 'the Major' had to be admitted to the workhouse:

Old Age – A Study at the Westminster Union by Hubert Herkomer. In the women's day-room, the old women sit on hard, backless benches. The women in the foreground are probably making new workhouse uniforms. (*The Graphic*, 7 April 1877.)

> The day came when the doctor called in the relieving officer. The old man was seriously ill; he had no relatives. There was only one place where he could be properly looked after, and that was the workhouse infirmary.... As soon as he realised where he was being taken, the old soldier, the independent old bachelor, the kind family friend, collapsed and cried like a child. He was beaten. But not for long. Before six weeks were over he was back in the parish and all his troubles were over, for he came in his coffin.[3]

For some elderly inmates, the workhouse really was a godsend, especially if they were seriously ill and needed hospital treatment. Eighty-two-year-old Mary Thomas was brought into the Lampeter Union Workhouse on 1 May 1896. The master recorded: 'She was in an awful state of filth and covered with vermin. We had to cut her things off with a pair of scissors and burn everything. She never recovered consciousness and died on the 4th instant, the immediate cause of death being paralysis.'[4]

LIVING CONDITIONS

In most union workhouses, the accommodation for the elderly differed little from that of the other inmates. The majority of aged inmates lived in crowded dormitories with little chance of any privacy. In 1889, one elderly male inmate told a visitor: 'I sleep in a ward with about forty men. Some of them snore terribly. When they do so, the next-door neighbour will catch hold of their clothes and pull them off, and at this there will be some hard words muttered.'[5] This was true communal living with 'no lockers for personal possessions'.[6]

One visitor commented on the tense relationships between elderly inmates: 'I could imagine how, in a large ward, with little variety of things to engage their thoughts, trifles could be magnified, and every word and movement bitterly criticised. The attendants have to be very firm sometimes in suppressing the bitterness of the inmates towards one another.'[7]

A SKETCH AT ST. PANCRAS.

An elderly female inmate at
the St Pancras Workhouse.
(*The Quiver*, July 1889.)

The old men and women had plenty of time for reflection, as work for the elderly was
not always insisted upon. Feelings of depression and resignation to their fate would have
been common, only alleviated, perhaps, by gossip. Such feelings cannot have boded well for
combating the 'sheer boredom of workhouse life' which was commented on by most visitors
to workhouses, including Charles Dickens and H. Rider-Haggard.[8]

Rider-Haggard recorded seeing:

> ...the old, old women lying in bed too feeble to move, or crouching round the fire in their
> mob-caps, some of them stern-faced with much gazing down the dim vista of the past,
> peopled for them with the dead, with much brooding on the present and the lot which it
> has brought them...[9]

At one workhouse visited by Dickens:

> ...some old people were bed-ridden, and had been for a long time; some were sitting on their beds half-naked; some dying in their beds; some out of bed, and sitting at a table near the fire. A sullen or lethargic indifference to what was asked; a blunted sensibility to everything but warmth and food, a moody absence of complaint as being of no use, a dogged silence and resentful desire to be left alone again, I thought were generally apparent.[10]

Once they were admitted to the workhouse, elderly inmates often became long-term residents. At Lampeter in 1891, the master recorded 'That Jenkin Davies aged eighty-one years, an Inmate died on the 11th instant the cause of death being debility and old age. He had been an inmate for eight years.'[11]

The elderly had to wear a uniform just like the other inmates and this differed around the country. In 1889 at St Pancras Union Workhouse, the elderly men wore a uniform of 'rough brown cloth with brass buttons and lightish corduroy trousers' while the elderly women were dressed in a 'white cap, small reddish plaid shawl, and blue cotton gown...'[12]

ACCOMMODATION FOR MARRIED COUPLES

In the majority of cases, elderly couples were separated on entering the workhouse. This was despite a ruling by the Poor Law Board in 1847 which required unions to provide separate bedrooms for couples over sixty, if requested. Many unions were slow to provide accommodation for married elderly couples because of the additional burden this placed on the rates.

However, when elderly married couples entered the workhouse together, it was often the case that one of them was too ill to be placed in the main ward and had to be admitted to the infirmary. It was therefore not possible for many married couples to be accommodated together. The fact that couples had to request that they remain together must have limited the numbers, especially at unions where it was known that separate accommodation was not available.

At one workhouse with over 1,000 aged inmates, it was usually the case that:

> ...couples who have been married as many as forty years are for the last four or five years of their lives practically separated from one another...there was only accommodation for twelve couples. Their quarters are called rooms, but in fact are simply divisions...about the same size as those seen in common lodging houses, with partitions...on the death of any occupant, these quarters are sought after...[13]

The Great Yarmouth Union solved the problem of finding the extra accommodation when, in 1881, they agreed to allow the married old men and women over the age of sixty to live together in 'rooms in a wooden building which could be fitted out for the purpose'.[14]

By 1895, only 200 married couples had their own rooms in the workhouse.[15] Six of these couples were at the West Bromwich Union where this level of provision was considered 'ample...for this humane regulation'.[16]

PAUPER BURIALS

In addition to the loss of independence, elderly inmates faced a fate that was commonly feared – a pauper burial. In the early years of the new Poor Law, the Poor Law Commission ruled that 'paupers be buried as cheaply as possible, and that the bells be not rung at the funeral, to save expense'.[17]

Rumours spread about the nature of such pauper burials. In Kent in 1836, an Inspector discovered that '…it was circulated in this county that the children in the workhouses were killed to make pies with, while the old when dead were employed to manure the guardians' fields, in order to save the expense of coffins.'[18]

At the Bromley Union in 1855, the guardians received a complaint about the coffin a pauper child had been buried in. The indignant clergyman who had conducted the funeral claimed that it was so disgraceful that 'any tradesman would be ashamed to send so rough a packing case for the most common articles.'[19]

Pauper burials were feared so much that 'working people were prepared to pay weekly contributions which they could often ill afford into a friendly society or burial club. Almost every middle-class investigator commented on the strength of this tradition among the working classes.'[20]

As well as the possibility of a pauper burial, under the Anatomy Act of 1832 medical institutions could request the bodies of unclaimed paupers for dissection purposes. Although unions had to give permission for this, and by no means all did, the elderly feared that 'their bodies would be turned over to medical schools for dissection' and therefore not receive a proper burial.[21]

PRIVILEGES FOR THE ELDERLY

Like the other inmates, the elderly were confined to the workhouse unless given permission to leave by the master. The frequency of leave of absence varied considerably across England and Wales. At the Dudley Union in 1872, the elderly inmates were allowed leave of absence once a week to visit friends or relatives.[22] The guardians of the King's Norton Union were less lenient, only allowing 'Leave of absence once a month for Inmates over sixty and of good conduct.'[23]

An elderly man whom Charles Dickens met at a London workhouse in 1850 begged for more liberty:

> I am greatly better in my health, Sir; but what I want, to get me quite round is a little fresh air, Sir. It has always done my complaint so much good, Sir. The regular leave for going out, comes round so seldom, that if the gentlemen, next Friday, would give me leave to go out walking, now and then – for only an hour or so, Sir!'[24]

Forty years later, a witness to the Royal Commission on the Aged Poor in February 1894 stated that 'it is the confinement that is the greatest evil'. In response to this, the following year the aged and infirm were allowed to 'attend their own places of worship' on Sundays but this was restricted to the 'well-behaved' only.[25]

Some unions were compassionate towards their elderly inmates from the early days of the new Poor Law. At the Dudley Union in 1860, when the chairman of the board of guardians complained about the amount of gas which had been used for heating, the Visiting Committee found that '…in consequence of the aged and infirm Inmates complaining of the coldness of the Dining and Bed Rooms some extra Gas has been burnt for warmth during the Winter Months.'[26] It is not known if this high consumption of gas was allowed to continue.

In the 1890s, elderly inmates benefited from extra privileges to make their lives in the workhouse more comfortable. This may have been due in part to the influence of the increasing number of women guardians on the board of unions across England and Wales. It was also as a result of the Local Government Board relaxing its draconian attitude towards elderly inmates. By 1896, the board instructed unions to abandon 'the policy of treating everyone in the workhouse alike'.[27] For the old men and women, this meant less restrictive meal times and relaxed hours for rising and going to bed. Most importantly, the board recommended that 'all but the most untrustworthy old people should be allowed to go out for walks'.[28]

Waiting for Dinner at the St Pancras Workhouse. (*The Quiver*, July 1889.)

However, disagreement between guardians about the treatment of elderly inmates still existed. In 1895, one of the guardians of the Wokingham Union proposed that 'overcoats be provided for all the aged men' who were fit enough to go out of the workhouse and that 'aged Inmates be allowed to go out every fine day instead of being kept in during four days of the week'. Both suggestions were rejected.[29]

Although prison inmates were frequently served tea and cocoa, workhouse inmates were not allowed dry tea or sugar to brew their own hot drinks. This rule was strictly adhered to until 1893 when the Local Government Board advised the unions that they could 'allow elderly inmates "dry tea", with milk and sugar, to brew their own drinks, without having to seek special permission from the Board, coffee and cocoa being added later.'[30]

In 1892, after a vigorous campaign by the authorities at Liverpool, the elderly men of that union were granted a small weekly allowance of tobacco. This right was extended to men and women over the age of sixty in all unions later that year.[31] At the Christchurch Union in 1895, the old men were granted a very special privilege: their own smoking room. This was a privilege denied to all the other inmates, especially 'the loathed able-bodied men'.[32]

WORK

Despite their age, the elderly were not excluded from completing work tasks at the workhouse if they were fit and able. In many cases, elderly inmates worked voluntarily to keep themselves occupied. It was reported that 'in nearly every workhouse could be found aged inmates who worked without compulsion: to act as nurse, wardsman, night porter, or even voluntary cleaner, was to salvage a fragment of identity and self-respect.'[33]

In 1889 at the St Pancras Union Workhouse, one of the old men complained: 'We have to pick oakum, and if we don't do our right amount we are put on bread and water. Between breakfast and dinner some go into the oakum shed, others go to tailoring or boot repairing.'[34] Elderly women were more likely to be set to work than the men as they could make themselves useful around the house with such tasks as repairing clothes, nursing or cleaning.

The Brabazon scheme, started in 1882 by the Countess of Meath, aimed to train the elderly in making handicrafts, which could be sold to obtain comforts for the makers. A kind of occupational therapy, it was usually supervised by members of a ladies' committee for the union. It is believed that this scheme was popular with the inmates because 'it was not run by the workhouse staff'.[35] It was also a welcome change from the more arduous labour of the workhouse. By 1900, 177 unions were participating in the scheme.[36]

Great Yarmouth was one such participating union. In 1903, Queen Alexandra paid five pounds for a bedspread at the Brabazon sale. The intricately designed bedspread had been made by two elderly inmates, Mrs Honour Girling and Mrs Elizabeth Ablett. By purchasing the bedspread, Queen Alexandra hoped to 'encourage the old people in their work'.[37]

In the 1890s at the Christchurch Union, it was the old men who were involved in the Brabazon scheme while the old women 'had their full employ in other work'.[38] The old men made a variety of goods such as baskets, rugs, wickerwork and woollen clothing which were sold 'to raise funds for new materials or to provide extras for the wards, for example, a gramophone'.[39] The men received payment in kind for their labours, usually extra tobacco.

REMOVALS

As mentioned in chapter 2, the laws of settlement were still strictly enforced under the new Poor Law. Allowances were rarely made for elderly inmates who were faced with removal to their settlement parish. In 1841, Alexander Repper, a sixty-five-year-old former marine, was a resident of the Helston Union Workhouse in Cornwall. It is believed that he was removed to Helston, the place of his birth, from London where he had lived prior to becoming a marine.[40]

Some unions were more compassionate. At Lampeter Union Workhouse in 1889, the master was directed by the board to remove Evan Evans, a pauper inmate, to the Llandeilo Union. He reported that:

> I made arrangements to remove the pauper, when he told me that he would not accompany me to Llandeilo. I informed him that in that case he had no alternative but to take his discharge but he said he would not leave the House unless he was compelled. As the pauper is an old man without any friends near Lampeter I have allowed him to remain in the House to receive the further directions of the guardians in the matter.

It is not known whether Evan Evans was removed to Llandeilo but he discharged himself from Lampeter three days later.[41]

CHARITY

From the 1850s, workhouses were opened up to visitors, and elderly inmates soon started to benefit from the greater contact with the outside world. Spearheaded by the Workhouse Visiting Society, visitors might bring books, magazines or flowers. More importantly, they brought news from outside, conversation and interaction with someone unconnected with the workhouse.

The women's day room or ward at the Hackney Workhouse, *c.*1900. (Ref. P3303. Courtesy of Hackney Archives Department.)

Later in the century, caring visitors might offer to take the elderly out of the workhouse for an afternoon, a privilege previously reserved for the children. In May 1896 at the Dudley Union, the guardians 'Resolved …that the application of Miss Bradley of Wolverhampton Street, Dudley to Entertain at Tea the Aged Female Inmates of the Workhouse at her Residence be granted'.[42]

CONTRIBUTIONS FROM RELATIVES

As with abandoned pregnant mothers and children, the guardians of all unions sought contributions from the relatives of elderly inmates to help meet the cost of indoor relief. In Norfolk in the 1880s, George Edwards paid 1s 3d per week as a contribution towards his mother's weekly 2s 6d poor relief.[43]

In many cases, it was extremely difficult for family members to contribute to the cost of their parents' poor relief, especially if they had large families of their own to provide for. In October 1850, Thomas Claggett, a grocer, was summoned to Southwark Police Court by the parochial authorities of St George's 'for refusing to contribute to the Maintenance of one of his Parents'. The defendant's mother, an aged widow, had applied for and obtained relief from the parish but her son 'had refused to contribute to her support, although a brother of his, who was only a shopman, and at very low wages, allowed her a trifle a week out of them, but not sufficient to defray her expenses.' Thomas Claggett, a well-dressed man responded that 'Appearances are deceitful; my expenses are considerable, and the profits on my business are very small; there is so much competition in the grocery line especially…I pay 45*l.* [rent] and taxes, and that is as much as I can do.'[44]

Fifty years later, in 1900, the guardians of the Aberystwyth Union wanted William Evans of Triorchy to increase his contributions towards his mother's maintenance in the workhouse. On 8 May, he wrote the following letter of protest:

Gentlemen, I have paid towards my mother the sum of 1/6 per week regularly. I cannot possibly pay more for the following reasons:

1) That I am married
2) That my wife is ill, and I am compelled to employ a servant
3) That my remit is 25/ per month
4) That my wages comparatively are small

Your Worships will please note that after deducting expenses, I have very little to spare… Your Worships may probably think that we, in the Rhondda Valley earn more money than we actually do.

It is so expensive to appear personally, but I hope this letter will satisfy you.

Yours obediently,

William Evans[45]

In rural unions, when children could not afford to make monetary contributions towards the relief of their elderly relatives in the workhouse, 'they might be able to supply vegetables from the garden or kindling from the fire'.[46] Elderly inmates did not like to be a burden to their family and it was commonly believed that '[The] Aged prefer a pittance from the parish (regarded as their due) to compulsory maintenance by children; compulsion makes such aid very bitter.'[47]

PENSIONS

The Old Age Pensions Act of 1908 brought in the first state pensions for men and women over the age of seventy. This was a non-contributory pension of five shillings per week for everyone over seventy who had an income of 'less than eight shillings per week from other sources'.[48] There was a reduced pension for anyone with an income of between eight and twelve shillings per week. However, anyone with an income of more than twelve shillings per week received nothing. There were many exclusions, including anyone 'who had been imprisoned in the previous ten years, or who had claimed poor relief in the last two or who was a drunk, or who had habitually failed to find work.'[49] Therefore, anyone who had frequented the workhouses in the previous two years, for whatever reason, was excluded from receiving the new state pension.

INTO THE TWENTIETH CENTURY

Towards the end of the nineteenth century, conditions for the elderly started to improve. In 1900, the Local Government Board ruled that outdoor relief be given to the 'aged deserving poor'. If indoor relief was necessary, it was recommended that the elderly be 'granted certain privileges which could not be accorded to every inmate of the workhouse'.[50] These privileges were to include 'flexible eating and sleeping times, greater visiting rights, and the compulsory provision of tobacco, dry tea (so that they could make a cup whenever they wanted) and sugar.'[51]

More concessions were granted to the elderly inmates, including the recommendation by the Local Government Board that separate day-rooms should be provided for those who had 'previously led moral and respectable lives.'[52] By the end of the nineteenth century, the majority of unions were implementing some kind of segregation on moral grounds, particularly for elderly inmates.

The Sheffield Union was even more enlightened. By 1897, they had built eight one-roomed cottages to accommodate elderly inmates 'either by a married couple, or by two men, or two women...' Only old men and women from Class A were entitled to be admitted to the cottages. These were inmates who were 'Aged and infirm over sixty years of age who have resided in the Sheffield Union for a period of not less than twenty years before applying for relief; who have not had relief during that time; whose character will bear the strictest investigation during that time, and who, through no fault of their own, have been unable to provide for old age.' Known as Firvale Cottages, there was a caretaker's house in the centre and 'all are connected together by a corridor, useful for exercise in bad weather, whence access is obtained to the bath-rooms and other conveniences.' As well as the high standard of accommodation, the occupants' 'dinners are cooked in the central kitchen by the Caretaker, but they prepare their other meals themselves...' They were 'quite free to pay visits to or receive visits from their friends'.[53]

At Maldon in 1901, twelve Windsor chairs were purchased for the elderly inmates and, in 1906, chairs were added to the bedrooms. The Maldon Board of Guardians also paid £3 to replenish the library and 'spent one shilling and four pence per month on "periodicals", for which later bound magazines, two halfpenny newspapers and a weekly local paper were substituted.'[54]

In general, conditions for the elderly inmates had changed beyond recognition by the end of the Edwardian period. A Poor Law Inspector commented that: 'The aged and infirm enjoy a large amount of liberty, they are only set to such light tasks as are sufficient to occupy them pleasantly and in all material conditions of feeding, housing and clothing they are much better off than the aged poor outside... I have often heard an aged inmate say that he had always declared that he would die rather than enter "the house", but if he had known that it was so comfortable he would have come there long ago.'[55]

THE INFIRM

In the nineteenth century, there was a very thin line between a family just getting by and poverty. Illness or an accident could strike at any time, immediately removing the breadwinner's ability to work and therefore earn wages to feed his or her family.

SICKNESS AMONG THE POOR

The labouring poor needing more than rudimentary medical treatment had two possible options. They could go to a voluntary, charitable hospital for free treatment or they could go to their local workhouse infirmary. However, voluntary hospitals excluded certain kinds of patients on 'social or medical grounds' including the truly destitute since they were 'viewed as having moral failings'.[1] Incurables, the chronically or mentally ill and those with infectious diseases were also rejected. While voluntary hospitals preferred to admit 'curable and interesting cases', they worked side by side with workhouse infirmaries to treat the poor. Once a voluntary hospital patient had passed the acute stage of illness, he or she was often discharged to a workhouse infirmary. In the same way, difficult surgical cases were often passed from the workhouse infirmary to a voluntary hospital.[2]

SICK CLUBS

Where labourers or more skilled craftsmen were in regular, well-paid employment, it was a popular custom to contribute to a sick club or friendly society. This was a kind of insurance scheme whereby if a member fell ill, he could expect to receive benefits of around 3s 6d to 6s per week during his illness. He could also expect to be attended by a club doctor 'at a fee of 2s 6d or so per member per annum.'[3]

One such society was the Friendly and Benefit Society of Butleigh in Somerset. In return for a contribution of four shillings per quarter, the society promised to provide for 'the comfortable relief of its respective members in cases of Sickness, &c.'[4]

The custom of contributing to sick clubs was widespread in the Dudley Union where, in 1855, the guardians reacted vehemently to the suggestion by the Poor Law Board that there should be an increase in the number of medical officers. They replied that 'the Board is decidedly of the opinion that additional medical aid is totally useless and uncalled for on these grounds; that sick Clubs and Benefit Societies exist so very generally in this district, and provide medical aid for a vast amount of the population.'[5] They added that in the district of Dudley and Netherton there were thirteen surgeons 'who are engaged either as Club or Colliery surgeons'.[6]

The Halifax Poor Law Infirmary, 1905.

WHO WENT TO WORKHOUSE INFIRMARIES?

For those of the labouring poor who could not afford to pay contributions to sick clubs or who were rejected for admission to voluntary hospitals, they had no option other than to seek help from their Poor Law union. Under the terms of the 1834 Poor Law Amendment Act, unions were required to appoint medical officers to tend to the union's sick. There was to be a medical officer for the workhouse itself and additional medical officers to look after the outdoor paupers in the districts of the union. In small unions, there might be one medical officer to cover both the workhouse and the district.

Male and female inmates who were sick and could not work to feed their families were placed in Class 1 and Class 4 respectively as they were 'infirm through age or any other cause'. The patients in workhouse infirmaries tended to be the elderly, the incurably sick, lunatics and epileptics and those with infectious diseases such as smallpox and venereal disease.

In December 1848, Sarah Bradford, a fifty-seven-year-old laundress, was admitted to St Marylebone Workhouse in London. Sarah had brought up her two children, Matthew and William Thomas, on her own following the death of their father, George Coombs in the 1830s. Her reason for admittance was illness, possibly some kind of mental illness. Sarah remained in the workhouse until 16 February 1851 when she died of cerebral disease, aged sixty. A fellow inmate, Mrs Elizabeth Mockford, probably nursed Sarah throughout her illness as she was the informant of Sarah's death. Elderly pauper inmates like Mrs Mockford were the backbone of the unpaid nursing staff in workhouses.[7]

ILLNESSES TREATED IN THE WORKHOUSE

Patients in workhouse infirmaries were usually afflicted with chronic illnesses or infectious diseases which excluded them from treatment in the better equipped voluntary hospitals. It was a cruel irony that paupers suffering with infectious diseases such as tuberculosis and scarlet fever were forced to seek medical treatment at the workhouse infirmaries, which were themselves hotbeds for disease. The haphazard arrangement of wards in older buildings with insufficient ventilation and a lack of accommodation to isolate infectious cases meant that workhouse infirmaries were rarely able to treat such patients effectively.

The West Bromwich Union Workhouse Infirmary (no date). (With thanks to Ann Gray.)

Such infectious diseases included ophthalmia, an infection of the conjunctiva which caused painful inflammation of the eye and, if untreated, could cause permanent blindness. This disease appears to have been particularly rife amongst workhouse children, although any institution housing children was susceptible to an outbreak of the disease. In fact, it was a court case resulting from two boys at a private school going blind from ophthalmia which inspired Charles Dickens to write *Nicholas Nickleby*.[8]

At the Dudley Union in 1862, thirty-six children were afflicted with the disease. The medical officer believed that 'probably the damp state of the School building may have been a predisposing cause of the disease...'[9]

Whilst scabies or 'the itch' was not a serious enough illness to warrant admission to a workhouse infirmary, it was another common contagious skin disease which thrived in the crowded wards of the workhouse. Caused by a parasite which burrowed in the skin, successful treatment was almost impossible unless the sufferers could be isolated. Both adults and children caught the disease but it appears that only children received medical treatment for it. This was 'possibly because the disease required long-term treatment, so that it was only children, permanently in the workhouse, who remained long enough to be cured.'[10]

Sufferers of venereal disease would have been summarily rejected by the voluntary hospitals on moral grounds. In the workhouse, they were admitted to the dreaded 'foul' wards and kept separate from the other inmates, again more on moral grounds than for health reasons. In 1843, Abraham Leach, the master of the Rochdale Union Workhouse, reported that 'the doctor finds great fault with the accommodation we have for the nasty ladies...'[11] These 'nasty ladies' were prostitutes who were regular 'ins and outs'. Every time they were admitted, they required medical attention for venereal disease.

Tuberculosis was 'one of the commonest causes which brought people to the workhouse infirmary.'[12] Between 1881 and 1890, one-ninth of the total death rate in England and Wales was due to tuberculosis.[13] A cruel, wasting disease, tuberculosis of the lungs, also known as consumption or phthisis, was easily contracted by malnourished paupers. A visitor to an East End workhouse in 1863 met a twenty-two-year-old widow of a sailor suffering from consumption who 'in appearance... was like a shadow.'[14] In 142 consecutive post-mortem examinations at an unnamed workhouse infirmary, almost one-third:

...were demonstrated to be due to tuberculosis of the lungs. In this class of society...the ravages of the tubercule bacillus seem to be even greater than in society as a whole.[15]

Liverpool was one of the more enlightened Poor Law infirmaries. Outside of London, it led the way in improving standards of nursing. In 1865, Agnes Jones, a disciple of Florence Nightingale, was appointed matron at the Liverpool Union Infirmary which housed almost 1,300 patients. Agnes had charge of sixty nurses plus 150 'scourers' and 'carriers'. She brought a rare 'spirit of kindness' to the whole workhouse, something distinctly lacking in many other union infirmaries. Agnes died just three years later after contracting typhus on the wards.[16]

CONDITIONS WITHIN THE INFIRMARY

As unions sought to reduce the burden on the rates, in 1840 only £150,000 out of a total Poor Law expenditure of £4.5 million was spent on medical services.[17] This meant that conditions in workhouse infirmaries were poor with neglect of patients caused by a lack of staff, trained or otherwise. In order to adhere to the principles of the workhouse test, it was always intended that conditions in Poor Law hospitals should be 'worse than those in the voluntary hospitals'.[18] Indeed, the workhouse infirmaries were 'intended only for the short-term use of the workhouse inmates and most were unable to meet the demands of the long-term sick who needed care.'[19]

What was it like to be a sick pauper in a workhouse infirmary? The *Dudley Herald* of February 1868 cited the Report of Edward Smith, a Medical Officer of the Poor Law Board, issued as a result of his visit to Dudley Union Workhouse on 16 March 1867. According to Smith, the infirmary lacked '...that air of comfort and convenience which should be found in sick wards.'[20] Smith noted that the ground floor was made of brick, which he thought would be cold for patients. There was a detached fever hospital but no padded room for lunatics and no proper lavatories. Smith observed there was also 'a want of chairs and other furniture'.[21]

The beds in workhouse infirmaries were generally not fit for their purpose. In 1861, a female workhouse visitor to a Bristol workhouse observed that:

> The same rough beds (generally made with one thin mattress laid on iron bars) which are allotted to the rude able-bodied paupers, are equally given to the poor, emaciated bed-ridden patient, whose frame is probably sore all over, and whose aching head must remain, for want of pillows, in nearly a horizontal position for months together.[22]

The *Leeds Mercury* reported that the sick inmates of the Huddersfield Workhouse infirmary slept on beds which were 'but bags of straw' and it was said that 'for twenty-three beds in that hospital, on the twenty-seventh of last April, there were but seven blankets, thirty sheets, twenty-one pillow-cases, and fifteen rugs.' In addition, 'still the practice obtains of placing two fever patients in one bed; that from the want of needful changes, the bed clothing, among which the fever patients have died, is obliged to be used for other patients, without being washed.'[23]

General hygiene in workhouse infirmaries left much to be desired. Robert Tatham, a medical officer, described the floors of the Huddersfield Workhouse infirmary as being:

> ...filthy. I don't think they had been washed down throughout the hospital, from the time of its being opened; marks of uncleanliness presented themselves nearly everywhere; cobwebs hung from the ceilings; the coverings of the beds were very deficient – mere rags some of them; some of the blankets would hardly hold together if you would shake them...[24]

The dreaded 'foul' wards were frequently in a worse condition than the wards of the main infirmary. Charles Dickens described the foul wards of Wapping Workhouse which housed sufferers of venereal and skin diseases thus:

The Park Hospital, Hither Green, one of London's fever hospitals, built in the 1890s.

They were in a building monstrously behind the time – a mere series of garrets and lofts… and only accessible by steep and narrow staircases, infamously ill-adapted for the passage upstairs of the sick or downstairs of the dead.[25]

At the foul wards of the Lambeth Workhouse, an inspector met a wardsman who kept a jug of salt under his bed. When asked what it was for, the wardsman replied 'that he could not do without it, for he used it to destroy the lice which he sometimes found in the beds.'[26]

In 1856, Louisa Twining, founder of both the Association for Promoting Trained Nursing in Workhouse Infirmaries and the Workhouse Visiting Society, visited the St Giles's Union Workhouse. She found:

…one poor young man there, who had lain on a miserable flock bed for fourteen years with spine complaint, was blind, and his case would have moved a heart of stone; yet no alleviation of food or comforts were ever granted him, his sole consolation being the visits of a good woman, an inmate, who had been a ratepayer, and attended upon him daily, reading to him to while away the dreary hours.[27]

QUALITY OF NURSING

Visitors to union workhouses across England and Wales all commented on the lack of paid nurses to tend to the sick. Where there was a paid nurse, unpaid paupers were used to supplement the nursing staff.

In the 1890s, a Poor Law inspector of workhouses in East Anglia recorded that:

The nursing was the weakest point. Not infrequently a single paid nurse was in charge of thirty or forty patients, and this meant that almost everything for the sick had to be done by pauper inmates. They had nothing to gain if they did the duty assigned to them well, nothing to lose if they did it badly…most of them were not disposed to take much trouble in attending to helpless old folk requiring assistance…[28]

In 1896 at the Clitheroe Union, the nursing was undertaken by one paid nurse and the matron, Catherine Lofthouse. When Catherine was confined to bed as a result of illness, this led to a 'drastic reduction in nursing capacity in the hospital and standards inevitably declined.'[29] A routine visit by a Local Government Board inspector revealed that two patients, Margaret Embley and James Bailey, had serious bed sores. An official inquiry followed which eventually led to the appointment of a night nurse.[30]

This situation was mirrored elsewhere. Louisa Twining claimed that 'the grosser evils of the previous decades had been replaced by passive cruelty.'[31] She observed that in many workhouses:

> ...the old and infirm were put to bed and kept there, for there was no-one to dress them, and the passive cruelty was general; the bed sores were frequent, though they were called 'eczema', and yet what could one nurse, much less an untrained girl, do with eighty or ninety cases under her care?[32]

OVERCROWDING

The fact that unions were frequently concerned about the high cost of the workhouse was reflected in the overcrowded state of a large number of workhouse infirmaries across England and Wales. Such conditions were hotbeds for disease and did not augur well for the retention or improvement of health. When infectious disease did occur, there were often no spare wards in which to isolate the victims, as in December 1879, when the children at the Dudley Union contracted scarlet fever.[33]

In February 1861, just under two years after the opening of the new Dudley Union Workhouse, it was reported that the infirmary was 'full and more room [was] required for the sick and lame'.[34] From this time on, various temporary accommodation was used to house sick paupers. This included 'a room intended as a shop for Industrial training,' obviously unsuitable for medical purposes.[35]

By June 1867, recommendations were made to enlarge the infirmary further by raising the two ends of the buildings.[36] When built, it was claimed that the new buildings would 'supply the necessary space for upward of a hundred additional Beds.'[37] As the infirmary would then be able to house 285 patients, and the Medical Officer reported that he had '331 cases upon his books' there was to be little reduction in the problem of overcrowding.[38] In addition, there were no safeguards for future overcrowding.

This rebuilding on existing sites and areas corroborates the argument that 'wherever possible ... old buildings were utilised for workhouse infirmaries, and when new building was unavoidable, specifications were pared to the absolute minimum.'[39]

DIET FOR THE SICK

It was the workhouse medical officer's responsibility to recommend specific diets for the sick which had to be ratified by the guardians of the union. In 1848 at the King's Lynn Union, there were different diets for the 'full sick', 'half sick' and 'low sick'. There were also diets for those with a fever. Women during confinement were allowed bread, dumplings and gravy while women suckling children were granted extra bread and sugar.[40]

REFORM OF WORKHOUSE INFIRMARIES

If Sarah Bradford, the laundress who died in St Marylebone Workhouse in 1848, had been an inmate after about 1870, she would have experienced a far higher standard of care. The appalling conditions within London workhouse infirmaries were highlighted by a report produced by the influential medical journal *The Lancet* between 1865 and 1866. This led to the founding of The Association for Improving London Workhouse Infirmaries in 1866 and an official government inquiry of the same year.

As a result, the Metropolitan Poor Law Amendment Act of 1867 allowed London Poor Law unions to set up Poor Law infirmaries separate from the workhouse. By 1882, London had six fever hospitals, four asylums and twenty infirmaries.[41] Although this new legislation did not apply to workhouses outside the capital, it did start to affect the way in which infirmaries were built around the country.

Under a memorandum from the Poor Law Board in 1868, it was recommended that 'care must be taken to avoid aggregating large numbers of inmates in a single block'. This was to encourage unions to separate the imbecile wards, schools, sick wards and isolation wards.[42] The new infirmaries were managed separately from the workhouse 'with a resident medical superintendent in charge of medical staff'.[43]

This undoubtedly had great benefits for the pauper patients. Under the previous arrangement, the infirmaries were managed by the master and matron in conjunction with the medical officer. Without a medical background and with the need to keep an eye on expenditure, the master and matron were not ideal managers of the infirmaries.

From the 1860s onwards, the majority of new workhouse infirmaries were built to pavilion designs which had separate ward blocks, pairs of windows opposite each other to provide cross-ventilation and two fireplaces to aid the circulation of air.[44]

AFTER THE 1860s

After the reforms of the 1860s, workhouse infirmaries were no longer exclusively for sick inmates. From this time onwards, people needing hospital treatment who lived in the parishes which the unions served began to be admitted straight into workhouse infirmaries. This meant that the parish medical officer did not have to travel so far to make visits. In fact, 'roughly one-third of Poor Law infirmary entrants were non-paupers'.[45]

A typical entrant to a workhouse infirmary was Thomas Preece. He was a fifty-three-year-old waggoner who drove for one of the railway companies. In 1885 he was admitted to the Kidderminster Workhouse infirmary suffering with pneumonia and died there shortly afterwards.[46]

In the same year, sixty-year-old Thomas Edgington was admitted to Oxford Union Workhouse. A labourer who worked on the railways, Thomas was also a professional cricketer. He died at the workhouse of 'paralysis', presumably meaning a stroke.[47]

Workhouse infirmaries did offer hope to the destitute poor. Smaller workhouses with few medical facilities often had extremely dedicated medical staff. In November 1900, the master of the Lampeter Union Workhouse recorded that 'Margaret Davies aged eighty-seven years from the Parish of Llanwren was brought into the House suffering from cancer on the arm… Dr Abel Evans and Dr E.C. Thomas performed an operation upon her and she is doing as well as can be expected'. Despite the success of the operation, Margaret Davies died two months later, the official cause being 'senile decay'.[48]

The standard of care in smaller workhouses had also improved. At the Sedgefield Union in County Durham in 1903, the master reported that:

A labouring Man named Thos. Burns was admitted into the workhouse on 13 January with the Medical Officer's order. The man was suffering from rupture & other complaints & was in the House seven days he had money & paid 7/6 for his maintenance.[49]

BIRMINGHAM AND MIDLAND EYE HOSPITAL,

295   CHURCH STREET, BIRMINGHAM.

CRANMER GELL, *Secretary*.

IN-PATIENT TICKET.
(AVAILABLE FOR FOURTEEN DAYS.)

ADMISSIBLE FROM

MICHAELMAS, 1894, to MICHAELMAS, 1895, only.

DAYS OF ATTENDANCE.

Mr. LLOYD OWEN ...   .   TUESDAYS AND FRIDAYS.
Mr. HENRY EALES ..   ..   WEDNESDAYS AND SATURDAYS.
Mr. WOOD WHITE ...   .   MONDAYS AND THURSDAYS.

I certify to the best of my knowledge and belief that

Name ....

Residing at ....

Age ....   Occupation .... *is a proper*

object for the relief afforded by your Institution, and recommend him or her for examination in order that, if duly qualified, he or she may be admitted as an IN-PATIENT of the Institution.

Dated the .... day of 189

Subscriber's Name ....

Address ....

PATIENTS ARE RECEIVED AT THE HOSPITAL EVERY MORNING (SUNDAY EXCEPTED) AT NINE O'CLOCK

**EYES EXAMINED AND SPECTACLES SUPPLIED FOR THREE OUT-PATIENT TICKETS.
AN ARTIFICIAL EYE IS SUPPLIED FOR AN IN-PATIENT TICKET.**

The Subscriber is earnestly requested not to give this Ticket of recommendation to any but a proper object for relief. The Secretary has received instructions to admit only such applicants.

(SEE BACK OF TICKET.)

(left margin) Subscribers of NOT LESS than £2 2s. 0d. per ANNUM, and residing more than FIVE MILES from the Hospital, can exchange Six of their OWN Out-patient Tickets for an In-patient Ticket, on application to the Secretary.

(right margin) Subscribers of not less than £2 2s. 0d. per annum can exchange an in-patient Ticket for Six out-patient Tickets, on application to the Secretary.

An in-patient ticket for the Birmingham and Midland Eye Hospital, 1894-1895. Union workhouses subscribed to specialist hospitals like this one and issued tickets to paupers needing specialist medical treatment. (Courtesy of Dr Paul Davies.)

SUBSCRIPTIONS TO SPECIALIST HOSPITALS

In addition to offering infirmary accommodation, most unions paid subscriptions to specialist hospitals in their local area. In some cases, these subscriptions were for workhouse inmates who needed more specialist treatment than the infirmary could provide. In other cases, the subscriptions paid for specialist hospital treatment for paupers receiving outdoor relief.

In January 1876, the guardians of the Dudley Union subscribed to no less than four hospitals plus a truss society for the following amounts:

Guest Hospital, Dudley   £6 6 0
General Hospital, Birmingham   £21 0 0

NOTICE.

The SUBSCRIBER or the PATIENT, previous to the latter coming into the Hospital, is particularly requested to ascertain from the HOUSE SURGEON if there is a BED VACANT, so as to prevent THE PATIENT being put to a USELESS EXPENSE; and In-patients should come provided with the necessary travelling expenses for their return home.

VISITING DAYS.

TUESDAYS and FRIDAYS, between 2 and 4 o'clock.

Patients must come clean and bring with them a change of clean linen, knife and fork, spoon, towel, comb, and pair of slippers.

Reverse of in-patient ticket for the Birmingham and Midland Eye Hospital, 1894–1895. (Courtesy of Dr Paul Davies.)

South Staffordshire General Hospital, Wolverhampton	£5 5 0
Birmingham Eye Hospital	£5 5 0
Dudley Truss Society	£10 10 0

The guardians explained that:

> ...each institution is opened for the reception of cases requiring special surgical treatment, either In or Outdoor, according to the class of tickets issued, which are found to be of great benefit to those cases where the several District Medical Officers are of the opinion that they can be better treated at the Hospital, than at their own homes.[50]

When the Local Government Board queried the subscription to the Dudley Truss Society, the guardians responded that the society 'has been of great advantage to a large number of poor persons who have been enabled to procure Trusses upon receiving a Ticket on the Society from the Guardians at a reduced price, which has been a considerable saving to the ratepayers of the Union.'[51] A truss was a surgical appliance worn to support a hernia, a common complaint amongst labourers whose work involved lifting heavy loads.

John Hobson, an inmate of the Dudley Union who was sent to the General Institution for the Blind in Birmingham, has already been mentioned in the chapter on children. Several years earlier, in July 1871, the guardians ordered that 'a further subscription of £1.1.0. be forwarded to the Eye Hospital at Birmingham in favour of John Hobson, an inmate of the Union Workhouse.'[52] Despite this treatment, it seems that nothing could be done to improve John's eyesight, as by 1875, when John was seventeen, the guardians had made the decision to send him to learn a trade at the General Institution for the Blind.[53]

INTO THE TWENTIETH CENTURY

Despite the reforms of workhouse infirmaries, conditions continued to be determined at a local level, particularly in the smaller workhouses. In 1901, the Cardigan Union Workhouse still had no proper infirmary for the sick, and the Ladies Visiting Committee suggested 'that a room fitted out as a sick ward is greatly needed as it is most distressing to see the sick and the dying in the same room, as the old people, who are only infirm.'[54]

In 1896, only eight Norfolk unions had separate infirmaries or infectious wards which were still administered by the workhouse rather than as a state hospital providing free medicine.[55]

In urban areas, in the larger towns and cities where Poor Law infirmaries were managed separately from the workhouse, conditions were undoubtedly an improvement on those experienced by paupers in the mid-nineteenth century.

In 1908, Elizabeth Brant, the fifty-eight-year-old widow of a canal boatman, was admitted to the Dudley Union Workhouse. It is probable that she was only admitted because she needed hospital treatment. Elizabeth would have experienced a far higher standard of care than that provided in the nineteenth century. It is not known how long she was in the workhouse infirmary before she died in August 1908 of cancer of the uterus and exhaustion.[56]

By the 1890s, the West Bromwich Union infirmary could accommodate 250 patients and it was 'so constructed as to be separate in its service and management from the other departments of the "house"...'[57] By this time, West Bromwich had a head trained nurse with five under-nurses and two night nurses to assist her. The fact that the infirmary was a distinct department made it:

> ...popular with the poorer stratum of society, for in case of illness the poor will willingly go to the Infirmary, whereas they would indignantly refuse to go to the Workhouse itself. By some curious attitude of the popular mind there is no 'disgrace' in accepting assistance from the poor rates through the Infirmary.[58]

THE LUNATICS

In the nineteenth century, the workhouse housed the mentally ill as well as the physically sick. Under the legislation of 1834, mentally sick paupers 'were not recognised as a separate group under the workhouse classification scheme and had no specialist accommodation assigned to them.'[1]

The definition of mental illness has changed markedly since the nineteenth century. The terms 'imbecile' and 'idiot' were used indiscriminately to describe anyone with a weak or feeble mind. Today, such people might be described as having learning difficulties. Epileptics and those subject to fits were also classed in this category with the genuine mentally ill.

After 1845, the Lunacy Commissioners held authority over all lunatics, wherever they were maintained, including workhouses. Their highly detailed, independent reports, written after their annual visits to each workhouse reveal the living conditions endured by the lunatics and the way they were treated by the workhouse staff. Whilst the unions were not legally obliged to enforce the Lunacy Commissioners' recommendations, the Poor Law Commission, and later the Local Government Board, tended to back up their suggestions. Even though the reports on the lunatics are so detailed, these inmates remained largely anonymous – very few are named.

INSANE INMATES

Lunatics were those inmates certified as being insane. It was the responsibility of the workhouse medical officer to notify the master of any pauper who was of unsound mind, and if he or she was violent or dangerous enough to warrant removal to the county asylum. Those paupers with acute cases of mental illness, regarded as curable, were accepted into county asylums for treatment.

The guardians of some unions were reluctant to send a mentally ill pauper to the asylum, unless he or she was a particularly violent or dangerous case. It was far more expensive to maintain paupers classed as lunatics in a county asylum than in the workhouse. In 1847, it cost the guardians of the Christchurch Union 2s 7½d per week to maintain a pauper in the workhouse, as opposed to an asylum patient who cost 12s per week.[2]

However, a delay in sending a dangerous lunatic to an asylum could have serious consequences for both the inmate and staff. At the Darlington Union Workhouse in 1890, the master recorded that 'Nellie Bell, during Monday night, cut her throat. Dr Middlemiss stitched up the wound, and she was out of danger. The occurrence had completely upset the nurse who was confined to bed. The Committee recommended that as Bell has made two attempts on her life and threatened the Nurse, Dr Middlemiss be requested to examine her as to her sanity.'[3]

Asylum, Denbigh

The Denbigh Asylum, 1909.

In 1842 at the Newton Workhouse near Warrington, it was reported that:

In one of the upper rooms in a most dilapidated state, a stout healthy looking young man about twenty-five years of age named Thomas Norman was chained to the floor. The man was a decided Lunatic, he had been in the workhouse upwards of a month whereas he ought not to have been in such a place one hour longer than it would have required to obtain his admission into a Lunatic Asylum.[4]

Some insane inmates, if considered manageable, remained in the workhouse. Unfortunately, where misdiagnosis or a sudden deterioration in mental state occurred, workhouse staff could be subjected to extreme danger. In 1877 at the small union workhouse in Lampeter, Mary Luke Davies attempted to strangle the matron. Afterwards, she was certified as insane and taken to the Carmarthen Asylum.[5]

Many workhouse inmates suffering with acute mental illness displayed such serious symptoms that they were unmanageable in the workhouse, being a danger to both themselves and the other inmates. In such cases, once certified by the workhouse medical officer, they were taken to the county asylum as soon as possible.

Alfred Woodhurst, a forty-nine-year-old former bonnet maker of Bethnal Green, was admitted to Middlesex County's lunatic asylum at Hanwell in July 1877. He had already spent sixteen months in Hoxton House Asylum following his release from Nottingham prison. His case notes reveal why he was not maintained in a workhouse. His disease was 'mania' and he was classed as both epileptic and dangerous. Whilst there were countless harmless epileptics maintained in workhouses, Alfred was considered dangerous to others. The asylum records describe his mental state on admission to Hanwell:

He is truculent & overbearing in manner and is incessantly grumbling about the quality of the food, clothing, bedding, etc. He says the attendants put chloroform in his tea & throw chloroform over his clothes: is under the impression that he is Lord Woodhurst, & rebukes those about him for not addressing him as 'My Lord'. Appetite good.[6]

Alfred's delusions of grandeur continued throughout his confinement at the asylum and, in September 1878, it was noted that he was 'continuing haughty, overbearing & very abusive to the officers. He believes he is a nobleman & is most irritable if argued with on the subject, & no persuasion in the world will induce him to wear one of the asylum caps, he rather goes bareheaded.'[7]

Alfred's general health remained good but his delusions continued, and developed into thoughts that he was being persecuted and murdered by others. Alfred was transferred to Leavesden Asylum in October 1910 and died there on 5 March 1915.[8]

IMBECILES AND IDIOTS

In 1849, the Poor Law authorities decreed that every inmate was either sane and should be treated as an ordinary pauper without a special diet or was insane and should be certified as a lunatic.[9] But what of the feeble-minded who did not fall into either category? These were the chronic or congenital cases who were maintained in the workhouse.[10] They 'could be seen wandering vacantly about the wards and yards of every rural workhouse … treatment was useless and physical restraint merely cruel.'[11] Such 'imbeciles' or 'idiots' were usually harmless but could be quite troublesome in an overcrowded workhouse.

In 1869, Mr Cleaton, the Visiting Commissioner in Lunacy to the Gressenhall Workhouse, reported that:

> There are at present eighteen inmates…who are classed as of unsound mind at this workhouse, and I have added to the list a man named John Jarrett, and a woman named Peace Pratt…Both are decidedly imbecilic. The latter has had two illegitimate children before she came into the house and is evidently unable to take care of herself. As she has no settled home she ought not to be allowed to leave the workhouse. The whole of these patients appear to be chronic and harmless, are reported to be easily managed in association with the ordinary inmates, and a fair number are usefully employed.[12]

As with workhouse infirmaries, there was a lack of staff to look after the ever-increasing number of imbeciles living semi-permanently in workhouses. In April 1898, Elizabeth Haywood, an imbecile at the Dudley Union Workhouse 'sustained injuries by throwing herself out of a window at the Workhouse during the temporary absence of the Nurse.'[13]

EPILEPTICS

Epileptics, or anyone suffering with fits from another cause, were placed with the imbeciles and lunatics in the workhouse, even though their mental state would usually have been sound and lucid.

Charles Dickens described meeting one such epileptic in a London workhouse in 1850:

> In another room…six or eight noisy madwomen were gathered together, under the superin-tendence of one sane attendant. Among them was a girl of two or three and twenty, very prettily dressed, of most respectable appearance, and good manners, who had been brought in from the house where she had lived as a domestic servant (having, I suppose, no friends), on account of being subject to epileptic fits, and requiring to be removed under the influence of a very bad one. She was by no means of the same stuff, or the same breeding, or the same experience, or in the same state of mind, as those by whom she was surrounded; and she pathetically complained that the daily association and the nightly noise made her worse, and was driving her mad – which was perfectly evident.[14]

Letter from the Corwen Union requesting payment for maintenance of Edward Evans at the Denbigh Asylum, 1868.

At the Newton Workhouse:

> Mary Johnson, a decent, respectable looking old woman was locked up in a bed room because, the Governor said, she was subject to fits and was in the habit of getting away and applying to her friends at Newton, he had therefore been told to lock her up. The poor woman complained of the hardship & being confined by herself during the day. I believe her only misfortune arises from weakness of interlect [sic] occasioned by old age.[15]

Epileptic inmates posed a very specific problem to union workhouses across England and Wales. As a result of the lack of paid attendants to look after these inmates, especially at night, countless lives were needlessly put at risk. As one Visiting Commissioner in Lunacy pointed out in 1891, 'epileptic patients are especially liable to death from suffocation caused by their turning on their faces in a fit, not necessarily severe, without making sufficient noise to attract the notice of any but a trained attendant specially watching the patients.'[16]

It is undoubtedly true that the more dedicated workhouse medical officers knew their lunatic patients better than the Visiting Commissioners in Lunacy who only saw them once a year. In such cases, disagreements could arise as to the best form of treatment for individual patients. This happened at the Dudley Union in March 1900 when the Visiting Commissioner recommended sending twenty-four-year-old Eliza Hill to an asylum. The guardians responded that:

> The Workhouse Medical Officer states that she has been subject to epilepsy from eight years of age, that she attempted to commit suicide some time ago, when living at home, and was sent for a short time to Winson Green Prison. Since her removal to the Union Workhouse she has been exceedingly quiet & well behaved, always willing to make herself useful, she is subject to fits, but the Medical Officer states that he has never seen her in one, but has on each occasion of his visit to the Imbecile Wards found her sensible and to all appearances in good health…[17]

Eliza was allowed to remain in the workhouse.

The Royal Albert Asylum at Lancaster. (With thanks to Ann Gray.)

Certain mental illnesses are hereditary. Esther Clarke, her younger sister Emma and her mother Ann Millner suffered periodically with mental illness characterised by periods of debilitating fits. In March 1850, twenty-one-year-old Esther was sent by the Coventry Union board of guardians with her mother to St Luke's Hospital, London, for treatment. She was discharged in August of the same year and sent home, although her mother remained at St Luke's until March 1851.

From this time onwards, Esther had regular periods of mental illness interspersed with good health. Her mental disorder was melancholia, said to be caused by religious delusions. Over the next ten years, she was admitted three times to Hatton Asylum by the Coventry Union, staying for six to eight months at a time. Esther's mother died in Hatton Asylum in July 1853.

When Esther was well, she was able to continue her work as a ribbon-weaver or silk-winder. In October 1864, Esther gave birth to her only son, George Fletcher Clarke. Between 1866 and 1873 she and George were regularly admitted to Coventry Union Workhouse. From September 1867 until May 1869, Esther was a patient again at Hatton Asylum. However, three-year-old George remained at the workhouse until he was taken out by his mother in May 1869. In 1870, Esther and George were re-admitted to the Coventry Union. Esther died of her illness in November 1873 at the workhouse aged just forty-four. George remained at the Coventry Union until he discharged himself, aged seventeen, in January 1882.[18]

TREATMENT OF THE MENTALLY ILL

The quality of life for mentally ill paupers depended to a large extent on how they were viewed by the workhouse medical officer. If they were considered to be non-medical cases, they were likely to be left in the 'dubious care of pauper nurses'.[19] In Leicester Union Workhouse, the medical officer visited the insane only once a quarter, and elsewhere 'the doctors attended the insane only if they became physically ill'.[20]

In the majority of cases, the medical staff of workhouses did not attempt to treat or cure imbeciles or idiots. However, at Kidderminster in 1840, Henry Webb, a boy who was an 'idiot… from birth' due to inflammation of the brain, was successfully treated by the workhouse medical officer. The treatment was 'bleeding, placing him on a "low diet" and keeping him quiet'. The guardians were pleased that Henry's health had improved as they were spared the expense of sending him to a lunatic asylum, which they had previously considered.[21]

Wherever possible, it was recommended to give the lunatic inmates activities or work to occupy the mind, and to take them for regular walks in the workhouse grounds. Some unions took the idea of work tasks for imbeciles to the extreme. In 1900 at Aberystwyth Union Workhouse, the Visiting Commissioner in Lunacy stated that the bathing of the lunatics 'cannot be done by the porter, for the inmate who performs that duty is classed as, and is, an imbecile.'[22]

A visit to the Powick Asylum in 1864 by the guardians of the Dudley Union reveals the kind of activities undertaken by the lunatics in asylums:

> We visited the different Workshops, such as Carpenters, Shoemakers etc. and witnessed the Lunatics at Work at their various trades. Altogether we think great credit is due to Dr Sherlock and the other Officers for the admirable way in which the Institution is managed.[23]

It was simply not possible to provide such varied activities for lunatic inmates in the workhouse because of the lack of staff. The women were usually involved in sewing, knitting, carrying out domestic duties and working in the laundry while the men were less well occupied. In many workhouses, whenever possible, the lunatic inmates were taken out for walks in the grounds while in others, illustrated publications and cheap prints were put in the wards. At one workhouse, on the advice of the Commissioners in Lunacy, a musical box was bought for the female lunatics which 'gives much pleasure to the women and is occasionally lent the men who are not well provided with means of either occupation or amusement.'[24]

LIVING CONDITIONS

Accommodation and facilities for lunatics, imbeciles and epileptics varied considerably from workhouse to workhouse. At the small Lampeter Union Workhouse in 1900 where there were five inmates classed as imbeciles, the Visiting Commissioner in Lunacy was 'glad to find that the imbeciles all have flock beds above the straw mattresses' and that 'the patients are kindly treated and properly cared for.'[25]

At the Samford Union in Suffolk in 1898, it was reported that 'the imbeciles are well treated and have sufficient diet, getting four meat dinners weekly. The dormitories and bedding are in proper order…All of both sexes are bathed weekly.'[26]

However, such excellent care was not evident everywhere. The main problem faced by the lunatic pauper in a workhouse was a severe lack of personal space. Overcrowding in the imbecile and lunatic wards was common in most medium to large workhouses, mainly because the county asylums themselves were overstretched and had insufficient beds to meet the demand.

The Colney Hatch asylum was opened in 1851 solely to cater for pauper patients from the London unions. By 1867, it had 'turned down 3,800 applications, due to lack of vacant beds'.[27] The Medical Officer of the Poplar Union commented that 'it has become a perfectly hopeless matter to obtain admission for a pauper…in any lunatic asylum in Middlesex.'[28]

Overcrowding in the imbecile wards was a major problem at the Dudley Union Workhouse. In 1880, Mr Cleaton, the Visiting Commissioner, described the effect on the imbeciles:

> Dr Higgs the Medical Officer…accompanied me through the Wards and….evidently takes great interest in these patients. All were tranquil and orderly in behaviour notwithstanding

the serious overcrowding but I observed some black eyes among the men, the result of quarrels such as often happen among patients of this class who have insufficient day space.[29]

Mr Cleaton also remarked that:

> …the beds are so close that they touch each other at the sides and the patients have to climb into and out of their beds over the bottom. Apart from the insufficient space it can be easily be imagined how objectionable it must be for insane patients, many of whom are of dirty habits….to sleep in beds actually touching each other at the sides.[30]

A year earlier, it was reported that: 'One of the beds so arranged is occupied by an idiot lad who not only is prone, like many other idiots, to invade his neighbours' beds, but is strongly inclined to bite.'[31]

The problem of overcrowding at Dudley was eventually resolved by converting the old schools into accommodation for the imbeciles. The difference in living conditions for the imbeciles was marked. In February 1888, Mr Bagot, Commissioner in Lunacy reported that 'Remembering what the old Special Wards were I cannot too strongly express my satisfaction with the great improvement which has been effected in the accommodation for the imbecile wards…'[32]

Members of a visiting committee, made up of a group of guardians from the board of every union, would have regularly visited their lunatic poor in the county lunatic asylums. Such visits were often invaluable as they allowed an opportunity for guardians to talk with trained staff accustomed to providing a high standard of care for lunatics. The guardians could observe the lunatics at work and leisure and the superintendent of the lunatic asylum invariably offered suggestions and recommendations which they could then implement in the workhouse.

A visit by members of the Visiting Committee of the Dudley Union to Powick Asylum near Worcester prompted the guardians to review the bedding and sleeping arrangements for the lunatic paupers at the workhouse:

> We recommend the Guardians to continue the use of Iron Bedsteads in the Dormitories at our Workhouse and to have a few made with sides to attach for the use of patients subject to fits. We also recommend that Flock Beds and Straw Mattresses about two inches thick be procured for each patient…[33]

It can be assumed that prior to the visit there were no beds with sides attached to prevent epileptic patients from falling out during a fit. It is not known what kind of mattresses were in place before flock beds and straw mattresses were purchased, but it is likely they were of an inferior quality and not suitable for their purpose.

In addition to overcrowding and a lack of personal space, lunatic paupers could also suffer when there were insufficient members of staff to look after them. Many unions employed insufficient paid attendants, relying on assistance from unpaid sane pauper inmates. In 1878 at Dudley, there was one paid male attendant with two sane pauper helpers by day and night. The female attendant only had one such helper by day, but a second helper slept in one of the two ward dormitories at night.[34] This lack of paid medical staff mirrored the situation in the workhouse infirmaries.

Generally, the lunatics and imbeciles had separate male and female day rooms and dormitories from the other inmates. However, at smaller, more rural workhouses, accommodation was less segregated. In 1863, 'only four workhouses in Norfolk had separate lunatic wards, and a further five segregated the mentally deficient from the other paupers.'[35]

Even in workhouses where the lunatics and imbeciles were properly segregated, there was little to occupy the mind. On visiting one workhouse in September 1890, Dr Albutt, the Visiting Commissioner in Lunacy, complained that:

Not a book or a newspaper was to be seen on the wards. Many of these inmates are undoubtedly incapable of reading books but far more of such persons are able to amuse themselves, especially with illustrated books and papers, than inexperienced observers would anticipate.[36]

The boredom and monotony felt by imbeciles in the workhouse was highlighted by a Commissioner in Lunacy to one union in 1889. He commented that:

....in the men's yards I noticed some pigeons, which are much petted by the imbeciles and clearly afforded them some pleasure and these afflicted men, especially those who cannot be walked out, sadly need something to enliven the dull monotony of their lives.[37]

RESTRAINT

At times it was necessary to restrain mentally ill inmates who were a danger to both themselves and others. Restraint could only be used when sanctioned by the medical officer and a record of each occasion had to be made in the Register of Mechanical Restraint. At the Dudley Union in 1896, a Visiting Commissioner disapproved of the restraint jacket as 'being of a type that we do not permit fastened by numerous leather bands and buckles. Proper light canvass [sic] jackets with closed sleeves ends and tapes will have to be provided according with the recently published Commissoners' Rules.'[38] By their very nature, workhouses were not designed to accommodate the special needs of lunatics or imbeciles. In 1892, a Visiting Commissioner in Lunacy to one union workhouse complained that 'there is no padded room for noisy turbulent cases dangerous to themselves.'[39] Despite the criticism, very few workhouses would have had padded rooms fitted out especially for lunatics at this time.

CONTRIBUTIONS FROM RELATIVES

Wherever possible, the families of lunatic paupers admitted to asylums were asked to contribute towards the cost of maintenance. This was invariably difficult for the families, and in January 1873 the guardians of the Dudley Union 'resolved that the necessary proceedings be taken against Josiah Lee for repayment of the cost of maintenance of his Wife Eliza Lee at the Worcester County Lunatic Asylum.'[40]

In some cases, where paupers had money of their own, the guardians of workhouse unions took steps to use the money to pay for their maintenance in the asylum. In March 1854, the guardians of one workhouse union discovered that Eliza Neale, an inmate of the Powick Asylum in Worcester, had 'money in her own right in a Bank.' They decided that 'at least the interest of such money be appropriated towards repaying the parish the expense of her support in the Asylum.'[41]

RECOVERY

Mental illness is not always permanent. Many of those afflicted enjoy periods of good health. A good proportion of those who were sent to an asylum from the workhouse were deemed treatable and were expected to make a recovery. As already mentioned, every union appointed a visiting committee to regularly visit the asylums which housed their lunatic poor. This enabled them to check on how many lunatics were chargeable to their union and to discuss each individual case with the asylum superintendent. If a pauper was deemed well enough to

LUNATICS IN WORKHOUSE.

CERTIFICATE

TO BE GIVEN BY THE MEDICAL OFFICER OF THE WORKHOUSE, UNDER
SECTION 20 OF THE 25 & 26 VICT. CAP. 111.

I, *Thomas Thompson*

the Medical Officer of the *Sedgefield*

Union Workhouse, do hereby certify, pursuant to the provisions of the 25 & 26 Vict.

c. 111, s. 20, that in my opinion,

Jane Valks

aged *45 years* years, a Pauper Lunatic, is a proper person to be kept in

a Workhouse, and that the accommodation of the *Sedgefield*

Union Workhouse is sufficient for h*er* reception.

Dated this *28th* day of *Nov.* 18*81*

Thomas Thompson
Medical Officer.

120a. Lunatics in Workhouse. Medical Certificate.

A certificate confirming that it was appropriate for forty-five-year-old Jane Valks, a pauper lunatic, to be kept in Sedgefield Union Workhouse, 1881. Jane died in the workhouse in 1894. (U/Se 114. Reproduced by permission of the Durham County Record Office.)

leave the asylum, he or she did not necessarily return to the workhouse. In many cases, such paupers were discharged to live with their family or friends who were subsidised to look after them.[42]

Forty-nine-year-old Amelia Boyd was admitted to the Surrey County Lunatic Asylum at Cane Hill by the Lambeth Union in November 1899. It is not known what kind of mental illness she was suffering from. By the time of the 1901 census she had been discharged and was living at home again. She was listed as an imbecile and it is likely her family were being subsidised by the Lambeth Union to look after her at home.[43]

In 1899, it was recommended by the medical superintendent of the Stafford County Asylum at Burntwood that 'Lizzie Davies be removed to her friends at Rowley Regis if she can be properly provided for and taken care of at home.'[44] Lunatic paupers in workhouses might also make partial recoveries. In 1874 at the Dudley Union, the Visiting Commissioner in Lunacy reported that:

> Thomas Wright, recommended at the last visit for removal on the grounds of being noisy and troublesome…has latterly and for many months past, we are informed, been much better and is easily managed. He is no doubt insane, and probably labours under delusions, but his case has now become chronic, and if he remains harmless and tractable his removal to an asylum may not be necessary. Should he however again become noisy or troublesome he ought to be sent to the Asylum.[45]

INTO THE TWENTIETH CENTURY

Imbeciles and idiots continued to be housed in union workhouses at the end of the nineteenth and beginning of the twentieth centuries with little improvement in conditions. In most workhouses, it was found that the weak-minded were 'useful in the laundry and other domestic work of the institution'.[46] By 1906 there were 11,500 inmates officially classed as of 'unsound mind' in the workhouses[47] and 'the sane and insane still continue[d] to be mixed up indiscriminately'.[48]

9

THE VAGRANTS

Perhaps one of the most difficult classes of inmates to deal with was the vagrant class, also known as tramps or casual paupers. Despised by the authorities, they were arguably the only class of inmate who did not experience a significant improvement in conditions during the Victorian and Edwardian period. They remained a thorny problem to unions throughout England and Wales.

The Poor Law Amendment Act of 1834 did not even mention vagrants as a separate class. Indeed, it was not until 1842 that guidance about how vagrants should be treated was issued. The Poor Law Commission ordered the unions to provide separate accommodation for vagrants and to 'detain them for four hours hard labour' before they could leave.[1]

If vagrants were fortunate, they might benefit from charity, but if they were caught begging or sleeping out in the open, they 'risked a fortnight's hard labour under the Vagrancy Act of 1824'.[2] Therefore, they had little option other than to seek refuge for the night in the 'casual' ward of a workhouse.

WHAT KIND OF PEOPLE TURNED TO VAGRANCY?

Like the workhouse inmates, the vagrants, or 'casual paupers', were divided into 'deserving' and 'undeserving'. The 'deserving' vagrants included genuine travellers in search of work or those whose occupation required regular travelling. This might include 'seamen who had spent their pay and were off to another port, navvies moving from gang to gang, and Irish seasonal labourers making their way home…'[3]

Unions in harvest areas, like Bromley in Kent, always experienced an influx of casual labourers in the summer. These seasonal migrants 'were not habitual wanderers, and…used the casual wards as a stopping place: these people usually travelled in family groups.'[4]

A March 1866 edition of the *Justice of the Peace* publication described the 'really deserving' vagrants as anyone '…who by dire misfortune, has fallen to the lowest level of destitution; amongst these will be found men, and women too, who have, in other days, been surrounded by every luxury and refinement…'[5]

One such 'deserving' vagrant was Captain Alexander Hall, a sixty-six-year-old former sea captain who was admitted to the casual ward of the King's Norton Union Workhouse on 29 March 1901 with his wife Rose Hannah. The master recorded that Alexander had '2/9 per day Pension.' As vagrants, both Alexander and Rose Hannah were required to complete a work task. Alexander picked oakum and his sixty-year-old wife cleaned the stair rail before leaving for their next destination, Worcester.[6]

A simple accident could force a man or woman into vagrancy. During his investigations into slum life, Jack London met a man known as 'Ginger' in the line at the Whitechapel casual ward. While employed by a fish dealer, 'Ginger' lifted a box of fish which was too heavy for him. His back was severely injured and his employer refused him 'a light job now and again'. His only chance to earn a living was by heavy work, but sadly, 'He is now incapable of performing heavy work, and from now until he dies, the spike, the peg, and the streets are all he can look forward to in the way of food and shelter.'[7]

The treatment of 'deserving' vagrants was always designed to be different from their 'undeserving' counterparts. Various regulations of 1848, 1868 and 1892 declared that genuine travellers looking for work should be differentiated from the professional vagrants and 'were to be excused their workhouse task or given tickets of way for the next workhouse on their route.'[8] At the Dudley Union in 1869, the guardians recorded that 'For the destitute & unfortunate but deserving wayfarers, who may require lodging in relief, the Committee would recommend that as far as possible every consideration and kindness should be shown.'[9] Despite such good intentions, the 'deserving' and 'undeserving' vagrants invariably spent the night under the same roof, 'sharing the often insanitary casual wards across England and Wales.'[10]

The 'undeserving' vagrants were the professional vagrants who had no intention of looking for work. In 1841, the Poor Law Commissioners described these casual paupers as '*mendicant vagrants*, who are known to be generally persons of dissolute character, to lead habitually a life of laziness and imposture, and not infrequently to resort to intimidation and pilfering.'[11]

In 1866, the *Justice of the Peace* publication featured the confession of an 'indolent casual' in London who revealed that after completing the work task and being discharged from the workhouse he:

> …betakes himself to a free reading room in Westminster, where, with a good fire, and amusing publications, he comfortably passes three or four hours; as the afternoon advances he lounges up towards the West End, and here he meets with others of the same class; they discuss the best means of imposing upon benevolent societies and individuals, the best soup kitchen, and how tickets are to be obtained…[12]

The vagrants' drying room at the Fir Vale Workhouse, Sheffield. (Courtesy of the Sheffield Teaching Hospitals NHS Foundation Trust.)

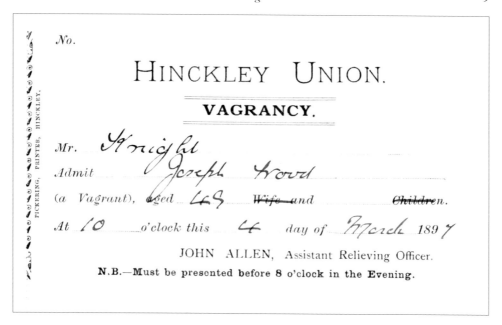

A vagrants' ticket issued in 1897 by the Hinckley Union. (Courtesy of Lyn Howsam.)

The 'undeserving' vagrants might also include 'such as are frequently seen at Police Courts and at the Central Criminal Court, thieves, pickpockets, area sneaks, and many much more desperate and of a darker dye…'[13]

Vagrants could be lone travellers, couples or even families and tramping was not limited to the young or middle-aged. Any vagrant who complained of being sick or injured on admittance to the casual wards would be examined by the workhouse medical officer. If serious enough, vagrants were admitted to the infirmary or sick ward of the main workhouse. Such illnesses could include general fatigue, lack of food or injuries to the legs and feet which would prevent the vagrant from continuing his or her journey.

In October 1895, Joseph Gwydr, a vagrant aged ninety-four years, was admitted into the Lampeter Union Workhouse by the medical officer 'suffering from a very bad foot.' He was discharged three weeks later.[14] Joseph was again admitted to the Lampeter Union the following winter and stayed for a month. He was discharged because he was 'able to go on his journey.' The last mention of Joseph in the casual registers of the Lampeter Union records his admittance for a week in May 1900. On that occasion, he was described as being a sweep born in 1802.[15]

There is no doubt that the vagrant wards of workhouses served as vital refuges for genuinely destitute or sick travellers and vagrants. A vagrant named Lucy Hannah Briggs, alias Parker, was in a very poor state when she was brought to the Clitheroe Union Workhouse late one night in 1895. She had spent a night lying on a heap of manure at a farm. The master reported that '…she was almost starving, having recently eaten nothing but wheat… Never having been married, she never in her life had a home of her own.'[16]

Female vagrants in the latter stages of pregnancy were often admitted to the main workhouse from the vagrant wards. In September 1886, Christine Higgins, a female vagrant and a native of Manchester, was admitted into the Lampeter Union Workhouse 'she being with child and her husband having deserted her.' She gave birth to a son named John in November 1886 'this being the first child born in the workhouse since the date of its erection in the year 1876'.[17] Christine was discharged with her son on 27 December.

The children of vagrants were also admitted to the vagrant wards, not the main workhouse, and slept with their mothers in the female vagrant wards. In order to accommodate the children, female vagrant wards were often larger than those for their male counterparts. This was the case at the Christchurch Union.[18]

Children who had been deserted by their vagrant parents were admitted to the main workhouse. In 1882, the five children of Samson and Eliza Price, who were travelling grinders, were admitted into the Lampeter Union Workhouse. The master recorded that 'Price and his wife were...taken into custody for drunkenness and the children were then left without any place to go or anyone to take care of them and they were brought into the house by P.S. Lyons.' Samson and Eliza Price were committed to Carmarthen Gaol for fourteen days and collected their children on their release.[19]

ADMITTANCE TO THE WORKHOUSE

Vagrants had to apply for admission to the casual ward, usually to the relieving officer for the union. From 1848, the Poor Law Board recommended that an experienced police officer should act as the assistant relieving officer. It was felt that if vagrants had to apply to the police for an admission ticket, the numbers of vagrants would decrease.[20]

The practice of appointing a police officer as the assistant relieving officer was abandoned after 1871. However, the assistance of the police was considered highly valuable for the staff of smaller workhouses like Lampeter. In 1896, T.J. Bircham, a Poor Law Board inspector, recommended that 'the police should be Assistant Relieving Officer for vagrants which might have a deterrent effect.' Discipline was difficult to enforce in these smaller workhouses and Mr Bircham also suggested that 'it would be very desirable to construct a few labour cells, in which the task of work could be performed separately and discipline would be more easily maintained.'[21]

On arrival at any workhouse, vagrants were searched for money and contraband items such as matches, tobacco and dangerous items such as knives. If they had no money, they were deemed to be destitute. While there were many vagrants who were genuinely destitute, others were known to hide money and valuables in hedges or ditches close to the workhouse. At Stafford, the vagrants had 'almost pulled down a hedge near the workhouse by hiding money in it.'[22]

Vagrants were only admitted to workhouses after a specific hour, usually 5 p.m. However, late admissions often caused problems for both the staff and inmates of the workhouse. In 1866, the master of Shifnal Union Workhouse complained that 'Tramps sometimes obtain orders from the relieving officer between six and seven o'clock, get them countersigned by the police-constable and then stop at public-houses in the town till between eleven and twelve, when they come to the workhouse and disturb the inmates by violently shouting and kicking at the outer doors.'[23] In 1874, after enquiring about the times of admittance in neighbouring unions, the guardians of the Dudley Union ordered that 'no Tramp or Vagrant shall be admitted to the union workhouse after 10 o'clock at night.'[24] It is not known if this rule was strictly enforced.

Late admissions were still problematic at the beginning of the twentieth century. At Lampeter Union Workhouse in 1903, the master complained that the:

> Casuals are admitted at any time from 5pm to 9pm & even 9.30pm. To be obliged to admit casuals at such a late hour as 9pm is very inconvenient, especially when they come in wet and their clothes have to be dried besides fire and lighting have to be kept going which means an extra expense.

The master suggested that the hours for admission from October to March be 5 p.m. to 6.30 p.m. and from April to September 6.30 p.m. to 8 p.m.[25]

THE INSCRIPTION ON THE PAVEMENT.—DRAWN BY KENNY MEADOWS.

The Inscription on the Pavement drawn by Kenny Meadows. (*Illustrated London News*, 27 January 1849.)

On admittance, vagrants were taken to a building separate from the main workhouse accommodation. From the early days of the new Poor Law it was deemed that it would be unsuitable for vagrants to mix with workhouse inmates. The guardians of the Dudley Union were adamant that '…a separate and confined Yard would be required, as Tramps or Casual Paupers should not…be permitted to have free intercourse with the other Inmates.'[26]

Under the Pauper Inmates Discharge and Regulations Act of 1871, it was ordered that 'every Casual pauper is, as soon as practicable after Admission, to have a Bath, with water of suitable temperature.' However, this seems to have been enforced for the male vagrants and rarely for the females.[27] It is possible that this was because the attendants of the vagrant wards tended to be male.

In the majority of unions, the vagrants had to use the same bath water (as was often the case in the main wards of the workhouse). Given the general lack of hygiene and the variety of contagious diseases carried by vagrants, going without a bath would probably have been less hazardous. In 1878, a reporter for the *Sheffield & Rotherham Independent* disguised himself as a vagrant to gain admission to the casual ward of the Sheffield Union Workhouse. The vagrants were ordered to strip to have a bath. The reporter wrote that: 'I had the good fortune to get out just as a man, black as a sweep, and suffering from the filthy disease known as the itch, came in. I was astounded to see that not only this man, but two others suffering from a far more loathsome complaint, were allowed – ordered in fact – to wash in the self-same water as the rest...'[28]

ACCOMMODATION

Most unions spent as little as possible on the accommodation for their vagrants. An observer in the 1840s noted that the buildings generally had:

> ...brick floors and guardroom beds, with loose straw and rugs for the males and iron bedsteads with straw ties for the females. They are generally badly ventilated and unprovided with any means of producing warmth. All holes for ventilation in reach of the occupants are sure to be stuffed with rags and straws; so that the effluvia of these places is at best most disgustingly offensive.[29]

With wild fluctuations in vagrant numbers throughout the year, it was difficult for unions to plan for the exact number of admissions. This could mean that the number of places for vagrants was sufficient for most of the year, but was vastly overcrowded at other times.

In unions with overcrowded casual wards, the guardians had the power to give vagrants 'just enough out-relief to enable them to buy a night's lodging in a common lodging house.'[30] This would probably have been the preferred option for most vagrants, and it was certainly the case at the Clitheroe Union. In 1894, the Local Government Board's Inspector noted that 'You are unable to accommodate them all, so issue tickets for lodging houses and I think in these circumstances, many apply who know full well they will not be sent to the workhouse.'[31]

When the new legislation of 1871 was passed, unions had to reassess their provision for vagrants. At the Dudley Union, the guardians recorded that 'The Ward for Male Tramps is able to afford accommodation for twenty-eight during the night, and that for Females for about half this number...' However, 'occasionally as many as from thirty to forty Male Tramps have presented themselves for Admittance upon some special Evenings.' The guardians were also concerned that unless the number of vagrants was considerably reduced as a result of the legislation, the present staff of officers would not be able to efficiently meet 'the requirements of the Government Board, as to Searching, Bathing and keeping of the necessary Registers.'[32]

Under the new legislation, unions were required to provide 'separate cells, beds or compartments...so that not more than one pauper, excepting in the case of a mother with an infant, or children, shall sleep together.' It was also ordered that 'The Clothing, when wet is to be dried, and if thought necessary, disinfected, and others supplied for the night, or time being.'[33]

Whilst unions sought to fulfil their obligations under the new legislation, by necessity, the accommodation for the vagrants was to remain basic to act as a deterrent. In 1887, a young writer named James Craven posed as an unemployed mechanic to investigate the conditions at the casual ward of the Keighley Union in Yorkshire. He found that the bedding was 'alive with vermin'. In his opinion, 'the general treatment of vagrants [was]...a disgrace to any civilised country...'[34]

DIET

Like the accommodation in the casual wards, the diet for vagrants varied across England and Wales. At the Dudley Union in 1869, male vagrants were given 8oz of bread or 6oz of bread and 1 pint of gruel for supper. Female vagrants and children between the ages of seven and fifteen were given 6oz of bread and 1 pint of gruel for supper. Children under the age of seven received 4oz of bread and half a pint of gruel. Breakfast for all the vagrants was exactly the same as supper, with half the quantity of bread before the work task and the other half given on its completion.[35] The same monotonous diet was doled out at the Ecclesall Bierlow Union in 1896 where vagrants had 6oz of bread and a pint of gruel for breakfast. This was repeated at supper time.[36]

WORK TASKS

Every vagrant, male or female, had to perform a work task before being allowed to leave the workhouse. The exception was if the day fell 'on a Sunday or a religious festival such as Good Friday, which was a day of rest.'[37] The work tasks were specifically designed to be a deterrent and were therefore both arduous and monotonous. Male vagrants were usually given the task of stone-breaking or oakum-picking.

The Casual Poor Act of 1882 set out several possible work tasks for male vagrants. They included breaking up to thirteen hundred weight of stone, pounding up to two hundred weight of stone, picking four pounds of unbeaten or eight pounds of beaten oakum, or spending nine hours undertaking such duties as chopping wood, grinding corn or pumping water.[38] Vagrants were not meant to be given work tasks 'beyond their age or strength' but, in practice, unless a vagrant refused to work, the medical officer was 'rarely consulted.'[39]

Most workhouses had a specific yard for stone-breaking. At the Christchurch Union, there were six 'cells' in the male vagrant ward with cubicles next to them in which they had to complete their work task.[40]

Oakum-picking was often completed in the casual ward itself or in a vagrant's own cell. In 1899, the master of Sedgefield Workhouse in County Durham recorded that 'There is little profit in Oakum-Picking but the task in teasing the Rope deters many men from entering the Casual Ward, who would otherwise apply for admission.'[41]

The reporter for the *Sheffield & Rotherham Independent* who went undercover at the Sheffield Union Workhouse described the task of picking oakum, which had to be completed before breakfast, in these terms:

> …each man was given a portion which consists of old strips of rope of various lengths and thicknesses. These pieces are so soaked with pitch that they are as hard as close grained wood, and our task was to reduce it by picking with the fingers to fine fibre….in spite of all our efforts, it took the greater part of us four hours and a half to pick our portion, so that it was half-past eleven before the porter came in to weigh and remove each man's lot, and then breakfast was served.[42]

Oakum-picking may have been a deterrent for some vagrants but regulars of the casual wards may have become accustomed, and even adept, at the task. This was especially true if a vagrant had ever been detained in prison where oakum-picking was a regular chore.

Female vagrants were also given work tasks, usually oakum-picking or cleaning. In 1860, the guardians of the Dudley Union ordered 'that each Female Tramp do pick one pound of Oakum after having received a night's lodging and breakfast.'[43] At the Bedford Union, the women had a more diverse list of tasks, including, 'cleaning and scrubbing the casual wards, washing and mending the clothes of other vagrants, or serving food to vagrants.' Some women were also given the harsher tasks of breaking stones or oakum-picking.[44] Under no circumstances would the female vagrants have been asked to clean in the main workhouse, as vagrants were considered to be a real contaminating influence on the other inmates.

In many unions, even the children of vagrants had to complete a work task before leaving the workhouse. In 1901, at the King's Norton Union, Walter Cornick, a cycle maker and his wife, Martha, were admitted to the vagrant wards with their three children. The children undertook cleaning work with their mother. However, the work task for children does not seem to have been strictly enforced. When Martha Cornick was re-admitted to the King's Norton Union vagrant ward later that year, with two of her children but without her husband, she was 'allowed to go, having a family'.[45]

Before the passing of the Casual Poor Act of 1882, vagrants could discharge themselves before eleven o'clock on the morning following their night's stay. After 31 December 1882, vagrants were required to be detained until nine o'clock on the second day after admission.[46] Vagrants could be detained until the fourth day if it was his or her second application to the same union within one month. However, the new regulations were not rigorously enforced in every union. Certain unions would not detain a vagrant for two nights 'if it were cheaper to send him away unfed the day after arrival'.[47] There was so much disparity between the unions that, in 1886, a Poor Law inspector complained that 'only half the unions observed the requirements of detention for an extra day.'[48]

COMMUNICATION BETWEEN VAGRANTS

In 1834, the Poor Law Commissioners had feared that the new workhouses 'built an easy day's tramp away from each other, might be seen as an attractive proposition to vagrants.'[49] In theory, the treatment of vagrants in workhouses was supposed to be the same throughout England and Wales. However, the system was flawed because in practice, both the accommodation and work tasks differed. Regular vagrants who tramped in particular areas had a very efficient form of communication: the 'bush telegraph'. They could therefore communicate with each other about the virtues of individual workhouses including the quality of the food, the difficulty of the work tasks and the lack of the discipline.

At one workhouse, the supply of oakum ran out so that the vagrants were excused their work task. The number of vagrant admissions 'rose in a fortnight from twenty to forty-five and then soared to seventy-five.'[50] However, once stocks of oakum were replenished, admissions dropped dramatically to their former level.

Vagrants also communicated through graffiti messages left on the walls of the vagrant wards, particularly in the Midlands. In 1865, a message praised Much Wenlock Workhouse: 'A stunning workhouse for a good supper and breakfast; Much Wenlock, lads, that's the place.'[51]

VAGRANTS STAYING IN THE WORKHOUSE FOR WORK

At smaller workhouses where staff and resources were limited, it was not uncommon for vagrants to be admitted to the main workhouse where their skills could be utilised. This was with the consent of the vagrant and it could last for several weeks. This may have appealed to some vagrants, especially in the tough winter months. George Bowes, the master at Sedgefield Union Workhouse, was particularly enterprising with regard to setting the vagrants to work. In June 1905, he proudly wrote that: 'I have had the whole of the outside woodwork of the workhouse painted with Two Coats of Paint, the labour has been done by Painters taken from the Casual Ward.'[52]

DISRUPTIVE VAGRANTS

Some disruptive vagrants committed criminal offences at the casual wards. Such offences might include escaping from the workhouse before completing their work task, refusing to take a bath, destroying or stealing workhouse clothing, refusing to complete the work task or disobeying the master. If caught, vagrants were always brought before the local magistrate and, depending on the offence, jailed for anything from one week to several months.

Dudley Union Workhouse which became Burton Road Hospital. (Courtesy of Ian Beach.)

At the Lampeter Union in 1891, the master recorded that John Spencer 'a casual pauper was given into custody…for refusing to perform his task of Stone-Breaking and also for assaulting me and was sentenced to fourteen days hard labour.'[53]

There were many occurrences of vagrants deliberately destroying workhouse clothes or other workhouse property, despite the consequence of such actions being imprisonment. Why? There are two possible explanations. Deliberate acts of vandalism or violence could be seen as a protest against the poor conditions and accommodation offered to vagrants. In 1889, a tramp named George Lofthouse was charged with tearing up his clothes at the Clitheroe Union Workhouse. When brought before the magistrates, he explained that:

My clothes were very bad and I asked for a needle and thread to mend them. My request was refused and I therefore tore them up. Those I was given were also very bad and were not worth a shilling altogether, and I refused to wear the vest.

George was committed to prison for seven days.[54]

To other vagrants, prison, with its more generous diet, was an attractive alternative to the vagrant wards, especially during the winter. In 1878, the reporter for the *Sheffield & Rotherham Independent* who went undercover in the casual ward at the Sheffield Union workhouse met a vagrant known as 'Prison Jack'. Jack regularly tramped around the country until the cold weather set in. It was reported that:

…his habit was to seek shelters, for the winter months, and this he did by insulting the 'Screw' as they called the workhouse governor while staying in the 'Spike' – the workhouse; or, if opportunity did not serve for this, a favourite plan was to tear up his clothing, or burn the oakum he was set to pick; any of which vagaries would result in his being taken before the 'beak' and 'quadded'...[55]

According to the *Justice of the Peace* publication of March 1866, 'at Pentonville Prison a convict gets 140oz of bread a week, and at Millbank Prison 150oz, so that, as regards "the staff of life", the convict has the advantage over the pauper.' In addition, the maximum amount of meat given in any London workhouse to 'able-bodied paupers' was 'below the minimum given in any London convict prison, that minimum being 30oz.'[56] Given that vagrants were fed an even worse diet than the workhouse inmates, prison was clearly an attractive proposition to many regular vagrants.

It is unclear whether an incident at the casual ward of Sedgefield Union Workhouse was deliberate or accidental. The master recorded that on 10 August 1892:

> Six Casuals were picking Oakum in their Bathroom, one of them named Jas. Wheelan aged sixty-five Years struck a match that he had hid in his Coat linings to light his pipe & set fire to 8lbs of Oakum worth about 1s 3d, the fire might have been very serious. The man named had all his Whiskers burnt off, another had his arm badly burnt...[57]

INTO THE TWENTIETH CENTURY

Conditions within the casual wards had changed little by the beginning of the twentieth century. In 1909, a campaigning journalist named Everard Wyvall posed as an out-of-work clerk walking from London to Portsmouth so that he could investigate the 'spikes'. At one casual ward, he was 'locked in a small cell with barred windows' and then spent a day stone-breaking, which left him 'with hands almost raw' and 'aching and sore in every limb'. Afterwards, he spent a second night in a communal ward 'where he was shut up for thirteen hours in an unlighted room with ten other men, with only hammocks between them.' At dawn, their breakfast of dry bread was brought in 'and thrown on the floor as though they were animals.'[58] Although as a soldier, Wyvall had slept out in the rain behind enemy lines, he wrote that 'nothing will ever compare with that horrible night....Even now I find myself shivering at the thought of that dreadful experience.'[59]

Female vagrants fared little better. Mary Higgs, Secretary of the Ladies Committee of Oldham Union Workhouse, was a well-known advocate of vagrancy reform. In 1904 and 1906 she disguised herself as a tramp and, with a companion, spent the night in the casual wards of several Northern workhouses. The accommodation was:

> ...uniformly cheerless and prison-like and the food even worse: saltless, or appallingly over-salted, gruel, dry bread and cheese, with no water allowed except at mealtimes....Everything possible seemed to be done to degrade women vagrants who were given no facilities to dry damp clothes and were strictly forbidden – even if put to work in the laundry – to wash their own dirty garments.

During her investigations, Mary Higgs quickly dispensed with 'the prevailing idea in my class of society...that tramps as a class were so incorrigible that...the only thing was to severely penalise vagrancy.'[60]

THE MASTER AND MATRON

Without a doubt, the duties and responsibilities of the master and matron were the most onerous and difficult of all the workhouse officers. Inevitably, as the managers of the workhouse, their work, personalities and approach directly affected the living conditions and treatment of the paupers within it. A kindly, compassionate master and matron could help to make a stay in the workhouse bearable, even comfortable. On the other hand, a sadistic master or matron could create a climate of fear, making the inmates' lives a living hell.

TYPES OF APPLICANT

No specific qualifications were required of candidates for the post of master except that they had to be over twenty-one years of age and able to keep accounts. At many workhouses, the 'commonest source of recruits were former policemen and army NCOs.'[1] This was certainly the case in Northamptonshire unions which preferred to appoint 'former prison, army or police officers' for their workhouse masters. The Poor Law inspector for the area believed that these were 'just the men to detect fraudulent applications'.[2]

When the new workhouse was finally opened in the Lampeter Union in 1877, the applicants for the post of master and matron included a station master, a police constable and a member of the fire brigade.[3]

It is not known what the previous occupations of the Aberystwyth Union's master and matron were. However, in 1900, a visitor was highly impressed with them after an unexpected visit to the workhouse. He wrote to the guardians that they were 'a credit to Wales – most humane officials I have ever come in contact with. Devoid of Military Officialdom that is generally to be found in our workhouses.'[4]

Applicants for the post of matron were considered better suited to the role if they were a trained nurse[5] or had experience in midwifery. Later in the nineteenth century, larger unions would not consider applicants for the post of master and matron unless they had considerable experience in the Poor Law service.[6]

Smaller unions, which could not attract high calibre applicants, were not so concerned about previous experience. The first master and matron of the Lampeter Union were John Harris and his wife who were evidently inexperienced in Poor Law administration. They undertook that they 'would go for a month to some of the neighbouring workhouses in order to obtain information as to the duties of the offices of Master & Matron.' Unusually, the couple also agreed 'to perform the duties of Porter at this workhouse or pay the Salary of such Officer should a Porter be hereafter required.'[7]

Louisa Twining, a prominent workhouse reformer, described workhouse masters and matrons as people from the 'low and uneducated middle-class'.[8] She questioned 'why the appointment of master should not invariably have been given to a man of superior position…

the post being one that requires great discretion and powers of government, such as we might expect to find in retired officers...'[9]

The reason was simply that the long hours and onerous duties were not compensated for with a reasonable salary or living accommodation. The *Guide to the Management of Workhouses* of 1870 stated that the master 'should devote the whole of his time to the discharge of his duties, and he cannot be an efficient officer if he devotes himself to pleasures or even to duties away from the workhouse.'[10]

William James Gilpin, master of West Bromwich Union Workhouse between 1871 and 1896. (Courtesy of Ruth Piggott.)

MARRIED COUPLES

The vast majority of master and matron posts were jointly held by married couples because they would have to work in close partnership to ensure the smooth running of a workhouse. When recruiting for these posts, most unions advertised specifically for a married man and his wife, without dependent children. This was despite the fact that 'the Commissioners did not rule that the matron must be the master's wife'.[11]

In December 1843, an advertisement in the *Norfolk Chronicle* sought to:

...elect a Married Man and his Wife, between the ages of twenty-five and forty years, as MASTER and MATRON of the Gressenhall Workhouse...at the following salaries....the Master £100, the Matron £25 per annum, with Board, Washing and Lodging in the workhouse. Qualifications and Testimonials to Character to be forwarded to the Union House... The party elected will be required to enter into a Bond, himself in £150 and two sureties in £100 each.[12]

Fifty years later at the Darlington Union, the guardians advertised for a new master and matron. The salaries were £55 and £35 per annum respectively and it was stated that:

Candidates must be fully competent to accurately keep the books and accounts, and to perform all the duties prescribed by the Regulations of the Local Government Board and the Guardians... The persons appointed must be man and wife, without encumbrance.[13]

An ambitious clerk, assistant master or schoolmaster might be highly experienced and ready for the role of workhouse master, but if he was unmarried his application would have been overlooked in favour of joint applications from a married couple. This was the dilemma faced by twenty-four-year-old William James Gilpin in 1871. At the time employed as the Assistant Master at Hackney Union Workhouse, he wanted to apply for the vacant post of master at West Bromwich Union Workhouse but it was only open to married couples. Luckily for William, the Assistant Matron at Hackney, Emma Brooks, was of the same mind and they agreed to apply for the post together, stating they would be married by the time they took up the posts, if appointed:

William and Emma arranged for their contracts with Hackney to end on the same day, 6 September 1871, and next morning were married at South Hackney Church after which they took the train to West Bromwich. By the evening they were installed in the Master's Lodge. William's initial salary was £85 and Emma's £40 per annum, plus rations and furnished apartments but within eight weeks these were raised to £105 and £55 respectively.[14]

William and Emma managed the West Bromwich Union Workhouse from 1871 to 1896. One of the earliest developments during their tenure was the setting up of the Wigmore District Schools in May 1872. William was instrumental in joining with the Walsall Union to form the new School District, a particular passion of his as 'To William, good education was the keynote to success in life.'[15] Children over the age of four were sent to the Wigmore Schools which were under the control of a Superintendent and Matron. It was believed that 'after that age it is well to endeavour to remove them as far as possible from all the contaminating influences and taints of concentrated pauperism.'[16]

When William Gilpin died in 1897, a year after retiring from the workhouse, the guardians paid him this generous tribute:

He always displayed a kind consideration for the inmates, who under the circumstances seemed happy and contented, by his tact and energy. Mr Gilpin no doubt saved many women from falling amongst the lowest of the low – women who were now married and happy mothers of families.[17]

DUTIES

Broadly speaking, the master was responsible for the male paupers whilst the matron was responsible for the females. On admission, the master and matron had to make sure the paupers were searched, cleansed and clothed before they were placed in the correct ward according to their classification.[18] They had to make routine visits to the sleeping wards at eleven o'clock in the morning to check they were clean and ventilated, and also at nine o'clock every night in Winter, and ten o'clock every night in Summer to check that all the paupers were in bed.[19]

The master and matron were also required to hold a daily roll-call of the paupers and provide employment for the able-bodied 'and to allow none who are capable of employment to be idle at any time'.[20]

In addition, both the master and matron had specific duties relating to their domain of the workhouse. The matron was in charge of the kitchen, the workhouse linen and clothing, and the cleanliness of the workhouse as a whole. She was to superintend the making and mending of linen and clothing, making sure that the clothing was 'properly numbered and marked on the inside with the name of the Union'.[21] The matron also had to ensure that every pauper had clean linen and stockings once a week and that the beds and bedding were kept 'in a clean and wholesome state'. She was required to take proper care of the children and sick paupers and, 'to provide the proper diet for the same, and for women suckling infants…' A further duty of the matron was to 'pay particular attention to the moral conduct and orderly behaviour of the females and children, and to see that they are clean and decent in their dress and persons.'[22]

The master had responsibility for security, ordering provisions and keeping all manner of books and accounts. He had to superintend the distribution of food at mealtimes, say grace before and after meals, and also read prayers before breakfast and after supper every day. In order to keep the workhouse secure, he was required to receive the workhouse keys from the porter at nine o'clock every night and deliver them back to him at six o'clock every morning. Whenever a birth or death occurred in the workhouse, the master had to make sure it was registered by the Registrar for Births and Deaths and also that it was entered in the workhouse register.[23]

The master was required to 'take care that no pauper at the approach of death shall be unattended either during the day or the night' and he had to arrange burial for all dead paupers whose bodies were not removed by relatives.[24] It was the master's responsibility to send for the medical officer for any pauper who was taken ill or became insane, and 'in the case of dangerous sickness, to send for the Chaplain, and any relative or friend of the pauper…whom the pauper may desire to see.'[25]

The master's most onerous duties probably related to the books and accounts he had to keep which were rigorously scrutinised by the guardians at every board meeting. He had to keep 'nine different account books, including minute details of food wasted in cooking.'[26] As well as recording births and deaths, he had to write reports in the master's book, make records in the Workhouse Medical Relief Book and record admissions and discharges. In addition, he had to receive all the provisions for the workhouse, match them up with the relevant bills or invoices and submit them to the guardians for approval.[27]

The master had to be a highly efficient manager and needed excellent interpersonal skills. One of his main duties was to 'enforce industry, order, punctuality, and cleanliness and the observance of all regulations for the government of the workhouse by the paupers, and the several officers, assistants, and servants…'[28]

The efficient management of a workhouse would have been impossible without assistance from the inmates. In a Memoranda for the Guidance of Masters and Matrons on Workhouses in Sir John Walsham's District of 1861, it was stated that:

Emma Gilpin (*née* Brooks), matron of West Bromwich Union Workhouse between 1871 and 1896. (Courtesy of Ruth Piggott.)

The first care of the Master and Matron (after providing adequately for the necessary wants in the several wards under their superintendence) should be to select from among the inmates a suitable Wardsman or Wardswoman who should be held at all times responsible to the Master and Matron for the cleanliness and order of their respective wards.[29]

This was a good idea in theory but very small unions found it extremely difficult to put it into practice. The matron of the small Sedgefield Union Workhouse was Hannah Lambert, the widowed cousin of the master, George Bowes. In October 1888, she wrote to the board of guardians asking for a paid assistant to be appointed. Her letter gives a valuable insight into the onerous duties she had to undertake, without other staff to help her:

As Matron of the Workhouse I wish to bring under the notice of your Honourable Board the necessity of granting me some assistance so that I can carry out the regulations of the Local Government Board more efficiently. At present there are only two able-bodied women in the House & both of them suffering from debility which renders them unable at all times to do much household Work. Consequently all my time is taken up in Cooking & looking after the Sick. I have had no time for making up new Articles of Clothing for the Stores for over six months & that is needed very much it is a well known fact that no Single Woman can carry out the duties allotted to her & discharge them efficiently as requested by the Local Government Board Inspector…[30]

This indicates that the only paid members of staff in the workhouse were the master and matron, with assistance from pauper inmates, when available. The situation did not improve and by June 1889 Hannah herself was ill 'and unable to follow her duties'. Subsequently the master wrote that:

> Consequently the Sick have not had their proper dietaries cooked for them the washing, bedmaking &c has been omitted thro the want of Women. I have tried to engage the services of a Nurse for the Matron & the Sick but have failed.'[31]

SALARIES

Advertisements for posts of master and matron appeared in local newspapers and in publications such as the *Poor Law Unions Gazette*. There were vast differences in salary across England and Wales, as the amount offered depended to a large extent on the size and wealth of the union.

Between 1860 and 1914, the Aberayon Union, a tiny workhouse, paid just £30 per annum to its master.[32] Dudley, an industrial union, opened its new workhouse in 1859. The master was appointed at a salary of £80 per annum while the matron was to receive £30.[33]

Higher salaries were offered by larger unions. In 1869, the Liverpool Union paid the master £350 per annum to reflect the fact that there were 3,500 inmates within the workhouse. In the same year, Birmingham Union housed 1,994 inmates, offering a salary of £250 per annum without rations whilst the Manchester Union offered £240 per annum to manage 1,894 inmates.[34]

Larger unions were also able to offer a higher standard of living accommodation. It has been argued that as servants and lodging were provided free, 'the master and matron of a large institution could live very comfortably'.[35]

Inevitably, because of the disparity in salaries and working conditions, smaller unions had problems recruiting and retaining workhouse masters, as the most efficient and trustworthy holders of the posts sought career progression within a larger workhouse.

ACCOMMODATION

In the Dudley Union, the employment package for all resident staff included 'Officers Rations, Laundry and Furnished Apartments'.[36] Prior to 1881, these rations had included beer, but after several cases of insobriety were discovered among senior staff at an official inquiry this was discontinued.[37] At larger unions, the master and matron might have had their own house separate from the workhouse.

DEATH, RESIGNATION OR DISMISSAL OF MASTER OR MATRON

Once appointed, masters and matrons held their post until they died, resigned or were removed by the Commissioners.

In many cases, when a workhouse master died he might be replaced by his own son. This was often because the family was known and trusted by the guardians. In other cases, working for the Poor Law service as a workhouse master was a family tradition, as it was for three generations of the Ditchburn family. Luke Ditchburn was a chemist and medical dispenser before becoming the master of the Winchfield Workhouse in Hampshire. His wife Elizabeth was matron. From there, they moved to the Chesterfield Union Workhouse, taking up their duties on 2 October 1880.

Luke's sister Jane and her husband George Leaton were matron and master of the Thetford Union Workhouse. Luke's son, Matthew Ditchburn, followed his parents into the Poor Law

MERIDEN UNION.

ELECTION OF MASTER AND MATRON.

THE Board of Guardians of this Union will at a Meeting to be held at the Union Workhouse at Meriden, in the County of Warwick, on Tuesday, the 17th day of April next, proceed to the Election of a Man and his Wife as MASTER and MATRON of such Workhouse. The Salary of the Master will be £40 per Annum, and that of the Matron £20 per Annum, with Board, Lodging, and Washing in the House.

The Persons Elected must be able to keep all the Books and Accounts, and conform to the Orders prescribed by the Poor Law Board, and will be required to enter upon their Duties on the 24th April next, and the Master must give approved Security to the Amount of £50 for the faithful Performance of his official Duties.

Applications in the Handwriting of the Parties, stating their respective Ages and present Occupation, and the Number and Ages of their Children (if any), with recent Testimonials inclosed, must be sent to me on or before Tuesday, the 10th day of April next, marked "Meriden Union."

A Personal Canvass of the Guardians will be considered a disqualification.

No Candidate will be required to attend on the day of Election or at any other time, unless officially written to for that purpose, and no Payment on account of Travelling or other Expenses, or as a compensation for loss of time of parties so invited, can be made.

By order of the Guardians,

Coventry,   HENRY J. DAVIS,
28th March, 1866.   Their Clerk.

Advertisement for master and matron at the Meriden Union Workhouse. (*Justice of the Peace*, 31 March 1866.)

service. He began his career as the master's clerk of St George's Union from 1894 until 1898 when he worked for the St Pancras Union in the same capacity. He and his wife Adelaide were soon appointed master and matron at the Horton Union Workhouse in Bradford where they stayed until 1909, when they moved to Birmingham to manage the workhouse there.

Matthew's second son, Douglas, was also destined for a working life within Poor Law. With his wife Doris, he was master of the County Infirmary in Cambridge from 1934 onwards.[38]

The guardians of the Lampeter Union were so keen to retain the services of their matron when the master died that they were happy to appoint an inexperienced master. In January 1901, the master Evan Jones died. His wife Anne continued as matron and, two months later, she remarried. Her new husband James Evans was appointed as master.

The Local Government Board Inspector, T.J. Bircham, commented that: 'When the new master has learnt to keep his books it will be easier for him. No doubt he will get the assistance from the Clerks Office or he might see the Tregaron master.'[39]

Although unions preferred their masters and matrons to be married couples, if a master was particularly valued and his wife died the guardians would not insist that he resign. This happened in the case of Harry James Bristow, the master of the Midhurst Union Workhouse, who was appointed in 1868. His wife, Jessie, was appointed as matron. With nursing and midwifery experience, she was well suited to the role. When Jessie died in June 1888, the guardians were reluctant to lose Harry as a valued member of staff. He was asked to continue as master for six months and Ellen Westbrook was elected as matron to work with him. Harry's appointment was extended and he continued as master until September 1899.[40]

SUCCESSFUL PARTNERSHIPS

At the Dudley Union, Thomas William Stillard was the master from the time of its opening in 1859 until his death in 1873.[41] Thomas had previously been the relieving officer for the Tipton district.[42] His wife, Maria, was the matron.

Thomas and Maria Stillard were highly valued by the Dudley board of guardians. When Thomas died, the guardians recorded that 'the Board has lost an able and efficient officer, the Poor a kind and considerate friend and the Ratepayers a faithful and honest Servant.'[43]

Maria Stillard continued as matron until 1875.[44] When she resigned, the board proposed to grant her a Superannuation allowance due to the 'long and faithful services rendered by Mrs Stillard and her late Husband.'[45] This was not, in fact, allowed to go ahead, largely due to the Local Government Board's objections that Maria Stillard was still able to work, with or without four dependent children, but the intention on the part of the guardians was clear.[46]

George Bowes was the master of the small Sedgefield Union Workhouse in County Durham from around 1876. A farmer's son from Yorkshire, he was twenty-five when he was appointed with his first wife, Elizabeth, as matron. When she died, George's widowed cousin Hannah Lambert took over the post. Some time later, George re-married and his wife Emily became matron. In 1891, George requested a testimonial as he intended to apply for the post of master at the Darlington Union.[47] However, he was either unsuccessful or changed his mind about applying as he remained the master at Sedgefield for at least thirty years.

The Bowes' long service as master and matron at Sedgefield had a very positive impact on the workhouse as a whole. In 1899, one visitor recorded that 'The general condition of the workhouse and inmates is a great credit to Mr and Mrs Bowes.'[48]

George took a special interest in the welfare of the inmates, especially the children. He personally visited the children who were apprenticed, sent into service or boarded-out. Many of the children who left the workhouse wrote regularly to him and others chose to come back for their holidays. In April 1906, George Bowes recorded that 'Henry Sutheran, one of our Boys spent a day with us last week, he likes his situation and is comfortable and happy, he looked well and was spotlessly clean, is a credit to himself and the Board.'[49]

George's wife Emily, who acted as matron, was also kind and compassionate. In 1902, George reported that, 'The Matron asks permission to take four of the Women in the House to Redcar on Saturday first for the days outing, the expenses will be partly paid by themselves, the Matron will make up the rest.'[50]

In 1891 at the Bromsgrove Union, Mr and Mrs Barrows were elected master and matron at the salaries of £60 and £30 respectively. They stayed until July 1900 and, on leaving the union, the guardians recorded that 'in the opinion of this Board, Mr and Mrs Barrows possess many qualities fitting them for the positions they hold and the Guardians are glad to know that they leave Bromsgrove to enter upon a greater sphere of usefulness and responsibility in the management of a larger workhouse.'[51]

At the Cardigan Union in 1906, Captain and Mrs Richards retired as master and matron. The guardians recorded that 'each one of the occupants expressed their deep regret at the fact of losing two such exceptionally good, kind-hearted officials.'[52]

Another successful partnership was that of Daniel and Eleanor Pickett who were master and matron of Stratford-on-Avon Union Workhouse from 1896 to 1927. On their retirement, the *Stratford Herald* published an article about their life and work which provides some interesting insights into the role of workhouse masters and matrons. The reporter claimed that Daniel Pickett 'seems to regard his position as that of a patrician householder.' He went on to ask: 'Does "Oliver Twist" make you weep? Then visit Mr Pickett and his charges, and you will soon be happy again. Compared with Mr and Mrs Bumble, he and his kindly wife are as alkali to acid…'.

When asked about the punishment of paupers, Daniel replied:

The new Risbridge Union Workhouse at Kedington, Suffolk. (*Illustrated London News*, 2 April 1859.)

Well, I'm empowered to put a man on bread and water, but I never do without consulting the doctor. Really, I don't think I have punished half-a-dozen people, or taken more than two before the guardians, during my forty years in poor law service. I don't believe in too much power being allotted to one man.

Despite suffering with the constant pain of gout in his legs, Daniel was able to superintend the workhouse from a bath chair with the help of Eleanor and assistance from other members of staff. In his interview, Daniel went on to pay tribute to his wife Eleanor: 'You have no idea how important it is that the matron of an establishment like this should possess sympathy and the gift of organisation, and so I must pay a tribute to the wonderful way in which my wife has helped me…'[53]

COMPLAINTS ABOUT MASTERS AND MATRONS

It was, perhaps, inevitable, that with the great power the master held over the paupers, some chose to abuse it. It has been argued that the master's '…greatest power was his control over the minutiae of the house; his greatest temptation his relations with local tradesmen.'[54]

In the early years of the new Poor Law, lurid reports of excessive punishments by masters and matrons were regularly printed in the press, particularly *The Times*. In 1841, the master of the Hoo workhouse was investigated for flogging some of the young, female inmates.[55] In 1840, at the Bath Workhouse, Rebecca Collett, a woman 'heavy with child' was confined to 'a damp, stone dungeon, without even straw to lie on.'[56]

Sometimes, the guardians and the Poor Law Board were slow to weed out miscreant masters or matrons. George Catch was the notorious master of the Strand, Newington and Lambeth Workhouses where there were numerous complaints about his harsh treatment of the inmates. Catch was finally dismissed when he was found guilty of cruelty to the able-bodied women under his care. It was reported that he had:

…terrified one of the disreputable women so much that she fled; thinking she had hidden up a chimney, Catch and the medical officer tried to smoke her down with a burning mixture of chloride of lime and sulphuric acid. Since she was not there, the mixture fortunately did no more than choke nurses and other paupers in the room.[57]

John Pringuer and his wife Rebecca were the master and matron of the Faversham Union Workhouse. In 1841, the guardians were concerned about the high number of Faversham inmates being sent to prison, compared with those of neighbouring unions. It was discovered that the master had on occasion 'shown harshness of manner.' The guardians instructed him 'in future to be kind, but at the same time firm.'[58]

The master's house at the Christchurch Union Workhouse, now converted into housing. (Courtesy of Carl Higgs.)

Masters and matrons could also be guilty of mismanaging the accounts and taking advantage of their position in ordering the supplies for the workhouse. In November 1881, the guardians of the Dudley Union were forced to dismiss their master, matron, assistant matron and porter at the same time. An official inquiry revealed 'grave irregularities…both in regard to the management and the conduct of some of the officers.'[59] In particular, 'the accounts of the consumption of provisions in the workhouse were kept in a grossly irregular and careless manner.'[60]

INTO THE TWENTIETH CENTURY

Towards the end of the nineteenth century and the beginning of the twentieth, masters and matrons were still expected to work excessively long hours and discrimination against officers with families remained a significant issue.[61] In many larger unions, with the increased workload of record-keeping, a clerk or assistant master was appointed to assist the master in keeping the books.

The Poor Law Officer's Superannuation Act of 1896 provided a much-needed pension scheme for all Poor Law officers, including masters and matrons. This was a contributory scheme whereby officers had a sum deducted from their salary to put towards their pension. Officers could also apply to the guardians for an extra sum to be added to their superannuation based on the number of years of service. Although the superannuation scheme was undoubtedly a breakthrough for all Poor Law officers, it affected the mobility of masters and matrons as 'superannuation payments were not transferable.'[62]

THE SCHOOLTEACHERS

The schoolteacher had one of the most arduous jobs in the workhouse. As with the majority of officers' posts, the schoolteacher was required to live in, the remuneration usually being board, washing and rations. The workhouse schoolteacher had to be on call at all times to look after the children in his or her care. Unlike schoolteachers of Board or National schools, the officers' duties with regard to the children did not end when the schoolday finished.

DUTIES

The duties of the workhouse schoolteacher were many. First and foremost, he or she was required to instruct 'the boys and girls who are inmates of the workhouse…for three of the working hours, at least, every day….in reading, writing, arithmetic, and the principles of the Christian religion….and train them to habits of usefulness, industry, and virtue.'[1]

Schoolteachers were also expected to 'regulate the discipline and arrangements of the school, and the industrial and moral training of the children, subject to the direction of the Guardians.'[2] This was no mean feat at many unions where a teacher might have sole charge of up to eighty children.

Another duty of the workhouse schoolteacher was to 'accompany the children when they quit the workhouse for exercise, or for attendance at public worship, unless the Guardians shall otherwise direct.'[3] This last duty naturally increased the schoolteacher's working hours and encroached on the little free time he or she had.

At times, the schoolteacher's role was one of surrogate parent to the workhouse children as he or she was the adult with whom they were in most contact. This extended to keeping 'the children clean in their persons, and orderly and decorous in their conduct.'[4]

A final duty was to 'assist the Master and Matron respectively in maintaining due subordination in the workhouse.'[5] This duty did not refer specifically to children, so unions could interpret it in such a way that the schoolteacher was expected to help keep order throughout the workhouse, including the adult wards.

Teaching in a workhouse school was not an attractive option, and so recruitment and retention was a perennial problem for the guardians of workhouse unions. Reading the following extract from a Poor Law Board Circular in 1870, it is easy to see why:

> Suppose a young man, after serving an apprenticeship to his profession and passing two years in a training college, accepts a charge of a workhouse school: he soon discovers that teaching is the least part of his duties. He has to rise at six o'clock in the morning to see his boys washed before breakfast. He has to attend three times a day in the dining hall, to superintend bathing, combing, scrubbing floors, making beds etc; to take the boys out for exercise and to see them to bed at night. So that if he does his duty conscientiously he is fully engaged from

six in the morning till eight at night. This unpleasant course of duty goes on day after day without intermission or change. Saturday is no holiday and Sunday is no day of rest...[6]

There must have been countless schoolteachers like Joseph Wakelam, the schoolmaster at the Dudley Union, who felt the need to leave the workhouse for a few hours' respite. In November 1871, just a month after being appointed, he was informed by the guardians that:

...his frequent absence from the Workhouse after the discharge of his duties cannot in future be allowed, but that his Absence from the Workhouse must be in future restricted to two Nights Weekly on the understanding that he returns to the Workhouse not later than ten o'clock p.m.[7]

It should be noted that Joseph left the workhouse 'after the discharge of his duties' but he was still expected to be on call. The issue seems to have been resolved because Joseph's salary was increased from £30 to £40 per annum in August 1872 and he stayed in the post until November 1874.

The 'inability ever to feel off-duty' certainly contributed to the high turnover of teaching staff across England and Wales.[8] One inspector commented that:

It appears to me quite unreasonable that a schoolmaster of thirty years of age should be compelled to be within the walls at nine o'clock or half past nine every night, or that he should on every occasion be obliged to ask leave of the master of the workhouse before he can go outside.[9]

Children at the Gressenhall village school, taken before 1912. Children from the Mitford and Launditch Union Workhouse attended the school, and can be identified by their shaven heads and distinctive uniforms. (Courtesy of Gressenhall Farm and Workhouse – The Museum of Norfolk Life.)

SALARIES

As with other workhouse posts, salaries varied across England and Wales, again fluctuating according to the size of the union and the number of children to be taught. In 1846, in a bid to attract better qualified applicants and retain them, an Act of Parliament was passed which provided £30,000 to increase the salaries of workhouse teachers. This was to amount to a grant of no more than £30 per teacher. In addition, workhouse schoolteachers were to be housed in better accommodation and were to be exempt from menial service. School attendance registers were to be kept and workhouse schools were to be regularly inspected by the Committee of Council on Education.[10]

If the HMI Inspector was not satisfied with the standard of teaching, he would not issue a certificate. Without a certificate, unions could not apply for the government grants to fund their schoolteachers' salaries which left the guardians with a choice. They could either dismiss the teacher and appoint a new one, or they could pay the teacher's salary from union funds. A surprising number of guardians disagreed with the HMI inspectors' judgement about the capabilities of the teachers at their union, as at Droitwich in 1862. The guardians were convinced by the chaplain that the inspector's criticism of their schoolmistress was unfair. They paid her salary from union funds and, it seems, the chaplain was justified in his actions, as the following year the HMI inspector stated that 'the children appear to me to have improved and made progress since my last visit, several can read and write fairly, and were correct in their sums.' A certificate was duly issued and a grant was paid.[11]

By 1849, the average salary for a workhouse schoolmaster was £26 per annum with £16 per annum for workhouse schoolmistresses. Fifteen years later, the Bromsgrove Union advertised for a schoolmistress at £25 per annum 'subject to such increase as may be awarded by the Committee of Council on Education, with Rations, Lodging, and Washing in the Workhouse.'[12]

Nineteen-year-old Alexander Frizelle was appointed schoolmaster to the Dudley Union in 1874 at a salary of £40 per annum.[13] Despite his youth, Alexander appears to have been an extremely competent teacher as, eighteen months later, the guardians decided to increase his salary from £40 to £60 per annum. They justified their decision to the Poor Law Board by stating that:

...since Mr Frizelle's appointment at the Dudley Union the general management of the school has considerably improved, and that he has taken great pains to forward the education of the children, and also having taken into consideration the amount of salary paid to similar officers in adjacent Unions and the amount of remuneration paid to qualified Teachers generally, the Guardians consider Mr Frizelle fairly entitled to receive for his services a Salary of £60 per annum.[14]

In 1877, Alexander married the schoolmistress, Esther Anne Mason, and together they regularly received Certificates of Efficiency in the First Division.[15] Alexander and Esther were considered valuable assets to the Dudley Union Workhouse. When the Poor Law Board queried the fact that Alexander and Esther had a son living at the workhouse, the guardians responded that they 'would regret to lose the services of Mr & Mrs Frizelle. The amount received from parliamentary grants have for several years repaid the guardians the annual amount of their salaries.'[16] It was agreed that Alexander should pay 2s 6d weekly 'for the Maintenance of his Child in the New Schools at the Workhouse...'.[17] Alexander Frizelle retained his post as schoolmaster at the Dudley Union for nearly twenty-three years, long after the death of his wife.

Where there were large numbers of children to be taught without extra assistance, there was usually a large turnover of staff to match. There are countless examples of schoolteachers leaving their posts due to ill-health, probably caused by stress and fatigue. Twenty-four-year-old Lucinda Gould was appointed schoolmistress to the Christchurch Union in 1843. Prior to her appointment the children were 'cared for by an inmate.' Lucinda Gould was considered an effective teacher, as, in 1849 she was awarded 'a Certificate of Competency in the First Division from the Committee of the Council of Education.' In her final years in the post however, Miss Gould's teaching was badly affected by her ill-health, and a school inspection of 1869 records that the children were 'deficient in liveliness' and did not show 'much intelligence.'[18]

INFLUENCE OF THE CHAPLAIN

In many unions, the chaplain held a position of power over the teaching staff. It was considered important that the chaplain 'should be responsible for the day-to-day administration of the workhouse school…because he would then be able to comment on religious aspects of the school curriculum.'[19] Inevitably, this could lead to conflict between the chaplain and the schoolteacher.

Many chaplains took their responsibility for the school very seriously. At Kidderminster in 1844, the chaplain recommended that 'it would be as well for them [the children] to continue school till half past four for this month instead of running about the yard wearing out shoe leather and making a great noise.'[20] Although these longer hours were a contravention of the regulations issued by the Poor Law Commission, the schoolmistress was expected to comply with the chaplain's recommendation and work the new hours.[21]

ACCOMMODATION

In smaller workhouses, such as Sedgefield in County Durham and Lampeter in Cardiganshire, the children were sent to the nearby village or Board school. It was simply not economical to employ a dedicated member of staff to teach the children. At the industrial Dudley Union, a schoolmaster and schoolmistress were appointed as part of the core staff when the new workhouse was opened in 1859. The schoolmaster was to receive £30 per annum and the schoolmistress £20 per annum. Both were to receive workhouse rations in addition to their salary.[22] As the schoolteachers were required to live in, the post at Dudley also offered 'furnished apartments at the workhouse.'

Whilst the term 'furnished apartment' may sound grand, it may have been little more than a poky room. In the early years of the New Poor Law, accommodation for schoolteachers was little better than the wards the inmates slept in. The Assistant Commissioner Ruddock stated that between 1834 and 1844, the workhouse schoolmistresses were 'generally pent up in a small closet boarded off from the common sleeping apartment of the children.'[23]

QUALIFICATIONS AND TRAINING

Although the education of workhouse children was considered essential to help them out of the poverty trap, in the early years of the New Poor Law qualifications for workhouse schoolteachers were not necessary and 'any literate person' could apply for a schoolteacher's post.[24] In 1847, the former occupations of Norfolk workhouse teachers included 'hairdresser, tailor, saddler, parish clerk, workhouse porter…, dressmaker, housekeeper and lady's maid.'[25] In Worcestershire, only two of the schoolmasters appointed between 1834 and 1871 had previous teaching experience.[26]

It has been argued that when it came to recruiting schoolteachers 'the second-rate man had to be accepted because few trained people were willing to work for Poor Law salaries.'[27]

This picture illustrates the instruction of pauper children in the South Metropolitan District School, Sutton. This district school was set up in the early 1850s to house children away from the workhouse. The children are being taught tailoring skills. (*Illustrated London News*, 4 May 1872.)

At the Faversham Union in 1836, the guardians appointed Thomas Fukes, a pauper inmate, and his wife Frances as schoolmaster and schoolmistress. Thomas Fukes was able to write his name but his wife signed with an X on her marriage certificate. When Thomas died in December 1843, there was much wrangling between the guardians and the Local Government Board. The guardians wanted to retain Mrs Fukes as schoolmistress at £10 a year and appoint Thomas Elvey, a local grocer, as schoolmaster.[28]

In July 1844, the Local Government Board argued that the 'existing arrangement…appears to be a most disadvantageous one for the girls…Under the present arrangement the education of the girls is not carried far enough.' They urged the Faversham guardians to appoint another more qualified schoolmistress but retain Mrs Fukes as an assistant at the present wage as 'she is useful amongst the girls attending to their personal habits and to train them in needlework.'[29]

The Faversham guardians assented to the idea and decided to choose a schoolmistress 'competent to teach the girls reading, writing and arithmetic' from nine until noon each weekday and on Sunday, religion during the same hours. However, the Poor Law Commission in London was insistent that the appointed schoolmistress should 'reside at the workhouse and devote her whole time to the duties of the office.' In November 1844, almost a year after the death of Thomas Fukes, the Faversham guardians appointed Jane Wallington, a married forty-six-year-old from Faversham who had previously been the mistress of a National School for four years. Jane Wallington remained in her post for twenty years.[30]

The pupil-teacher system was at the heart of teacher training in England, having been started spontaneously by a thirteen-year-old boy called William Rush who took over the teaching in the Mitford and Launditch Union when the teacher became ill. William developed his teaching skills further when he was sent by the guardians to the model pauper school at Norwood, and from there to the Battersea Training School. He emerged as a fully trained teacher and, in 1849, he received a salary of £60 per annum to teach at the Walsingham Union, 'which was the highest salary of any Norfolk workhouse teacher.' William Rush left the Poor Law service 'to teach at the National School in Broadstairs, Kent, where he died shortly afterwards from tuberculosis.'[31]

Sir James Kay-Shuttleworth and the Committee of Council on Education further developed the English pupil-teacher system in 1846. State grants were available to pupil-teachers who undertook a five year apprenticeship under an experienced teacher. Successful trainees could then compete for a Queen's Scholarship to a training college. This was all well and good in theory, but in practice few workhouses employed suitably qualified teachers with a certificate of competency or efficiency to supervise potential trainees.[32]

WORKHOUSE EDUCATION

The education provided by workhouse schoolteachers varied across England and Wales. The minimum, according to Article 114 of the Consolidated General Order, was a grounding in reading, writing, arithmetic and religion. However, in 1846 at the Martley Union, the guardians refused to teach writing because:

> ...pauper child inmates of the workhouse received as good an education as that generally given in the country and they do not feel themselves justified in going to any expense whereby they [inmate pauper children] might receive advantages that are not attainable by the children of those who support their families without parochial relief.[33]

The Poor Law Commission insisted that the pauper children should 'receive such an amount of instruction as will fit them for good situations in after life.'[34]

The HMI inspections assessed the schoolteachers' intellectual competency, defined by the Privy Council Committee on Education in 1849, as the ability to 'read fluently, write from dictation and from memory, [and] work sums in the first four simple and compound rules of arithmetic.' There is no evidence to suggest there was any 'attempt to estimate teaching ability.'[35]

Learning was therefore mainly by rote. As a result, in the 1870s, when workhouse children were examined at the same time as elementary schoolchildren, 'they did worse in subjects which required independent thought.'[36]

COMPLAINTS ABOUT SCHOOLTEACHERS

As with any official workhouse post, the schoolteacher could abuse his or her power. Complaints about schoolteachers regularly came to the attention of the Poor Law Board.

One Assistant Commissioner commented: 'There is no class of officer of whom such continual complaints are made...I need not call to your recollection the numbers you have been obliged to dismiss for drunkenness or other immoralities.'[37]

At the Kidderminster Union in 1869, the schoolmaster was accused 'by an inmate, near confinement, of having connexion with her.' The schoolmaster admitted that the accusation was true and he was promptly dismissed from his post. The man later applied for the post of master at the Pershore Union but his dismissal from Kidderminster meant he was debarred from the post. The man's name was added to a central register of dismissals 'kept to ensure that offenders were not employed in the Poor Law system again.'[38]

Despite the existence of this central register, the Poor Law Board was often 'slow to weed out unsatisfactory teachers, especially if they were trained.' In 1871, they finally refused to sanction the appointment of Mr W. Robinson as schoolmaster because he had 'worked in five unions in five years, and left all of them under a cloud.'[39]

One of the 'scattered homes' for pauper children of the Sheffield Union. (Courtesy of the Sheffield Local Studies Library.)

The schoolmaster who prompted John Rowlands (later to become the explorer Sir Henry Morton Stanley), to run away from St. Asaph Union Workhouse near Denbigh was James Francis, a sadistic former collier who had lost a hand in a mining accident. He was 'soured by misfortune, brutal of temper, and callous of heart', yet the children always received good results when examined by HMI inspectors, undoubtedly through learning by rote.[40]

SUCCESSFUL TEACHERS

Not all appointments of schoolteachers were unsatisfactory. At the Romford Union, the guardians were delighted with their schoolmistress, Miss Pepper and 'her kind and able treatment of the children, as evidenced by their excellent demeanour and their advancement in learning.' Miss Pepper received a salary of £20 per annum and in 1842, the guardians proposed to 'present her with a gratuity of Ten Pounds.'[41] Miss Pepper later resigned to look after her sick and ageing father.

Mary Hancox, an unmarried twenty-seven-year-old from Penn in Staffordshire, was appointed schoolmistress at the Dudley Union in May 1860.[42] Mary had previously been a governess to the family of Thomas Meyrick, an architect and surveyor to the Board of Health in Wolverhampton. She had looked after six children: five daughters and one son, ranging from eleven years old to less than one month. That she had teaching experience was not in doubt. However, it was a very different teaching situation at Dudley Union where, for the remuneration of £20 per annum, she was expected to teach seventy girls and attend to their industrial training as well.

Mary appears to have been a conscientious teacher, if a little overzealous, and in December 1862 she was called before the guardians after a complaint about punishing one of the girls. She was 'informed that the Corporal Punishment of female children is prohibited by Art:138 and that the Master should be informed of all cases where punishment is required.'[43]

When Mary applied for a fortnight's leave in July 1862 she was given permission by the guardians only 'on the condition that her sister who is accustomed to tuition shall take her place in the school during her absence.'[44]

In February 1864, Mary Hancox applied to the guardians for a rise in salary. Her request was referred to the Visiting Committee who discovered that she has 'double the number of children in the School in comparison to the number when she was engaged four years ago.'[45] As it was pointed out that Mary also had to undertake the industrial training of the children in her care, her salary was duly increased from £20 to £28 per annum.[46]

ADVANCEMENT

For many workhouse schoolteachers, especially those in large unions, the post was a springboard to one of greater responsibility within the Poor Law service: the coveted role of a master or matron. As the majority of unions preferred married couples to fill their most responsible posts, courtships were often played out among the lower ranks of staff who held lofty ambitions for advancement in the Poor Law service.

Many a workhouse officer married another in order to obtain promotion. Mary Hancox did just that. In March 1866 she resigned from the Dudley Union to take up a post as matron at the smaller Ludlow Union.[47] The master was none other than George Kirby, who had been appointed at Dudley as assistant master on the same day that Mary was appointed schoolmistress.

George Kirby had resigned his post at Dudley in 1860, and it is not known where he was working before his appointment as master at Ludlow. Perhaps they had been planning to apply for a master and matron partnership while they were both at Dudley. Perhaps the idea only came to fruition during the three years George was away from Dudley. However it happened, their marriage and partnership must have been a successful one as they were master and matron at Ludlow for over thirty-five years.

Another ambitious schoolmaster at Dudley Union was James Silvester Chance. He stayed at Dudley for three years before becoming the master of the King's Norton Union Workhouse in Birmingham. At some stage he must have moved to London as his widow was the matron of the Epsom Union Workhouse in 1881.

In 1862, the HMI Inspector, T.G. Bowyer, described workhouse teachers as 'a very respectable, hard-working and conscientious class of persons, who make up by diligence and dedication to their duties, for deficiencies under which many of them labour in regard to ability and instruction.'[48]

There were many workhouse teachers like Miss Pepper and William Rush who devoted themselves to their teaching, to the benefit of the workhouse children, until ill-health forced them to resign. Other equally hard-working workhouse teachers like Mary Hancox and James Chance were rewarded for their labours through promotion to senior positions at other workhouses.

INTO THE TWENTIETH CENTURY

Workhouse schoolteachers were a rare breed at the end of the nineteenth and beginning of the twentieth century. Generally, by this time there was a move towards sending children out of the workhouse to so-called 'district' schools, specialist institutions or cottage homes. Other unions boarded their children out with local families.

The Bakewell Union Workhouse (no date).

In unions where children remained in the workhouse, there was a trend towards sending them to local schools. In many cases the schoolteachers were replaced by 'industrial trainers' who, in theory, had the important job of trying to equip the children for the world of work outside the workhouse and giving them the tools to work their way out of poverty. In practice, they were often simply unemployed seamstresses, shoemakers or tailors.

At the Darlington Union in 1892, the female industrial trainer was required:

> ...to take charge of the Infants; to take charge of the other Children maintained in the Workhouse, when not at School; to see that the Children are kept clean and tidy; to be responsible for the cleanliness of that part of the Workhouse occupied by them; to instruct them in Sewing and Domestic Work; to Teach the Girls to Cut Out and Make up Clothing; and also to assist the Matron when required.[49]

The boys at Darlington were not neglected either. The guardians appear to have tried to kill two birds with one stone by choosing an industrial trainer for the boys to fill a vacant baker post in the workhouse. The boys' industrial training was therefore only in baking and the trainer was to undertake all the baking for the union.[50]

The 1905 Royal Commission heard evidence that the salaries and holidays of the remaining workhouse schoolteachers did not compare favourably with those of elementary schoolteachers and 'they were still expected to work long hours as the children's attendants.'[51]

Workhouse school teaching had changed little by 1908 when the Board of Education criticised Poor Law Schools where 'Rows and rows of fat, clean, well-shod infants sat bored and listless, [and] recite in unison what they do not understand...'[52]

THE MEDICAL OFFICER

Under the terms of the Poor Law Amendment Act, all unions had to appoint a medical officer to take care of the sick in the workhouse and those receiving out-relief. In small unions, the post could be held by the same person. In larger unions there was a medical officer for each district within the union and a workhouse medical officer. The posts were non-residential.

TYPES OF APPLICANT

In the social hierarchy of the workhouse staff, the medical officer had a lowly status. In most cases he combined his role in the workhouse with private practice and he was 'generally regarded as no better than a struggling tradesman.'[1] Young, newly qualified doctors might take a post as a workhouse medical officer 'in order to help build up a practice in a district…'[2]

A letter to the *Yarmouth Independent* of 1879 signed 'A Surgeon, But Not A Candidate' described the problems of appointing a newcomer to the area as a district or workhouse medical officer: 'There are already at least seventeen medical men in practice in Yarmouth, each of whom would theoretically have to give up a share of his practice to a new comer.'[3]

QUALIFICATIONS

Applicants for the post of both workhouse medical officer and district medical officer had to possess a diploma or degree as a surgeon from a Royal College or University in England, Scotland or Ireland. In addition, he needed a degree in medicine *or* a diploma or licence of the Royal Physicians of London *or* a certificate to practice as an apothecary from the Society of Apothecaries of London. He was also qualified to apply if he had 'been in actual practice as an apothecary on the first day of August one thousand eight hundred and fifteen' or if he had a warrant or commission as surgeon or assistant-surgeon in Her Majesty's Navy, Her Majesty's Army or the Honourable East India Company prior to 1 August 1826.[4]

As qualifications in both surgery and medicine were a prerequisite, it has been argued that 'paupers were looked after by a better qualified doctor than the typical rural practitioner who treated the independent poor.'[5]

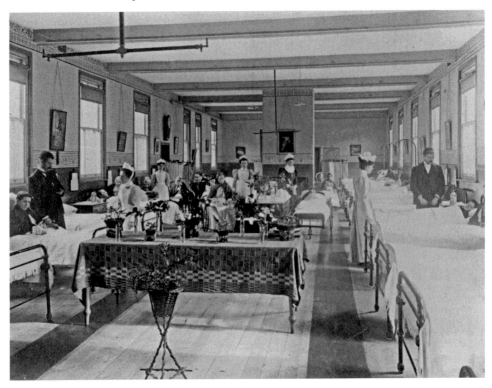

An infirmary ward at the Fir Vale Workhouse, Sheffield. (Courtesy of the Sheffield Teaching Hospitals NHS Foundation Trust.)

DUTIES OF THE WORKHOUSE MEDICAL OFFICER

The duties of the workhouse medical officer were many and varied. He was to 'attend duly and punctually upon all poor persons in the workhouse requiring medical attendance and according to his agreement to supply the requisite medicine to such persons.'[6] The fact that the medical officer had to supply and pay for his own drugs for the use of the paupers remained a bone of contention throughout the Victorian period and well into the twentieth century.

It was the medical officer's responsibility to examine the paupers in the receiving ward on admittance to the workhouse. If any pauper was 'labouring under any disease of body or mind', the medical officer had to direct the master to place him or her in the sick ward.[7]

Under the Consolidated General Order, it was intended that the sick ward or infirmary was the medical officer's domain. He was to 'give directions and make suggestions as to the diet, classification, and treatment of the sick paupers, and paupers of unsound mind.'[8]

The medical officer also had specific responsibilities with regard to the children. He was to vaccinate any children who were not vaccinated and to give instructions as to their diet and treatment. Women who were suckling children were also to be given specific diets by the medical officer.[9]

With regard to the paupers of unsound mind, the medical officer had to decide whether they were fit to stay in the workhouse. If he deemed them to be too dangerous, he had to give the order to send them to a lunatic asylum, and report to the guardians accordingly.[10]

The living conditions of the inmates obviously had an effect on their health so the medical officer also had to 'report in writing to the Guardians any defect in the diet, drainage, ventilation, warmth, or other arrangements of the workhouse, or any excess in the number of any class of inmates, which he may deem to be detrimental to the health of the inmates.'[11] Despite this duty set down in the Consolidated General Order, observations made by the medical officer to the guardians often fell on deaf ears. For example, at the St Faith's Union in the 1840s, the medical officer made suggestions for the:

> …provision of piped water to the bedrooms and of clean towels; the practice of bathing entrants to the house in the same water was condemned for spreading vermin and disease; and the bad ventilation and overcrowding in the wards were alleged to be affecting the health of the paupers.[12]

His suggestions were met by 'a wall of indifference.'[13]

These observations were extended to include any defects in the 'arrangements of the Infirmary, and in the performance of their duties by the Nurses of the sick.'[14] When relationships between the medical officer and nurses were strained, this could have a knock-on effect on the care offered to the inmates and cause a high turnover of nursing staff. When Dr Joseph Rogers became the medical officer for the Strand Union Workhouse in 1856, he found that the pauper nurses were rewarded with beer or gin allowances. Their liquor ration was issued at 7 a.m. and so they 'began the day drunk.'[15] Dr Rogers reported that they 'only in exceptional instances paid any attention to what I said.' He 'suffered particularly at the hands of one called Charlotte who 'invariably treated me with supreme indifference, not unmingled with supreme contempt'.[16]

TRIMDON. *Colliery*

Oct 7 1905

I hereby certify that *Richard Poole*

residing at T.C.

is **unable** *to follow his employment* on account of *Epileptic Convulsions*

Hugh Russell
M. D.

Thomas Russell
Physician & Surgeon

A medical certificate from 1905 confirming that Richard Poole, a miner at Trimdon Colliery, was unable to work because he suffered from epilepsy. The certificate would have entitled Richard to apply for poor relief. (U/Se 41. Reproduced by permission of the Durham County Record Office.)

In addition to these duties, medical officers had to issue medical certificates for every sick pauper, record the death of any pauper who died in the workhouse and keep meticulous records regarding the diet of sick paupers.[17]

DUTIES OF THE DISTRICT MEDICAL OFFICER

The district medical officer also had specific duties. He was to:

> ...attend duly and punctually upon all poor persons requiring medical attendance within the District of the Union assigned to him, and according to his agreement to supply the requisite medicines to such persons...[18]

It was important that he only attended paupers 'with a written or printed order of the Guardians, or of a Relieving Officer of the Union, or of an Overseer.'[19]

Like the workhouse medical officer, he also had to keep meticulous records for the guardians of the medical relief he had provided and make sure he informed the relieving officer of 'any poor person whom he may attend without an order.'[20]

SALARIES

It was not until 1842 that the Poor Law Board decreed medical officers should be appointed on a salaried basis.[21] Before then, medical officers were appointed on a contract basis, just like the tradesmen who supplied goods for the workhouse. Many penny-pinching boards of guardians were keen to secure 'the services of local doctors willing to make the lowest bid.'[22]

In 1857, the guardians of the Dudley Union objected vehemently to the suggestion by the central authorities that they appoint medical officers on a lifetime basis, like the other workhouse officers, to which they had 'an insurmountable objection...'.[23] Two years later, the guardians were still arguing about the Poor Law Commission's suggestion. They argued that 'the annual appointment of all medical officers can be the only sure guarantee for securing really efficient Medical Relief to the Poor.'[24]

When James Hester was appointed the workhouse medical officer at the Abingdon Union in 1835, he was to be paid £110 per annum. This was 'to include all cases of casual poor, accidents, surgery and midwifery, and to supply medicines, ointments, bandages and leeches.'[25]

At the Samford Union in 1860, Dr Albert Fleming was appointed medical officer for the Holbrook District at a salary of £61 17s 8d and an extra £35 for duties in the workhouse. He had to attend at the workhouse on Mondays, Thursdays and Saturdays.[26]

When the Dudley Union Workhouse was first opened in 1859, the medical officer received the top salary of £90 per annum. This was to include 'operations of every description. All confinements and cases of childbirth and every kind of medical and Surgical treatment... together with all medicines.'[27]

Ten years later, Dudley's workhouse medical officer, Mr Haden, applied for an increase in salary. When he was first appointed in 1859, there were between 160 and 165 beds. Now there were an additional 120 beds. The Visiting Committee reported that:

> The Medical Officer has 331 cases on his books – there have been as many as 360. He is paid £90 a year which with extras would probably increase the amount to £100, out of which he has to provide all Drugs, Instruments & Appliances. Upon comparison with ten other Unions in the district, whilst he is paid very much less, the Medical Officer of the Dudley Union has (with the exception of Birmingham) very many more beds & patients under his care...that in several of them all & in others, part of the Drugs required are paid for by the Guardians.[28]

Mr Haden's salary was duly increased by £20 per annum to £110 per annum.

George Middlemiss was the workhouse medical officer for the Darlington Union and also for the South and East Darlington districts from July 1882 until June 1911. Towards the end of his service for the union, his salary was £115 per annum which was made up of £70 for the workhouse and home, £35 for his district work and £10 for tending to the sick at the Boys Home.[29]

In May 1890, Thomas Frederick Higgs, another medical officer for the Dudley Union, applied for an increase in salary. He was appointed in 1871 at a salary of £110 per annum and since then 'increased accommodation has been provided at the workhouse, by the conversion of the Old Schools into Imbecile Wards and the erection of detached School Buildings and the duties of the Medical Officer have in consequence been increased.' The Visiting Committee recommended that his salary be increased to £150 per annum 'to include the cost of Drugs, Instruments, Medical Appliances, Fees for Midwifery etc.'[30] The guardians agreed and his salary was duly increased.

Ten years later, Thomas Higgs' salary was increased again from £150 per annum to £200 per annum and it was stated that 'the cost of Drugs to Mr Higgs is about £60 per annum.'[31] The issue of drugs for the workhouse remained a thorny one, and in May 1903 Dr Higgs wrote to the guardians 'asking to be furnished with a supply of Drugs and Surgical Instruments for use at the workhouse.'[32]

The salaries of the district medical officers varied according to the size of the district, but the average was £65 per annum towards the end of the period.[33]

In 1879, the guardians of the Great Yarmouth Union had problems recruiting a new medical officer for the workhouse. A letter to the *Yarmouth Independent* from 'a surgeon, but not a candidate' suggested that this was due, at least in part, to the low salary offered which was £105 per annum. The writer explained more fully how a medical officer's annual salary might be spent:

> …we will imagine that twenty patients have been attended daily. Of these twenty at least twelve would have medicine supplied, and allowing that the least possible amount was expended in drugs – viz, two pence per head – this alone would amount to 36*l.* 10s. per annum. …35*l.* per annum would be a low estimate for the original cost of drugs alone. Then it would be necessary to have a surgery, and supply bandages and other surgical appliances. Add 10*l.* a year for this. Deducting 15*l.* from 105*l.* would leave 60*l.* to pay for the work done, in round numbers 23s. per week, or two pence per patient. And at this rate the Yarmouth Guardians value the services of a gentleman who must…be more than twenty-one years of age, have spent four years in time, and hundreds of pounds in money on his studies and have passed the necessary examinations…I think…that it is certain no medical man could live on the salary alone…[34]

From the 1840s, unions were authorised by the central authorities to 'pay the district medical officers an extra fee for three types of treatment: smallpox vaccination, midwifery, and certain surgical operations.'[35] However, workhouse medical officers were not to be paid extra for operations. It was considered that, where possible, surgical cases should be sent to voluntary hospitals.[36] As already mentioned in the chapter on the infirm, many unions paid large subscriptions to specialist hospitals for precisely this reason.[37]

SUPPLY OF DRUGS AND MEDICINES

The medical officer had to supply drugs from his own salary, a requirement which was a thorny issue throughout the nineteenth century. To compensate, medical officers often recommended extras like food and beer to provide nourishment for the sick paupers under their care.

The Camberwell Infirmary, also known as St Giles Hospital, Camberwell, early 1900s.

At the Select Committee on Medical Relief in 1854, the Reverend C. Oxenden of Barham in Kent reported that the medical officer for his parish would not provide 'such an expensive class of medicine as quinine for cases of fever but would prescribe wine instead, since the Poor Law guardians were compelled to supply meat, wine, spirits and porter for patients on the doctor's recommendation.'[38]

At the Dudley Union, the workhouse medical officer certified that 'Phebe Chapman is suffering from Typhus Fever – six pints of Ale a week will be necessary for this patient.'[39]

Not all guardians acted on the medical officer's recommendations on food for the sick. At Basford, the medical officer was forbidden 'to order more than tea and gruel as 'extras' for the sick until a board meeting had sanctioned further extravagance.'[40]

In an attempt to ensure that inmates received the best possible medicines, a circular letter of 1865 issued by the Poor Law Board recommended that 'Cod Liver Oil, Quinine, and other expensive medicines, shall be provided at the expense of the Guardians.'[41]

In 1898, when Dr Fraser of the Clitheroe Union was asked to state the annual cost of prescribed drugs to the workhouse, he replied: 'I have no idea what they would be likely to cost. I do not keep drugs separately for the workhouse as the inmates are treated with the same ones I use for my own patients. The prescriptions are dispensed at my own house…'[42]

In the same year, a Local Government Board Inspector visited the Clitheroe Union and commented that: 'The arrangement by which the Medical Officer supplies all medicines etc., is somewhat out of date. The more usual practice is for the Guardians to find all drugs and medical appliances and to fit up a surgery at the Workhouse, where the Medical Officer can dispense.'[43] Despite this assertion, it was only in the larger unions where the guardians were prepared to fund the drugs themselves and provide a dispensary at the workhouse.

LONG-SERVING OR SUCCESSFUL MEDICAL OFFICERS

Despite the often low salaries and poor working conditions, some unions had long-serving medical officers, who perhaps saw the role as a vocation and genuinely wanted to provide the best possible treatment for the poor. Thomas Frederick Higgs started working for the Poor Law service as the district medical officer for the Kingston Union when he was twenty-four years old. From there, he moved to the Dudley Union, becoming a medical officer for the Dudley North district in 1860. After eleven years, he was appointed as the workhouse medical officer.

In 1900, the guardians recorded that:

> Mr Thos. F. Higgs has been in the service of the Guardians as Workhouse Medical Officer for twenty-nine Years, during which time there has been no complaint against him, either as to his conduct towards the sick, or as to the quality of the Drugs supplied by him. That it would be more desirable to consider the question of the supply of Drugs in connexion with…new Appointments, when it might be thought desirable to have a Resident Medical Officer.[44]

Despite his advancing age, Thomas Higgs remained the workhouse medical officer until at least 1908, by which time he was seventy-three years old.

Dr Joseph Rogers, who has already been mentioned in the chapter on the infirm, was a crusading workhouse medical officer keen to reform the injustices of workhouse infirmaries. In 1856, he took up his first post as a workhouse medical officer at the Strand Union Workhouse where the notorious George Catch was the master. The nature of the medical officer's role meant that he was subservient to the master, and lacked the power to implement the changes he believed necessary. It was therefore inevitable that in many union workhouses a power struggle was played out between the master and the workhouse medical officer.

Joseph Rogers and George Catch clashed immediately, as evidenced by this report:

> When the doctor ordered extra food for a nursing mother, Catch would put her back on the 'house diet'. When a woman was confined, Catch would delay calling in the doctor until nine days later, when he no longer qualified for an extra 'childbirth' fee. When the doctor took a day off, Catch reported him to the Board for being absent, although he had in fact appointed a locum…[45]

As a leading figure in the Association for Improving Workhouse Infirmaries, Joseph Rogers went on to become one of the campaigning forces behind the reforms of London's workhouse infirmaries in the 1860s.

COMPLAINTS ABOUT MEDICAL OFFICERS

District medical officers had the difficult task of visiting paupers in their homes to administer medical relief at the same time as attending to patients from their own practice. With a large geographical area to cover it was often difficult to meet the demand. As a result there were frequent complaints about the non-attendance or neglect of district medical officers.

Dr John McNab Ballenden was the medical officer for the First Sedgley district in the Dudley Union. In April 1877 a case of alleged neglect of duty was made against him 'by Joseph Edwards residing at Gornal Wood, for not having given proper Medical Attention to his wife Mary Edwards during her confinement.' It was alleged that he had only attended to Mary Edwards on one occasion and she had died as a result.[46]

The Matron Miss Lawson and staff at the Fir Vale Workhouse, Sheffield, 1900s. (Courtesy of the Sheffield Teaching Hospitals NHS Foundation Trust.)

The guardians suspended Dr Ballenden while investigations were carried out. An inquest into the death of Mary Edwards confirmed that she had 'died from exhaustion, consequent upon the weak state of the Heart, the laceration of the peritoneum and Vagina consequent on the cross-birth and protracted Labour.'

Dr Ballenden wrote to the guardians explaining his actions. His evidence gives an illuminating insight into the way in which Victorian doctors treated difficult cases of childbirth:

> …I carefully examined the case and after visiting some time left, as it was a case where manual interference would be improper and dangerous. I prescribed some opium Pills, and gave a Saline mixture with Tartrate of Antimony, and left the case in the charge of a midwife, to whom I gave the necessary directions, and told her if any alteration took place, to send for me again. Having had a very extensive midwifery practice extending over many years and amounting to about 9,000 Patients, the case presented no difficulty to me, it was one requiring time, and medicine to allay irritation and help natural relaxation…I knew the woman having attended to her previously, and would most certainly not have administered chloroform to her under any circumstances…the administering of chloroform would be most dangerous with such Lungs and Heart as the P.M. disclosed. During my evening Surgery hours I had been told that another Doctor was attending Mrs Edwards…

Had he returned to attend to Mary Edwards, Dr Ballenden had intended to carry out a procedure known as a craniotomy, something he termed 'breaking up the child'. He objected to comments made by a doctor at the post-mortem which stated that 'the operation of breaking up a child (Evisceration &c) is one of the most dangerous in Surgery, nothing but the ignorance of the operation can make it at all dangerous.'

He himself later explained:

> My plan of treatment in such cases is when sufficient dilation has taken place, and I find turning dangerous – To simply break up the child and run no risk of injuring the Mother, this I have done over and over again, in from ten minutes to half an hour, without inflicting the smallest pain or injury to the Mother – I would not, when it is necessary, hesitate to sacrifice the child to save the Mother…Any man of experience with common sense would say in such a case, use every means to increase the natural dilatation and diminish the bulk of the object to be passed through.

After hearing Dr Ballenden's arguments and reasons for not attending to Mary Edwards a second time, the guardians wrote to the Poor Law Board:'…the Guardians are of opinion that from the explanation given to the Board by Dr Ballenden as to his conduct, his suspension should now be removed.'[47] Dr Ballenden continued as the district medical officer for the First Sedgley District until 1894 when he resigned.[48]

Complaints about workhouse medical officers were less common than those about district medical officers. Such complaints were usually about the number of visits made to the workhouse, or insobriety on the part of the medical officer. At the Samford Union in 1895, the guardians received complaints from the master, the matron, the nurse, the porter and the relieving officer about the medical officer, Dr Fleming. It was alleged that the doctor 'often turned up drunk.' The guardians quickly asked for his resignation as surgeon and physician to the workhouse and as medical officer for the Holbrook District.[49]

INTO THE TWENTIETH CENTURY

As the Poor Law infirmaries developed and expanded to cope with the increased demand, more and more unions realised they needed to appoint full-time medical officers. This was particularly true in the larger towns and cities. However, in 1900 'only forty-four unions had resident medical officers.'[50] It is not clear how many unions had full-time non-resident medical officers.[51]

13

THE NURSING STAFF

Before the 1860s, nursing was not officially recognised as a profession. Consequently, the nursing in workhouses was provided by a combination of paid, untrained nurses and unpaid pauper inmates. Nurses were required to live-in at the workhouse and therefore unmarried women or widows without dependent children were preferred by the guardians of most unions.

DUTIES OF WORKHOUSE NURSES

In the early years of the New Poor Law, one of the duties of workhouse nurses was to attend to the infirm in the sick and lying-in wards. It was also their responsibility to administer medicines to their patients, under the direction of the medical officer. For this reason, all workhouse nurses had to be able to read the written directions on medicine bottles.

However, some workhouse unions were lax in checking that applicants could read. At the Samford Union in 1868, Nurse Goldsmith undertook her duties for a month before the guardians realised she could not read the written directions left by the medical officer.[1]

As the medical officer was not necessarily in daily attendance upon the wards, the workhouse nurse was required to inform him 'of any defects which may be observed in the arrangements of the sick or lying-in ward.'[2] She also had to ensure there was a night light in the sick ward.

Workhouse nurses were subject to the orders of the master, matron and medical officer. The supplies to the infirmary were controlled by the workhouse master, and the matron was in charge of the nurses. The relationship between matron and nurses was akin to that of 'housekeeper to servants' and, despite the responsibilities of the workhouse nurse, she 'had the same status as other pauper servants.'[3] Her role was therefore distinctly undervalued considering the work she was expected to undertake.

Power struggles between a workhouse nurse and the master or matron were not uncommon. Maud Newbury, the Superintendent Nurse at Dudley Union Workhouse, was suspended from her duties in September 1901. The guardians wrote to the Poor Law Board: 'It will be difficult to maintain efficient management and discipline necessary should Miss Newbury be permitted to resume her duties…' In particular, the guardians stated she was:

…unable to accept the position of being subject to the control of the Master & Matron in all matters other than treatment of the sick…as evidenced by the complaints of the Master of her insubordinate behaviour both to himself and the Matron, which weakens their authority and tends to disorder.

WANTED, at the Manchester Workhouse at Crumpsall, an active unmarried Man, who has had some experience in the care of imbeciles, as an ATTENDANT in the Imbecile and Epileptic Wards.   Salary £26 a year, with rations, washing, lodging, and uniform, to be increased by annual increments of £2 to a maximum salary of £32 if the duties are satisfactorily performed.   The salary and emoluments will be subject to such deductions as are required by the Superannuation Act.   Applications, marked outside "Male Attendant," stating age and occupation, and enclosing copies of testimonials, to be sent to me not later than 2 30 p.m. on Wednesday, the 15th inst.   Information as to the duties may be obtained from the Master of the Workhouse.—By order,

GEO. MACDONALD, Clerk to the Guardians.

Poor Law Offices, New Bridge-street,
Manchester, 3rd October, 1902.

SALFORD UNION.—Female Imbecile Attendant. — WANTED, by the Guardians of this Union an ASSISTANT ATTENDANT in the Female Lunatic Wards at the Union Infirmary, Hope, near Eccles, to take alternate Day and Night duty when required.   Salary, £20 per annum, increasing £1 yearly to £25, with rations, uniform, and residence in the Infirmary.   Candidates must be single, or widows without encumbrance, and preference will be given to one who has had previous experience.   Form of application will be forwarded on receipt of stamped addressed envelope, and the application must be sent to me on or before Tuesday, 14th October, 1902.— By order,

F. TOWNSON, Clerk to the Guardians.

Union Offices, Eccles New Road, Salford,
3rd October, 1902.

Advertisements for attendants to the imbeciles at the Manchester (Crumpsall) and Salford Union Workhouses. (*Manchester City News*, 1903.)

The Local Government Board refused to sanction a dismissal and Maud Newbury insisted on an official inquiry on her treatment by the guardians. After the inquiry, the guardians wrote again to the Local Government Board requesting 'an Order, relieving the Master & Matron of the Duties of making morning and nightly visits to the sick and lying-in wards of the Workhouse.' Maud also issued an apology.[5] Unfortunately, these measures did not solve the problem and after four nurses threatened to resign, the guardians formally requested Maud's own resignation. She finally left the Dudley Union in January 1903.[6]

SALARIES

The salaries of workhouse nurses varied throughout England and Wales, again according to the size of the union. In 1859, Fanny Dalby was the nurse appointed as part of the Dudley Union's core staff when the new workhouse was opened.[7] She was a twenty-seven-year-old widow from Stourbridge. Fanny was appointed on a salary of £15 per annum with board and rations and she was the only paid nurse to the workhouse. Her role would have been to nurse the sick and elderly, plus the imbeciles, with only the help of unpaid attendants chosen from the pauper inmates. In May 1860, just a year after being appointed, the guardians agreed that 'the salary of Mrs Fanny Dalby the Nurse be for the future £20 p.a. being an advance of £5, until a Male Nurse is appointed.'[8]

WANTED, at the Manchester Workhouse at Crumpsall, an active Unmarried Man, as ASSISTANT SUPERINTENDENT of INFIRM MEN. Salary £25 a year, with rations, washing, lodging. and uniform, to be increased by annual increments of £1 to a maximum salary of £30, if the duties are satisfactorily performed. The salary and emoluments will be subject to such deductions as are required by the Superannuation Act. Applications, marked outside "Assistant Superintendent," stating age and occupation, and enclosing copies of testimonials, to be sent to me not later than 2 30 p.m., on Wednesday the 15th instant. Information as to the duties may be obtained from the Master of the Workhouse.—By order,

GEO. MACDONALD, Clerk to the Guardians.

Poor Law Offices, New Bridge-street, Manchester.

3rd October, 1902.

Advertisement for attendant of infirm men at the Manchester (Crumpsall) Union Workhouse (*Manchester City News*, 1903.)

In 1850 at the Mitford and Launditch Union in Norfolk, the nurse's salary was just £10 per year. This had increased to £20 per year by 1856.[9]

In the late nineteenth century, many unions advertised a starting salary which would be increased each year until a maximum salary was reached. This measure was designed to encourage nurses to remain in their posts for longer, indeed, at the Darlington Union in 1894, the guardians advertised for a certified nurse at a salary of '£28 per annum with an addition of £1 yearly, until a maximum of £30 be reached.'[10]

The problem of the wide disparity in salaries was not resolved during the Victorian period, and indeed carried on into the twentieth century. As a result, the turnover of paid nursing staff in many unions was high, and recruitment and retention of nurses remained a thorny issue for most unions throughout the Victorian period.

LIVING CONDITIONS

Fanny Dalby's working life, like that of every other workhouse nurse, would have been arduous in the extreme. Her hours were long and she was expected to be on call day and night because 'few unions made separate arrangements for night nursing.'[11] In the early years, most unions employed only one paid nurse so Fanny would only have had assistance from unpaid pauper helpers.

It is not clear what Fanny's accommodation at the Dudley Union Workhouse was like but, in some unions workhouse nurses 'had no separate quarters, but ate and slept in the ward with the patients.'[12] This was the case at the Christchurch Union where, before the new nurses' home was opened in 1902, the nurses 'were having to sleep in the infirmary.'[13]

The nurse at the Cirencester Union Infirmary had better accommodation. In 1890, there was one trained nurse under the authority of the matron. She had 'a sitting room & bedroom' and it was added that 'a bell communicating with her apartment hangs in each sick ward...'[14]

Given the lack of facilities, opportunities and respect offered to workhouse nurses, it is hardly surprising that there are countless examples of individuals being dismissed for misconduct and drunkenness. Like pauper servants, workhouse nurses 'could be rewarded with extra rations.'[15] Although it was forbidden for pauper nurses to be rewarded with alcohol in lieu of monetary payments, this was often sanctioned by union guardians. In many unions, it was well-known among the paupers that it was 'in their interests to bribe the nurses to secure the minimum of attention'.[16]

In December 1850, the guardians of the Mitford and Launditch Union recorded that:

> Susan Wright is brought before the Board charged with depriving the pauper patients in the Old Men's Ward of certain Wine and other articles allowed them as Extra Medical Relief – she being then employed as Nurse in the same Ward and with having unlawfully introduced wine and spirits into the Workhouse. Ordered that Susan Wright be brought before a Magistrate to be dealt with according to law and that she be forthwith discharged from her Office as Nurse.

For her crime, Susan Wright was imprisoned for fourteen days at Wymondham Bridewell.[17]

The Local Government Board refused to sanction the appointment of Adelaide Wilkinson as a night nurse to the male and female infirmaries at the Dudley Union Workhouse.[18] This was because 'she had been in four other situations after leaving Birmingham in 1888, and that apparently she did not produce any testimonial from any one of the Institutions where she was employed.' On further investigation, the matron at one of the institutions, the Bedfordshire Hospital Trained Nurses Institute, stated that 'She is an excellent nurse, but unfortunately given to taking alcohol, I have been wanting her address for some time as she is owing money to several tradesmen here.'[19]

WHO BECAME WORKHOUSE NURSES?

Workhouse nurses were 'bound to the workhouse routine, without family life, without status…'[20] so what kind of women chose to nurse in workhouses? Whilst the majority of workhouse nurses were unmarried or widowed, others had husbands who were working elsewhere.

Sarah Grace Hannam became a nurse at Knaresborough Union Workhouse shortly after her second marriage in 1892. Her husband, Matthew, was at various times a hawker and a stone mason. It is likely that Sarah needed to work because Matthew's income was sporadic. Matthew also found employment at the workhouse in the capacity of stone mason, although it is not known how regular this was. As a workhouse nurse, Sarah would have lived-in at the Knaresborough Union and one of her daughters, Annie, was born at the workhouse in 1893. By the time of the 1901 census, Sarah and Matthew were living out of the workhouse although Sarah continued to work at Knaresborough for many years. She died at work in April 1932 when she was seventy-eight years old.[21]

Another nurse with a family was Charlotte Evans who was employed at the West Ashford Union Workhouse between 1881 and 1891. It is not known when she was first appointed but her connection with the West Ashford Union began when her husband, John, was 'Master of the Vagrant House' in Tufton Street, Ashford. They lived at the vagrant house with their young daughter, also called Charlotte.

During her time as nurse at West Ashford, it is highly likely that John had employment elsewhere. As previously stated, the post of workhouse nurse was usually residential and Charlotte was required to live-in at the workhouse. As the only nurse, her job would have been both strenuous and exhausting, especially considering her advancing age. Charlotte died the following year in 1892 aged seventy-five at the home of her daughter in Bristol.[22]

Fanny Dalby remained the nurse at the Dudley Union for four years until June 1863. The fact that the infirmary was constantly being described as overcrowded by both the Visiting Committee and the Visiting Commissioners in Lunacy probably played a large part in Fanny's decision to leave. Only after she resigned did the Dudley Union decide to appoint a male

The nurses' home at the Fir Vale Workhouse, Sheffield, *c*.1900. (Courtesy of the Sheffield Teaching Hospitals NHS Foundation Trust.)

and female nurse. Fanny moved on to posts of greater responsibility, although not at other workhouses. At the time of the 1871 census she was the matron of the Sparkhill Sanatorium in Yardley, Birmingham, while in 1881 she was in charge at the Industrial School in Coventry.

Fanny's successor was Sophia Siddons, who had been a nurse at the Wolverhampton Union Workhouse. It is not clear why Sophia left her previous post at Wolverhampton where there was an assistant male nurse and a superintendent for both the male and female insane inmates, in addition to Sophia herself. Perhaps she wanted more responsibility. If that was the case she would have found it in abundance at Dudley. Although a male nurse was appointed at the same time as Sophia there was no other paid assistance.

Sophia Siddons and Thomas Shipton, the male nurse, must have worked well together, because in April 1866 the guardians recorded their decision that 'the application made by the Nurses at the Union Workhouse to be allowed to marry and to reside in the House be granted.'[23] They continued in their posts until 1876 when they both died within a week of each other.[24]

PAUPER NURSES

Many unions, mindful of the burden on the ratepayers, resisted appointing paid nurses for as long as possible. This was even more evident in rural unions like Norfolk where, in 1844-5, the twenty-two unions only had four nurses between them.[25] In the 1850s, the central authority in London was reluctant to insist that unions employ 'professional nurses for work which they regarded as part of the inmates' duties.'[26] There was some increase in the number of paid workhouse nurses after the reform of workhouse infirmaries in the 1860s. However, it was not until after 1897, when unions were forced to find alternatives to pauper nurses, that the number of paid nurses significantly increased.

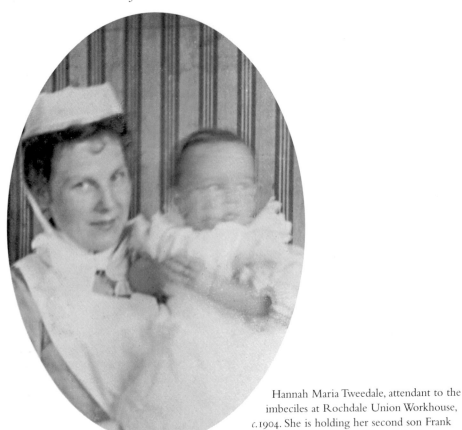

Hannah Maria Tweedale, attendant to the
imbeciles at Rochdale Union Workhouse,
*c.*1904. She is holding her second son Frank
Tweedale. (Courtesy of Judith Hawkins.)

Throughout the nineteenth century, unpaid pauper nurses were used to supplement the
paid staff. They were usually drawn from the able-bodied and elderly female inmates of the
workhouse. As mentioned in the chapter on the infirm, in 1851 Elizabeth Mockford nursed
Sarah Bradford at St Marylebone Union Workhouse and was the informant on her death
certificate. She was a seventy-six-year-old widow who had been an inmate at Marylebone for
at least ten years.

Although it was distinctly frowned upon to pay pauper nurses for their services, there are
frequent instances of guardians rewarding their pauper attendants in this way. In August 1844,
the guardians of the Mitford & Launditch Union ordered that 'five shillings be given to Mary
Ann Nichols and Lucy Loveday for their services in the Union Workhouse in nursing eighty
children sick in measels [sic] and typhus fever.'[27]

Many unions, like Dudley, resisted appointing sufficient paid nurses and continued to
use pauper attendants. In 1894, the Local Government Board wrote to the Dudley Union
reminding them that pauper attendants '...have little or nothing to lose by dereliction of Duty,
whereas a paid nurse is liable if found negligent to immediate dismissal, which might involve
the permanent loss of her livelihood...'[28]

It was not until 1897 that the Local Government Board passed an order forbidding the
employment of pauper nurses, but they were still allowed to work in the infirmaries under the
supervision of a trained nurse. In Norfolk, pauper inmates continued to be used unofficially
as sick attendants.[29]

ATTENDANTS FOR IMBECILES AND LUNATICS

From the 1860s onwards, unions were forced to provide extra staff to look after the ever increasing number of imbeciles housed in the workhouse. While the job had previously fallen to the paid nurse, this was no longer practicable with the increased workload in overcrowded infirmaries.

The reluctance of unions to appoint sufficient paid staff in the infirmaries was mirrored in the imbecile wards. Some workhouses decided to appoint just one member of staff for both male and female imbeciles with extra help provided by pauper inmates. Others struggled with two members of staff. The staff appointed were known as 'attendants' rather than nurses and they did not need the same qualifications as workhouse nurses.

A letter to the Poor Law Board written by the male nurse for the imbeciles at the Dudley Union in February 1877 gives a valuable insight into his working conditions. William Davies was in charge of thirty-six patients, sixteen of which were epilepsy cases. He was expected to give twenty-four hour care and he complained bitterly that he was not paid enough for his duties.[30]

Pressure was brought to bear on the unions to appoint sufficient staff by the Commissioners in Lunacy, who visited each workhouse annually to check on the lunatics and imbeciles housed there. However, it could take many years for unions to implement any recommendations.

In the majority of cases, attendants were required to be unmarried or widowed without dependent children. Unusually, in 1901 at the Rochdale Union Workhouse, the attendants for the imbeciles were two married couples. One couple was Hannah Maria and Walter Tweedale who had met while working at the Rochdale Union and married in 1900. They must have been considered valuable assets to the workhouse because they continued as attendants to the imbeciles despite having two children, Frank and Harry, in round 1901. During the Boer War Walter volunteered to serve with the St John Ambulance, returning to the workhouse at the end of the war. Sadly, Maria died of tuberculosis in 1907 aged just thirty-four, possibly contracted during her work at the workhouse. Walter re-married and went on to serve with the Royal Army Medical Corps in the Middle East during the First World War, for which he was honoured on returning home.[31]

THE REFORMS OF THE 1860s

As mentioned in the chapter on the infirm, the poor conditions of workhouse infirmaries in the 1860s were highlighted by the influential medical journal *The Lancet* and workhouse reformers such as Louisa Twining. Attention was also drawn to the lack of training and opportunities for workhouse nurses, an issue in which Florence Nightingale took an active interest.

Outside of London, Liverpool led the way in providing a model nursing service. In 1864, the Liverpool philanthropist, William Rathbone, paid himself for a staff of well-trained nurses for the Brownlow Street Workhouse superintended by Agnes Jones, the 'Florence Nightingale of the Poor Law'.[32]

From this time onwards, the Local Government Board encouraged unions to employ paid nurses only, but training was still not insisted upon. This was justified by the argument that:

> The nursing must be performed by a numerous staff of trained and paid officials, including special night nurses, under the superintendence of a person not specially experienced, but of good education and general social culture, for by such a chief only can proper discipline be maintained.[33]

A nurse and six young inmates at Hackney Workhouse, *c.*1889. The infants are being taken for a walk in their huge perambulator. (Ref. P3300. Courtesy of Hackney Archives Department.)

TRAINING FOR NURSES

Many unions resisted appointing trained nurses for as long as possible, arguing that 'the type of patient usually found in workhouses did not need specialised attention.'[34] For those unions wishing to employ trained nurses in their workhouse infirmaries, it was an uphill struggle to attract suitably qualified applicants. Workhouse infirmaries did not compare favourably with the expanding voluntary hospitals which offered higher salaries, better working conditions and superior accommodation.

From the 1870s onwards, the Poor Law Board encouraged the larger workhouse infirmaries to train nurses themselves by appointing probationers. The medical officer and head nurse would provide a year's training. Despite this initiative there was still a shortage of trained nurses. In 1879, Louisa Twining founded the Association for Promoting Trained Nursing in Workhouse Infirmaries which aimed to finance the training of workhouse nurses.[35]

In 1899, the Darlington Union advertised for a probationer nurse to take alternate day and night duty. The probationer was to 'receive instructions in Nursing from a fully Trained and Certificated Nurse.' The salary was £12 for the first year, £16 for the second and £20 for the third year.[36]

Those girls who applied to become probationers needed a little education to enable them to take and pass the written examinations. They came mainly from the lower-middle classes, 'daughters of professional men, farmers and shopkeepers.'[37] In 1873, the minimum age for candidates was twenty-five, but by 1900 this had been lowered to twenty-one.

Voluntary hospitals provided better quality, more thorough training than the workhouse infirmaries. As a result, applicants for probationer posts in union workhouses tended to be those who had lower expectations or who had been rejected by the voluntary hospitals.

This was still the case in 1913 when an Inspector reported from the South Midlands 'that there was such a shortage of trained nurses that the guardians employed partly trained girls who had been sent away from the schools because they were unfit.'[38]

Untrained nurses were 'more likely to be working-class girls who took the post in preference to domestic service.'[39] A large supply of probationers was needed because the nursing profession was made up of young women who could not continue their careers if they chose to marry. Even if workhouses were able to attract high calibre probationers, they were unlikely to stay nursing in workhouse infirmaries when more lucrative posts in voluntary hospitals or private nursing were available.

Smaller, rural unions continued to find it difficult to recruit and retain good nurses because of the 'boring work, social isolation and poor facilities.'[40] A Poor Law inspector commented that: 'The ordinary country workhouse, with perhaps fifteen to thirty inmates of the sick wards – mostly 'bad legs' or ordinary senility cases – does not provide work enough either to attract or to keep out of mischief a trained nurse on night duty.'[41]

INTO THE TWENTIETH CENTURY

Towards the end of the nineteenth century, both the training and accommodation for nurses started to improve. In 1897, the Local Government Board decreed that 'all infirmaries with a staff of three or more nurses had to employ a superintendent nurse' who could only be trained by an infirmary with a resident doctor.[42] The superintendent nurse had to have undergone 'for three years at least, a course of instruction in the Medical and Surgical Wards of a Hospital or Infirmary being a Training School for Nurses, and maintaining a Resident Physician or House Surgeon.' She had to hold a midwifery certificate and it was her responsibility to 'superintend, control and instruct the Probationer Nurses in the Infirmary…'[43] These new rules excluded infirmaries with less than three nurses so that 'in 1901 only sixty-three (of about 300) rural infirmaries had superintendent nurses.'[44]

Workhouses could also employ so-called 'assistant' nurses who only needed one year's training which could be provided by smaller infirmaries. However, the term was misleading as untrained women could still hold such posts. In larger infirmaries, there might also be 'charge' nurses who ranked between superintendent nurses and 'assistant' nurses. In 1902, a further qualification was required of workhouse nurses. The Midwives Act decreed that they needed a midwifery certificate in order to take charge of confinements.

The Local Government Order of 1897 which banned the use of pauper nurses in workhouses undoubtedly improved the standards of care offered to inmates. However, it presented another problem to the guardians of every union: that of providing accommodation for the extra nurses.

The Great Yarmouth Union was typical in having a small number of trained nurses prior to 1897. By 1901 they were employing twenty-three nurses and probationer nurses. The problem of accommodating the additional nurses was common to the majority of union workhouses. At Great Yarmouth, the isolation wards and box rooms had been converted into nurses' bedrooms to the extent that 'the sick inmates lacked isolation facilities and had to be screened from other patients.' However, many of the nurses' bedrooms were situated between the wards so that:

> …the great portion of air coming to them was from the sick wards. The air was naturally bad. Their windows adjoined the lavatories and there was constant traffic passing the nurses' bedrooms. They kept the gas on in their rooms to discourage the rats.

The living conditions caused much illness among the staff and 'at one time 25 per cent were off work sick.' Finally, in 1902, a purpose-built nurses' home was opened.[45]

The working hours of nurses at the Lambeth Union in 1906 were typical of most unions. They worked from 7.30 a.m. until 8 p.m. and went to bed at 11 p.m. They had just one half day off per week with alternate Sundays free from 2–11 p.m. The nurses were expected, 'To preserve order and decorum amongst the patients, to see that the rules are duly observed, to prevent loud talking, improper conduct or conversation, or smoking in the wards.'[46] In addition, it was ordered that 'Bedrooms are to be kept tidy, and the occupants are requested to avoid having too many knick-knacks, as they give extra work to the servants.'

By the beginning of the twentieth century, workhouse infirmaries were under even greater pressure, with an increasing number of beds and more acute cases which the voluntary hospitals had no room for. The duties of workhouse nurses continued to be challenging because so-called 'infirm' patients 'who were of little interest to a doctor could be difficult and time-consuming…' to look after.[47]

THE PORTER

One of the most lowly of workhouse officials was the porter. There was a very 'narrow gulf which separated [him] socially from the sad-faced creatures knocking on the gate for admission…', a fact of which the porter would have been all too well aware.[1]

DUTIES

The porter had a long list of duties to undertake, and although he was one of the lowest paid workhouse officers, the post did entail a great deal of responsibility.

First and foremost, he was required to keep the gate and to prevent any unauthorised person from entering or leaving the workhouse. The gate had to be manned at all times and at unions where there was no paid night porter, 'an inmate would usually relieve the paid porter at night.'[2] This was despite the fact that the central authorities 'objected more to the use of inmates as porters than as nurses…'[3]

Some degree of literacy was required from the porter as it was his responsibility to keep a register of 'the name and business of every officer or other person who shall go into the workhouse, and the name of every officer or other person who shall go out thereof, together with the time of such officer's or person's going in or out.'[4]

In November 1881, at the Dudley Union, an official inquiry was ordered into the management of the workhouse, amid rumours of insobriety and irregularities. It was discovered that the porter, Jesse Rushton, had 'made a false entry of the time of the Master's return to the workhouse',[5] claiming that the master had told him to do so.[6] It also appeared that a slate had been used in the porter's lodge instead of the register to record names of incoming and outgoing officers and visitors. This was specifically for the use of the inmate who looked after the gate when the porter's duties called him away from it. The porter insisted that he always copied down all the names from the slate into the register.[7] Despite his protestations, Jesse Rushton was dismissed and the master, the matron and the assistant matron all resigned.[8]

The porter was the first person any pauper seeking entry to the workhouse would meet. He had a certain amount of power over the paupers as he was authorised to 'search any male pauper entering or leaving the workhouse whom he may suspect of having possession of any spirits or other prohibited articles…'[9] If a porter believed that a female pauper needed to be searched, he had to call for the matron to undertake the task.

Such prohibited articles included alcohol, tobacco, dice, cards and matches. The porter could refuse entry to any pauper he suspected of having any such forbidden items and who would not give them up.

The porter also had the power to 'examine all parcels and goods before they are received into the workhouse, and prevent the admission of any spirituous or fermented liquors' and to 'examine all parcels taken by any pauper out of the Workhouse, and to prevent the undue removal of any article from the premises.'[10]

In terms of security, the duties were very specific. At every union workhouse, the porter was to:

> ...lock all the outer doors, and take the keys to the Master, at nine o'clock every night, and to receive them back from him every morning at six o'clock,...and if any application for admission to the Workhouse be made after the keys shall have been so taken to the Master, to apprise the Master forthwith of such application.[11]

The porter's duties might be extended because he had 'to obey all lawful directions of the Master or Matron, and of the Guardians, suitable to his office.'[12] At smaller unions, the porter might also be called upon to deputise for the master when he was away from the workhouse on business. In 1874 at the Samford Union, the porter named Dougherty took this duty to extremes by 'refusing to hand over certain keys to the Matron when the Master was absent...'[13]

In some unions, there was no paid porter at all. In April 1900, during a visit to the Aberystwyth Union, the Visiting Commissioner in Lunacy discovered that the porter was, in fact, an inmate classed as an imbecile.[14]

SALARY

Despite his onerous duties, the porter continued to be one of the lowest paid workhouse officials throughout the nineteenth and early twentieth centuries. In 1839, Francis Hobbs was appointed as porter at the Romford Union at '£15 a year and full board together with a coat and hat to the value of £5.'[15] By 1849, the 'average' salary for a porter was £18 per annum.[16] While salaries varied from union to union, the porter's salary had changed little by the end of the nineteenth century.

When John Evans was appointed porter to the Dudley Union Workhouse in 1890, his salary was just £20 per annum.[17] This was exactly the same salary as had been paid to the Dudley Union's first porter some thirty years earlier.[18] John's salary was increased to £22 per annum in 1897[19] and again in 1899 to £25 per annum 'in consequence of increased duties & late hours in the admittance of Tramps to the Union Workhouse.'[20]

Given the low salary and the long list of duties, it is perhaps unsurprising that few workhouse porters stayed in their post for long periods of time. While many applied for jobs which were not workhouse related, others went on to become schoolmasters or even masters of other unions. In February 1864, Edwin Jordan, the porter of the Dudley Union, resigned 'in consequence of his having been appointed to the office of Schoolmaster to the Hereford Union.'[21]

TYPES OF APPLICANT

The workhouse porter had to be physically strong as well as efficient. In February 1854, the guardians of one union recorded that the porter of the workhouse 'from Bad Sight & other Infirmity has become incapable of performing duties of Office.' They wrote to the Poor Law Board to ask to award the master of the workhouse an extra £10 per annum to perform the porter's duties.[22]

The role of a workhouse porter could be a dangerous one, given the sometimes violent nature of the people he had to deal with. In July 1846, the guardians of the Dudley Union 'ordered that Willm. Sidaway be prosecuted for an Assault upon the Porter of the Dudley Workhouse (Thos. Withers) whilst in a state of intoxification.'[23]

Joseph Mitchell, groom at the Fir Vale Workhouse, Sheffield, *c.*1900. (Courtesy of Margaret E. Towler, granddaughter of Joseph Mitchell.)

Alfred Lyons, who was the night porter at Lambeth Workhouse between July 1874 and July 1875, appears to have been well-qualified for the post. Before becoming the night porter, he was one of the early police constables with the Metropolitan Police Force, starting in September 1848. As a police constable, he was often called upon to maintain order in the Out Relief Hall at the workhouse. This experience seems to have stood him in good stead for coping with the discipline problems experienced by porters across England and Wales. As a night porter, Alfred was paid 20 shillings a week plus full emoluments of board, lodging and laundry. He resigned from his post in 1875 and later ran a beerhouse in Camberwell New Road.[24]

At first glance, John Evans, the porter at the Dudley Union Workhouse, appears to have been surprisingly young to fill the post. He was just twenty years old when he was appointed in October 1890.[25] However, Evans appears to have been well suited to the role, despite the challenges of looking after the male vagrant wards including the admittance of vagrants and the bathing, serving of meals and the performance of work tasks.[26] In 1905 Evans applied for the post of assistant master and storekeeper at the Dudley Union but his application was unsuccessful.[27] Despite this setback he continued as the workhouse porter until at least June 1905 with a service record of fifteen years.[28]

JOINT APPOINTMENTS

At some workhouse unions, the guardians preferred to make joint appointments of a husband and wife as porter and assistant matron or laundress. This was the preferred option of the Mitford and Launditch Union where, until 1865, a porter and assistant matron had a combined salary of £25 per annum.[29] This meant that when Thomas Butcher, the porter, was dismissed 'having been represented as inattentive to and neglectful of the duties of his office', his wife who was the assistant matron had to be dismissed as well.[30]

A SKETCH FROM LIFE IN ST. PANCRAS WORKHOUSE.

Above left: Henry and Amelia Boyd. Henry was the general man at the Lambeth Schools which housed children from the workhouse. (Courtesy of Sandy Norman.)

Above right: The old Gate Keeper at the St Pancras Workhouse. (*The Quiver*, July 1889.)

In January 1845, forty-one-year-old William Isted and his wife Sophia were appointed on a joint basis to the posts of porter and assistant matron at the Hailsham Union Workhouse. They were to receive a salary of £25 per annum.[31] William and Sophia's application may have caught the guardians' eye as William's cousin, Henry Isted, was the clerk to the Hailsham Union. Family connections were not a barrier to employment.

William had a background in farming, and in August 1857 he was appointed as Farm Superintendent at the workhouse. Sophia was to be the dairy maid.[32] Two years later, William and Sophia resigned at around the same time as Henry Isted, amid claims that there were irregularities in Henry's record-keeping.[33] The issue does not seem to have affected the way the guardians viewed William's service to the workhouse. They were happy to provide a glowing testimonial stating 'you have always, by sober, honest and respectable conduct, given...complete satisfaction.'[34]

COMPLAINTS ABOUT PORTERS

Appointments of workhouse porters were often short-lived, with frequent dismissals for offences ranging from drunkenness to abusing their power over the inmates. At the Bromsgrove Union in 1859, 'The master of the workhouse reported that Duffill the porter returned to the workhouse about 10 o'clock on the night of the 8th instant, intoxicated with liquor – that he had on other occasions come back drunk and that he sometimes used very bad language to the inmates.' Duffill refused to tender his resignation and was dismissed from his post.[35]

Improper relations between the porter and female inmates was also a common occurrence, with frequent pregnancies as a result. In October 1861, Benjamin Prince, the porter of the

Alfred Lyons, night porter at
Lambeth Workhouse, 1874–1875.
Alfred is pictured in his previous
occupation as a police constable
in the Metropolitan Police Force.
(Courtesy of Derek George.)

Dudley Union Workhouse, was dismissed after he made allegations of 'improper intimacy between the Governor – the Assistant Master – and Jane Lambert, an Inmate.' Evidence was taken from five different people and the charges were found to be 'unfounded and unjust' and the guardians stated that in fact it was the conduct of Benjamin Prince towards Jane Lambert that had been 'grossly improper and censurable.'[36]

At the Samford Union, Mr Tweed, the porter, was named as the father of an inmate's baby and quickly resigned to avoid dismissal. The union was efficient in pursuing him for the baby's maintenance and ordered Mr Tweed to pay two shillings per week. After his resignation, Mr Tweed insisted that 'as he was now temporarily out of work he could barely manage 1s. 6d.'[37]

INTO THE TWENTIETH CENTURY

Towards the end of the nineteenth century, most union workhouses had to employ extra staff to cope with the demands of looking after an increased number of inmates on multiple sites. Henry Boyd was employed as a general labourer at Lambeth schools, mainly the Old School, which accommodated children from the workhouse. At one time he was also a gardener at Lambeth Royal Infirmary. In 1899 fifty-four-year-old Henry was earning twenty-five shillings a week as the 'general man'.

Henry must have been a valued employee because when his wife, Amelia, was admitted to Cane Hill Lunatic Asylum in November 1899, the Lambeth Board of Guardians decided that 'Henry Boyd be not required to contribute towards the maintenance of his wife Amelia at Cane Hill Asylum.'

The main gate at the Grove Park Workhouse showing the porter's lodge. This picture was taken during the First World War when the site was a barracks for the Army Service Corps.

In July 1901, the matron reported that the night watchman was unable to carry out his duties due to ill-health. She added that Henry Boyd 'would be quite willing to do the Porter's duties on alternate evenings from 6 – 10.30' if his wages were increased. However, it was not until October that the Schools Committee reported:

> As to the performance of the duties of Porter at the Old School during the absence on leave of that officer on alternate evenings from 6-10.30. We recommend that H. Boyd, the General Man be directed to discharge these duties, and that his present weekly wage of 25/- be increased to 28/-.

Sadly, Henry was not to benefit from this increase in wages. He had become ill with chronic rheumatism and was unable to work. On 6 November 1901, he resigned and requested his pension. He was entitled to an allowance of 12s per week under the Poor Law Officers' Superannuation Act 1896. Again, Henry did not benefit from his well-earned pension as, just three weeks later, he died at home in West Norwood.[38]

In the late nineteenth century the duties of porters were extended to cater for the ever increasing numbers of vagrants frequenting the unions' casual wards. In March 1894, Darlington Union sought to appoint a porter and porteress to superintend the male and female casual wards. The candidates had to be 'man and wife, without children dependent upon them.' The salary was £20 and £15 per annum respectively 'together with Rations (without Beer), Washing and Furnished Apartments.'[39] An appointment such as this would have been extremely difficult with long hours.

THE CHAPLAIN

Although the post of workhouse chaplain was non-resident and part-time, his social status, influence and position as a spiritual pastor meant that he was 'the most influential workhouse officer.'[1] He was also the only officer to attend the weekly meetings of the board of guardians. The chaplain was regarded by many unions as an expensive 'kind of Sunday gaoler.'[2]

APPOINTMENTS OF WORKHOUSE CHAPLAINS

Each union was required to appoint a chaplain to the workhouse who would meet the spiritual needs of the inmates. The Poor Law Commission expected that a Church of England chaplain would be appointed, who was required to have the written consent of the Bishop of the Diocese.

However, many unions refused to appoint a chaplain as they could send the inmates to the local church for Sunday services at no cost to themselves. In unions where most of the guardians and inmates were Dissenters, there was an insurmountable objection to appointing a Church of England chaplain. In 1844, ten years after the passing of the Poor Law Amendment Act, the Poor Law Commission reported that 144 unions had still not appointed a chaplain. These unions were in areas where Dissent was strongest, such as Lancashire, the West Riding, Durham and Cornwall.[3]

In the 1860s at the Sheffield Union, there was no chaplain for the workhouse. Wesleyan ministers held services inside the workhouse and clergy from the Church of England visited the inmates at no cost. [4] Norfolk boards of guardians appointed an Anglican chaplain 'but allowed Dissenting ministers to visit members of their congregation who were in the workhouse.'[5]

In the end, the Poor Law Commission had to acquiesce and allow non-Anglican inmates to leave the workhouse on Sundays to attend service at their chapel since they 'accepted that no religious ceremony should be forced on paupers of other persuasions.'[6] This was despite the belief that if the inmates were allowed to leave the workhouse on a Sunday to go to church, 'all manner of evils would result.'[7] The guardians were expected to provide supervision of these inmates or to obtain a certificate of chapel attendance from the minister.

TYPES OF APPLICANT

At the majority of workhouses, the post of chaplain was 'usually undertaken by a curate keen to supplement his stipend.'[8] The chaplain in the anti-workhouse novel *Jessie Phillips* published in 1844, was portrayed as 'a harassed curate with six children to feed, who had taken the post on solely for the £25 a year salary, and hurried in once a week to gabble through the service, anxious only to get away in time for Matins at his own church, seven miles away.'[9] Although a work of fiction, it was not far from the truth in many workhouses. As the chaplain had to combine his workhouse duties with those of his own church and ministry, there was rarely enough time to carry out his duties properly.[10]

DUTIES

Under the duties laid down by the Poor Law Commission, the chaplain was required to read prayers and preach a sermon to the inmates every Sunday as well as on Good Friday and Christmas Day. He had a special responsibility towards the children. He was expected to 'examine the children, and to catechise such as belong to the Church of England, at least once in every month, and to make a record of the same, and state the dates of his attendance, the general progress and condition of the children…'[11]

The chaplain's influence over the spiritual life of the workhouse inmates was wide-ranging. At the Dudley Union in 1867, the Visiting Committee recorded that:

> We recommend the Board of Guardians to accept the offer made by the Christian Knowledge Society of Five Pounds worth of Books for Two Pounds and Ten Shillings for the use of the Inmates and that the selection of such Books, as would be most useful, be left to the Chaplain.[12]

A final duty of the chaplain, and perhaps the most onerous, was 'to visit the sick paupers, and to administer religious consolation to them in the workhouse, at such periods as the Guardians may appoint, and when applied to for that purpose by the Master and Matron.'[13]

SALARIES

The salaries of workhouse chaplains varied considerably across England and Wales. However, the importance of religion in the workhouse and the chaplain's social status usually ensured

A distant view of the Stourbridge Union Workhouse. During the First World War it was used as the 1st Southern Military Hospital. The picture illustrates the large site which would have included a chapel.

A volunteer from the charity, 'The Children's Home', knocking at the door of a typical East London family's home. The charity aimed to save destitute children from the workhouse. (*Highways and Hedges – The Children's Advocate*, 1898.)

that he would receive 'a salary which compared favourably even to the master's.'[14] This was despite the part-time nature of the post. This is borne out by the results of a survey from 1849 which compared the average salaries of workhouse officers. In 1849, the average salary for a master was £35 per annum and for a chaplain it was £46.[15]

However, such generosity was not evident in all workhouse unions. When the new Dudley Union Workhouse was opened in 1859, a chaplain was appointed as part of the core staff at a salary of £60 per annum, for which he was to 'fulfil the duties laid down in the Consolidated Order.'[16] While this was a high salary for a part-time post, the guardians must have valued the workhouse master more as he was paid £80 per annum.

Often, the salary depended to a large extent on 'local custom.'[17] One Yorkshire union only offered a salary of £10 per annum.[18] Basford, a textile union in Nottinghamshire, paid £24 per annum to its chaplain while Bridge, a small rural Kentish union, offered £50 per annum.[19]

MINISTERING TO THE SICK

The wording of the Consolidated General Order meant that unions themselves could decide at what hours, and with what frequency, their chaplain should visit the sick. In May 1868, the guardians of the Dudley Union discussed the duties of their soon-to-be appointed chaplain. They decided that:

> ...a Chaplain to the workhouse be appointed at the usual salary of £60 a year to give two services each Sunday, and one during the Week, with such a system of Visiting the Sick and Infirm as may be hereafter agreed by the Board at the time of appointment.[20]

In June 1868, the guardians decided that he should 'also visit the sick Inmates three days' weekly, devoting two hours each day to that purpose.'[21]

INFLUENCE OVER PAUPER EDUCATION

The chaplain's special responsibility with regard to the children meant that he had a great deal of influence in the schoolroom. This could lead to clashes with the schoolmaster or schoolmistress. In November 1875, the guardians of the Dudley Union received a letter from the chaplain, Reverend Tozer 'complaining of the conduct of Mr Frizelle, Schoolmaster.'[22] The nature of the complaint is not known, although at this time Mr Frizelle had only recently started his long workhouse career as schoolmaster at the Dudley Union.

Relationships between the chaplain and schoolteacher could also be harmonious. In 1848 at the Mitford and Launditch Union, the chaplain helped the young and inexperienced schoolmaster gain confidence in his teaching. Good reports from HMI about the boys' school quickly followed.[23]

In Norfolk, James Kay-Shuttleworth, a former Assistant Poor Law Commissioner and Secretary to the Privy Council on Education, recognised the value of the workhouse chaplain in improving pauper education. He worked hard to develop the role of the chaplain 'into a more active supervisory and advisory role.'[24]

INCREASING WORKLOAD

The onerous duties of the workhouse chaplain and his ever-increasing workload are clearly illustrated in an appeal from the vicar of Yarmouth and chaplain to the workhouse. In 1873, the Reverend Henry Nevill drew the attention of the guardians to his heavy workload and asked for a deputy chaplain to be appointed. His duties consisted of giving a full service with sermon in the chapel on Sunday mornings and afternoons, administering Holy Communion at least once a month, paying weekly visits to the boys' and girls' schools and visiting the sick and infirm twice a week.[25] Reverend Nevill pointed out that, in addition to these regular duties, 'a constant oversight has been kept over the fallen girls and women.' By his efforts, over the last ten years he had sent more than forty-five girls to refuges and houses of mercy where they had all done well. He believed that a deputy chaplain was needed because there were now 30,000 inhabitants in the parish and his salary as the workhouse chaplain was only £50 a year.[26] It is not known if a deputy chaplain was appointed or if Reverend Nevill's salary was increased.

Some extremely large metropolitan workhouses found it necessary to appoint a full-time chaplain. However, the work was usually 'still beyond the capacity of one man.'[27] The chaplain at the St Marylebone Workhouse had 1,600 inmates under his care,[28] making it virtually impossible for him to carry out the duties set out in the Consolidated General Order.

Workhouse inmates, possibly in the 1920s, although the uniform is similar to that worn in the 1900s. The inmates are from either the Ecclesall Bierlow Union Workhouse or the Fir Vale Workhouse in Sheffield. (Courtesy of the Sheffield Teaching Hospitals NHS Foundation Trust.)

DEDICATED WORKHOUSE CHAPLAINS

There were undoubtedly countless workhouse chaplains who took their role very seriously and, by their labours, contributed positively to the spiritual welfare of the inmates. In 1859, the chaplain to the Great Yarmouth Union, George Hills, resigned on being appointed as the new Bishop of Colombia. The guardians put on record that 'they had observed in George Hills an earnest zeal for the well-being of the poor people and their religious welfare and moral instruction. We have observed the bearings of his master mind and the good effect of his unostentatious piety.'[29]

Reverend Herbert Smith, the chaplain at the New Forest Union, has already been mentioned in the chapter about able-bodied women. In 1836, a quarter of the inmates were unmarried mothers and children. Reverend Smith took a great deal of time and care to minister and talk to the women with illegitimate children, in the hope of reforming their characters.[30]

The Reverend S. J. Tozer was appointed as the new chaplain to the Dudley Union in 1868. A native of Cornwall, he was the vicar of St John's Church in Tipton, one of the parishes which made up the Dudley Union. Reverend Tozer appears to have taken a keen interest in the welfare of the workhouse inmates. A year later, in May 1869, he applied 'to take the Workhouse School Children out for holiday in the month of June next.' His application was granted. The following year, he suggested that a box be placed at the Dudley Railway Station 'for the reception of used newspapers & books for the use of the Inmates at the Union Workhouse.'[31] The suggestion was agreed to and the plan adopted.

In May 1872, Reverend Tozer applied for an increase to his stipend which was not granted.[32] However, he was granted permission 'to reduce the Number of services on Sundays at the Workhouse during the Month of August.'[33] Four years later, Reverend Tozer's salary was finally increased to £80 per annum. This was because there were 250 patients in the infirmary 'who require almost constant visitation by the Chaplain.'[34]

A DREAM OF GREEN FIELDS.

Mr. Punch. "NOW, MISTRESS CHARITY, CAN'T WE MANAGE TO MAKE THE DREAM COME
TRUE—JUST FOR A FORTNIGHT?"

[The Children's Country Holidays Fund is in great need of assistance. The Hon. Treasurer is the Earl of Arran, 18, Buckingham St., W.C.]

A Dream of Green Fields. (*Punch*, 10 August 1901.)

INTO THE TWENTIETH CENTURY

The duty of the chaplain to visit the sick paupers and to 'administer religious consolation to them in the workhouse'[35] was undoubtedly the most onerous. The number of paupers and infirmary patients continued to rise so that, by the end of the nineteenth century, the work of most workhouse chaplains had increased considerably.

THE GUARDIANS

Under the terms of the Poor Law Amendment Act, every union had to appoint a board of guardians to oversee the day-to-day administration of the workhouse. The guardians had the difficult job of providing for the paupers of the union with one eye on the burden faced by the ratepayers.

TYPES AND QUALIFICATIONS OF GUARDIANS

The number of guardians for each union depended on the number of parishes within it, and of course this varied widely across England and Wales. The Gravesend and Milton Union in Kent had eight guardians to represent its two constituent parishes. With eighty-eight parishes, Louth in Lincolnshire had ninety guardians.[1]

It was considered important that every parish within the union be represented by a guardian. This was because 'the presence on every Board of a Guardian from an applicant's home parish was supposed to ensure that at least one member knew his circumstances and could speak up for him…'[2] In 1854, the ten guardians of the Dudley Union were made up of two gentlemen, two ironmasters, two mine agents, a draper, a chemist, a nail master and a glass manufacturer.[3]

At the Hayfield Union Workhouse in Derbyshire, the occupations of the guardians 'reflected the predominance of the textile industry in the area' with half of the sixteen guardians being connected with cotton or wool.[4] In rural Norfolk unions, four-fifths of the Poor Law guardians were farmers.[5]

There were two kinds of guardians, *ex officio* and elected. *Ex officio* guardians were local magistrates who were entitled to a place on the board without being elected while candidates who wished to stand for election as a guardian had to be a rate-payer, occupying property worth at least £25 a year.[6] Elections took place annually every April, and the voters were the ratepayers of the union.

Both elected and *ex officio* guardians shared the same duties and powers. The board of guardians for each union was to meet regularly, usually weekly. The post of guardian was 'not popular, and could be most time-consuming.'[7] Many guardians saw their election to the board as a necessary duty to the community as a whole and thus were conscientious in their duties and keen to make improvements at their union workhouse. A smaller minority with strong political views used their time as guardians to further their own personal cause.

In urban unions, self-interest was another possible reason for seeking election. This was because 'service as a Guardian offered a successful tradesman the chance to make useful social and business contacts…'[8]

Not all boards of guardians were enthusiastic about the task of Poor Law work. Some rural unions such as Freebridge Lynn and St Faith's in Norfolk 'sometimes failed even to achieve a quorum of guardians.'[9] However, in the neighbouring Mitford and Launditch Union, 'the typical board meeting had a higher attendance of twenty out of sixty-four guardians.'[10]

Left: John Whycliffe Wilson, one of the early guardians at the Fir Vale Workhouse, Sheffield, *c.*1906. Often referred to as the 'Children's Friend', he was instrumental in setting up the 'scattered' children's homes in the Sheffield Union. (Courtesy of the Sheffield Teaching Hospitals NHS Foundation Trust.)

Below: Proposed Plan 7 for the Lampeter Union Workhouse, showing the front and rear elevations, 1875. (Courtesy of Ceredigion Record Office.)

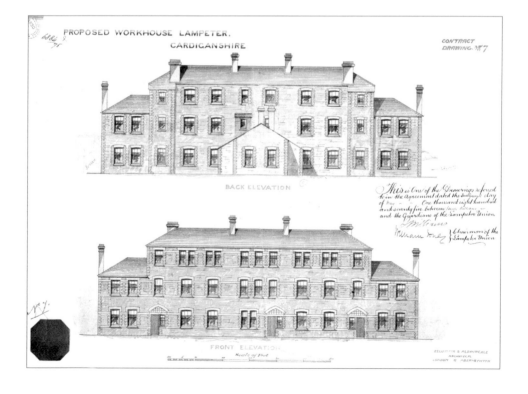

The guardians' building at the Stourbridge Union Workhouse. (Courtesy of Carl Higgs.)

BUSINESS OF GUARDIANS

Boards of guardians were required to meet regularly to discuss the business of the union. This might include 'the appointment and oversight of officials…, correspondence with other unions on questions of settlement and removal, approval of accounts and interviews of individual applicants for relief in the presence of the relieving officer.'[11]

As a board, the guardians of every union had to award contracts to suppliers for goods required at the workhouse. This included food, clothing, fuel, furniture etc. The clerk advertised for tenders in the local newspapers at periodic intervals throughout the year. The guardians then considered the tenders and awarded the contracts. In cost-conscious unions, contracts were often awarded to suppliers offering the lowest tender. Other unions were determined to find high-quality goods for the workhouse and awarded contracts accordingly. In theory, guardians were meant to be unbiased when awarding contracts to suppliers. In practice, contracts were often awarded to relatives of guardians or of other workhouse officers.

In addition to the main board, large unions had numerous committees covering various areas of the workhouse including finance, building and the boarding-out of children.[12] Each committee was made up of a group of guardians who would report back to the board. This added to the length of any meeting and also increased the responsibilities of each guardian.

LOCAL INTERESTS

It was undoubtedly true that boards of guardians understood local issues in their union better than the central authorities in London. Not all unions were 'driven by a mindless concern for economy.'[13] Many were anxious to ensure the kind treatment of destitute inmates and regularly questioned the orders of the Poor Law Commission.

A group of child emigrants at the Pinjarra Farm School, Western Australia, with Mr Kingsley Fairbridge, the head of the school. (*The Graphic*, 21 February 1914.)

In December 1845, the guardians of the Dudley Union treated their inmates to a Christmas meal.[14] Several months later, the auditor disallowed the expenditure and a dispute began between the guardians and the Poor Law Commission.[15] They argued that:

> ...the whole of the inmates of the several Poorhouses in the Union being either impotent, or aged and infirm adults or destitute children, the Guardians do consider the decision of the Poor Law Commissioners to be most arbitrary, oppressive and cruel – and more particularly so since the allowance of this small annual treat on Christmas Day has been customary from time immemorial, and also because the Guardians are convinced that in the whole Dudley Union comprising a population of 85,000 souls, there can scarcely be found a single ratepayer who would not vote for the continuance of the custom...[16]

The guardians continued the annual custom of a Christmas dinner for the inmates, despite the criticism from the Poor Law Commissioners.

Benevolent boards of guardians were reluctant to impose the workhouse test to the letter and continued to issue outdoor relief. The Norwich guardians believed that the 1834 Poor Law Amendment Act tended:

> ...to degrade the industrious artisan to the level of the indolent, and dissolute, were he to be compelled, when standing in need of temporary assistance from the failure of employment, to sell off his little furniture, the produce of his early industry, and become with his family the inmate of a workhouse.[17]

Generally, the guardians of Norfolk unions were 'increasingly confident that they could run the Norfolk Poor Law in their own way and with little external interference.'[18]

The guardians of individual unions also clearly understood the issues facing the ratepayers. In 1886, the guardians of the Newcastle Union stated that 'a considerable proportion of the rates are drawn from a class very little removed from pauperism, and... any considerable increase in their burdens would have the effect of causing them to become paupers.'[19]

A Pioneer in Embryo: A Scottish Recruit at the Farm School. A child emigrant at the Pinjarra Farm School, Western Australia. (*The Graphic*, 21 February 1914.)

WORKING CLASS GUARDIANS

The property qualification was reduced to £5 per year in 1892, and two years later it was abolished altogether. This opened the door for the election of guardians from the working classes who, arguably, understood the problems of the poor better than their middle-class counterparts.

William Crooks, who as a child became an inmate of a London workhouse, was elected to the board of guardians at the Poplar Union in 1892. He was the 'only former workhouse inmate known to have served on such a body.'[20] Mr Crooks was Chairman of the board from 1898 until 1906. He went on to become a Labour MP and the mayor of Poplar.

George Lansbury, 'a Socialist pure and simple'[21] was also elected a guardian at the Poplar Union. He described what happened after the first committee meeting:

…we were taken downstairs, where a seven course dinner was to be served. It was this which made me very disgusted with the middle-class men and women who controlled the institution; they could let little girls who they knew must be starved, stand and wait on them while they ate chicken, nice soups, sweets, etc., all at the expense of the rates.[22]

George Lansbury was 'determined to fight for one policy only, and that was decent treatment for the poor people…'[23]

FEMALE GUARDIANS

In the 1850s, unions across England and Wales began to allow members of a so-called 'Ladies' Committee' to visit women in the workhouse. Technically, women ratepayers who were eligible could stand for election as a guardian from the time of the Poor Law Amendment Act. However, it was not until 1875 that the first female guardian was elected in Kensington. Female guardians took a special interest in the welfare of the children, the inmates in the infirmaries, the elderly and the unmarried women.

Better Than the Workhouse: Two Brothers From a Sussex Union. These boys were child emigrants at the Pinjarra Farm School, Western Australia. (*The Graphic*, 21 February 1914.)

By 1885, there were fifty female guardians but it was not until 1894, when the property qualification was abolished, that the number increased dramatically. Just a year later there were more than eight hundred female guardians.[24]

Emmeline Pankhurst, the suffragette, was elected as a guardian to the Manchester Union Workhouse in the 1890s. She described what she found on entering office:

> When I came into office I found that the law in our district, Chorlton, was being very harshly administered. The old board had been made up of the kind of men who are known as rate savers. They were guardians, not of the poor, but of the rates and, as I soon discovered, not very astute guardians even of money.[25]

INTO THE TWENTIETH CENTURY

At the end of the nineteenth century and into the twentieth, the introduction of working-class guardians and the increase in women taking on the position gradually started to change the composition of the boards governing workhouses across England and Wales. Both female and working-class guardians were keen to make sweeping changes to improve the lives of the inmates, and their efforts slowly started to take effect.

THE CLERK

The clerk was usually the most educated of the workhouse officers, and often the most highly paid. He was 'the key official in any union'[1] because his wide-ranging role touched on every aspect of workhouse life. An efficient, trustworthy clerk was vital to the smooth running of a workhouse.

TYPES OF APPLICANT

While there were no specific qualifications set down by the central authorities, applicants for the post of clerk had to be over twenty-one years of age. Successful applicants were usually men of good standing in their local community, often with a legal background. In the larger unions, it was common for chief clerks to have legal training.[2] Even in smaller unions, solicitors were the preferred applicants for the post. The first clerk to the Westbourne Union was Daniel Smart, a solicitor at Emsworth.[3]

In the early years of the new Poor Law, some unions tried to save money by combining the role of master and clerk, a measure which was often encouraged by the central authorities.

This was the case at the Alton Union in Hampshire where, in March 1833, Matthew Heath Moss was appointed as 'Master of the Workhouse and Vestry Clerk' to the Alton Union in Hampshire. His previous occupation was as a pawnbroker, which also required careful record-keeping and handling of money. By the time of the 1851 census he had relinquished his responsibilities as master and devoted all of his time to the duties of clerk. His son, Matthew Hale Moss, followed in his father's footsteps, first as a brewer's clerk and then as clerk of the Alresford Union in Hampshire, a position he held for over forty years.[4]

Those penny-pinching unions which attempted to combine the roles of clerk and master soon realised their mistake. The two jobs 'required quite different qualities'[5] and there was more than enough work in each role to occupy one man.

As the post required handling money, clerks had to 'give a Bond, conditioned for the due and faithful performance of the duties of the office, with two sufficient sureties.'[6]

DUTIES

The clerk had a long list of duties to undertake which required excellent organisational and communication skills. One of the clerk's most important duties was to take minutes of the proceedings at every meeting of the board of guardians. The minute books would be audited so they had to be extremely accurate. He was also required to 'keep, check and examine all accounts, books of accounts, books, and other documents as required of him by the Regulations of the Commissioners.'[7]

Charles Prentice Barrett

Died at Eton - 6 May 1867 -

Charles Prentice Barrett, clerk to the Eton Union between 1836 and 1867. (Courtesy of Jill Barrett.)

It was the clerk's responsibility to 'peruse and conduct the correspondence of the Guardians according to their directions.' He was required to preserve all correspondence and the Orders of the Commissioners, as well as letters received and copies of all letters sent. He also had to preserve all letters, books, papers, and documents belonging to the Union 'and to make all necessary copies thereof.' The clerk was also responsible for placing advertisements in newspapers when new staff or supplies were required at the workhouse.[8]

The reason the clerk often had legal training was because another duty was to prepare all written contracts and agreements, and prepare all bonds or other securities to be given by any of the officers of the union. He also had to conduct all applications by, or on behalf of, the guardians to any justice or justices at their special, petty or general sessions. This was usually in connection with appeals against the settlement of particular paupers. He was also entitled to execute all the legal business connected with the union 'if he be an attorney or solicitor.'[9]

The clerk's financial abilities came into play with regard to the accounts of the union. He had the responsibility of countersigning all orders legally made by the guardians for the payment of money, and all orders legally drawn by the guardians upon the treasurer. Before every meeting of the board of guardians, he had to ascertain the balance due to or from the union. At the beginning of each quarter, he was required to lay before the guardians the non-settled poor accounts and non-resident poor accounts. The non-settled poor were the paupers who lived in the union but whose settlement was in another union, to which they were chargeable. The non-resident poor were the paupers who were living in other unions, but whose settlement was in the home union, to which they were chargeable. The clerk had to make remittances to other unions in the form of cheques or post-office orders as payment for the relief of the non-resident poor. He also had to send accounts requesting payment to other unions for the relief of their non-settled poor.[10]

Very large metropolitan unions appointed removal clerks to deal with removal and settlement orders. The Fulham Union advertised for a removal clerk in 1866 specifying that

An advertisement from 1841 requesting potatoes at the Hailsham and Hellingly workhouses, placed by Henry Isted, clerk to the union. (Reproduced by permission of the East Sussex Record Office, photograph courtesy of Bruce Isted.)

the successful applicant 'will be required to possess a thorough practical knowledge of the Law of Settlement, must be competent to take Examinations, prepare Depositions, Orders and Grounds of Removals and, if necessary, conduct Appeals, and will be expected to Remove the Paupers.'[11]

In smaller unions, dealing with removal and settlement orders was yet another duty of the clerk. Such work might include travelling to the alleged parish of settlement of a pauper to make investigations about his or her birth or marriage. It might also involve enforcing a settlement order by supervising the physical removal of a pauper to his or her settlement parish.

Another duty of the clerk was to communicate with, and to, all the officers engaged in the administration of poor relief so that they were all aware of the orders and directions of the Poor Law Commissioners. He also had to 'prepare and transmit all reports, answers, or returns' required by the Commissioners and to 'conduct duly and impartially, and in strict conformity with the regulations in force at the time, the annual or any other election of guardians.'[12]

The clerk also acted as a trusted advisor to the guardians on all matters connected with the workhouse. When the guardians of the Clitheroe Union discussed the appointment of a new workhouse clerk, one of them commented that:

> ...the Clerk has to advise the Guardians on many subjects which are not exactly routine duty. He has to be...a sort of head servant over the others. He is practically over the other Officers in the Workhouse, they look to him as the men of a regiment look to the Sergeant Major – to keep the non-commissioned officers in order. He has to fight their battles, more or less, outside the Union.[13]

Matthew Heath Moss with his wife Jane outside their cottage, *c.*1860-1870. Matthew was master of the Alton Union before becoming the clerk. (Courtesy of Derek Jenkins.)

SALARY

Like the salaries of the other workhouse officers, the amount of the clerk's salary depended on the size of the union, and therefore the amount of Poor Law work he had to undertake.

At the first meeting of the guardians of the Dudley Union in October 1836, Thomas Shorthouse was appointed as clerk at a salary of £150 per annum. It was recorded that 'it is expedient that he should in addition to the duties of Clerk, undertake the management of all Orders of removal arriving out of the parishes of Dudley and Rowley and the conduct of such business as is usually transacted by a Vestry Clerk.'[14] The high salary, compared with the other workhouse officers, was because of the vast number of duties.

LONG-SERVING CLERKS

In 1861, after twenty-five years as clerk to the Dudley Union, Thomas Shorthouse resigned. His replacement was twenty-seven-year-old Thomas Allen who was appointed on the same salary of £150 per annum. Thomas Allen came from a family of clerks. At one time his father had been the registrar of births, deaths and marriages in Dudley. In July 1865, Thomas Allen's salary was increased to £200 per annum.[15]

By the time Thomas Allen resigned in 1902, his salary had increased to £400 per annum with an extra £50 per annum for his services as clerk to the Union Assessment Committee.[16]

The reasons he gave for his resignation reveal how much he valued working for the Poor Law service:

> I have at times during the past several weeks been suffering from much nervous depression… The Board can well understand my feelings that after a lifetime association with Poor Law Work, Meeting Guardians and Officers Week by Week for so many years, how trying it is for me to give up 'official life', the several duties required to be attended to, believe me, having been to me a real pleasure than otherwise.[17]

At the Eton Union, the post of workhouse clerk was held for over a century by three generations of the Barrett family who were solicitors in the town. In 1836, Charles Prentice Barrett, at the age of twenty-two, was appointed clerk to the Eton Union at a salary of £140 per annum. As the author of *The Overseer's Guide* published in 1840, Charles took his workhouse role seriously. He continued in the role of clerk for over thirty years until his death in 1867, by which time the workload must have grown significantly. His son, Richard Henry Barrett, had been helping him for the last four years in the post of assistant clerk. When Charles died, Richard was appointed as clerk in his place, and Richard's elder brother, Charles J. Barrett, joined him as assistant clerk in 1871. Charles J. remained in this role until 1899 when Richard's son, Herbert L.C. Barrett took over the post. Richard continued as the senior clerk for forty-five years until 1912 when Herbert became clerk in his turn. He remained in the post for thirty-four years, with a break during the First World War.

It is not known if there were ever any allegations of nepotism about the successive Barretts who worked as clerks to the Eton Union. If any such allegations did occur, the guardians could simply have referred to their vast experience in the role. Each generation had completed a kind of apprenticeship as assistant clerk prior to becoming senior clerk, and therefore had superior knowledge of the complexities of Poor Law work.[18]

DIFFICULTIES OF KEEPING THE BOOKS

With such a heavy workload and all manner of books to keep meticulously, it is hardly surprising that some clerks were accused of irregularities and left the Poor Law service because of it. Henry Isted was appointed clerk to the Hailsham Union in April 1836 at a salary of £80 per annum. At the time of his appointment he was thirty-two years of age, and he had previously worked as a shoemaker/cordwainer. Unusually, he was also to be the boys' schoolmaster and his wife was to superintend the boys' clothes, 'and for these services he be allowed board and lodging for himself, wife and children.' The dual duties of clerk and schoolmaster were too onerous for Henry and it was difficult for him 'to give the requisite attention to the school department…particularly on Board days.' It appears that the master had to take charge of the boys on such days.[19]

In June 1838, the guardians decided that 'Mr Isted shall have such an assistant as may render it unnecessary for the Governor to take charge of the Boys when Mr Isted is otherwise engaged in the business of the Union.' However, Henry still had to undertake 'the superintendence of the Boys clothing and to see they were properly washed and cleansed, their heads examined and combed daily.'[20] By 1854, Henry and his family were living in Hawk(e)s Farmhouse in Hawks Road, Hailsham, close to the workhouse. Henry rented the property from the guardians for £15 a year.

Matthew Hale Moss, clerk
to the Alresford Union.
(Courtesy of Derek
Jenkins.)

Henry's twenty-three year workhouse career came to an abrupt end in September 1859 when the guardians decided that he was 'no longer to be trusted, from his gross neglect of his duties to the Board.'[21]. Henry himself wrote to the Poor Law Board informing them of his intention to resign because 'it appears that I no longer possess the confidence of a majority of the Board.'[22]

It seems that Henry had not kept the books correctly between 1854 and 1856, while during 1859 he had mislaid some accounts. As a result, Henry owed the Board the sum of £22, which was roughly the same as the average workhouse nurse or porter's annual salary at the time. Henry does not appear to have defended himself, so it can be assumed that the mistake had definitely occurred and the accusations were founded in truth.

The legal wrangling about the overdue account continued until June 1860 when the guardians decided they were 'willing to accept the balance of Mr Isted's account, provided he pays the legal expenses and gives up his lease.'[23]

INTO THE TWENTIETH CENTURY

Towards the end of the nineteenth century and at the beginning of the twentieth, it was more common for clerks to have a paid assistant to share the heavy workload. The number of books

Charles Prentice Barrett, clerk to the Eton Union talking to the master of the workhouse, dated before 1867. (Reproduced by permission of the Slough Museum and Jill Barrett.)

which the clerk was expected to keep generally increased throughout the Victorian period and the 'business of unions became more complex.'[24]

In January 1892, Mr Holloway, the Assistant Clerk to the Guardians of the Stourbridge Union, was appointed Clerk to the Bromsgrove Union at a salary of £175 per annum. A breakdown of his salary illustrates the many different committees the clerk worked for:

Clerk to Guardians £100 p.a.
School Attendance Committee Clerk £25 p.a.
Rural Sanitary Authority Clerk £25 p.a.
Clerk to the Assessment Committee £25 p.a.[25]

The Relieving Officer

In villages and towns across England and Wales, the human face of the new Poor Law was the relieving officer. Any person or family needing assistance from the union had to apply to him for poor relief or an order to enter the workhouse.

QUALIFICATIONS

Relieving officers had to be twenty-one years of age or over and fairly well-educated, as they needed to keep meticulous accounts. Large unions employed a number of relieving officers for each district. In smaller unions, where there were only one or two relieving officers, a larger geographical area had to be covered. The relieving officer was also required to 'reside in the district for which he may be appointed to act, devote his whole time to the performance of the duties of his office, and abstain from following any trade or profession, and from entering into any other service.'[1]

When Robert May applied to become a relieving officer for the Seisdon Union in 1879, he produced five testimonials to support his application. He had been both the assistant master and an assistant relieving officer at the Dudley Union for five years and now sought a more responsible post.[2]

DUTIES

Before any poor relief was granted, in the form of outdoor relief or an order to enter the workhouse, the relieving officer had to visit the applicant at home (if the house was situated within his district), and make 'all necessary inquiries into the state of health, the ability to work, the condition and family, and the means of such applicant.' He then reported back to the guardians at their next meeting when they would decide if relief was to be granted. He was also required to periodically visit the paupers receiving relief and report back to the guardians, these kinds of checks being intended to assess the validity of claims made by those who had applied for relief as a result of sickness and consequent inability to work. If the pauper had recovered, he was technically able to work and therefore was disqualified from receiving relief.[3]

If an applicant for poor relief was sick, or injured from an accident, and medical attendance was required, the relieving officer was required to give an order to the district medical officer to visit the applicant. He also had to regularly obtain from the district medical officer the names of any paupers whom he had attended without an order. Any pauper receiving medical relief was visited regularly by the relieving officer afterwards, who had the power to supply relief 'not being in money' on his own discretion, at least until the next meeting of the board of guardians.[4]

The Distress in Sheffield, dated January 1879. (Courtesy of Sheffield Local Studies Library.)

In the majority of cases, poor relief could only be granted after a decision had been made by the guardians. However, the relieving officer had the power:

> …in every case of sudden or urgent necessity, to afford such relief to the destitute person as may be requisite, either by giving such person an order of admission into the workhouse, and conveying him thereto if necessary, or by affording him relief out of the Workhouse, provided that the same be not given in money, whether such destitute person be settled in any Parish comprised in the Union or not.[5]

Once outdoor relief was granted, it was the relieving officer's responsibility to 'duly and punctually' supply the weekly allowances of the paupers within his district. He also had to visit, relieve and attend to the non-settled poor within his district 'according to the directions of the guardians… subject always to the obligation imposed on him in cases of sudden or urgent necessity.'[6]

The relieving officer had to keep meticulous accounts, as they were inspected each week by the clerk at the meeting of the board of guardians. They were also audited periodically. It was particularly important for him to keep a record of payments made by the non-settled poor as this would eventually be claimed back from the paupers' home union.[7]

The relieving officer's duties also extended to investigating the circumstances of potential pauper apprentices who were not in the workhouse, but in fact living within his district. This included examining 'the condition of the child, and of his parents, if any, and the residence of the proposed master, the nature of his trade, the number of other apprentices, if any, then bound to him, and generally as to the fitness of the particular binding…' If it was decided to go ahead with the binding of a pauper apprentice, and if the pauper was under fourteen years of age, the relieving officer had to take the child to the district medical officer 'to be examined as to his fitness in respect of bodily health and strength for the proposed trade or business…'[8]

A bill issued by the Chorlton Union for maintenance of Betsy Cope in the workhouse, 1896.

COMPLAINTS ABOUT RELIEVING OFFICERS

As the role of the relieving officer involved handling money, he was 'subject to constant temptation…'[9] Richard Hartill, a Relieving Officer for the Dudley district in the Dudley Union, was one who succumbed to the temptation. He was appointed in 1853 at a salary of £120 per annum and the guardians ordered that 'the security required be himself in £150 and two sureties in the like amount. That Mr Thomas Griffiths of Dudley, Gentleman and Mr John Darbey Shoe Manufacturer of the same place be accepted as his sureties.'[10]

Ten years later, following the revelation of Hartill's misdeeds, the guardians informed the central authorities that '…in reference to the Embezzlement by Richard Hartill the Relieving Officer for the Rowley District. Mr Hartill has been committed to the House of Correction for the space of nine months, with hard labour.'[11]

This was not an isolated case. At the Basingstoke Union, the chairman of the board of guardians wrote to the Poor Law Commission stating that:

One of our relieving officers carried on a system of fraud to a considerable extent…by producing forged vouchers…We suspended him from his office within half an hour…Our Clerk lost no time in applying to a magistrate for a warrant, but he has hitherto eluded the pursuit of the police and escaped.[12]

The other kind of complaint about relieving officers which was frequently received by guardians and the central authorities concerned their treatment of the poor. There is no doubt that the job was a demanding one, especially if a relieving officer had to cover a large geographical area. In such cases it was often difficult to meet the demands of visiting the poor and being available in times of urgency. Delays, or not having an order book at the time when the pauper applied for relief, could lead to unnecessary suffering and sometimes death.

At the Great Yarmouth Union in 1850, an inquest was held into the death of twenty-nine-year-old Sarah Augur. It was alleged that the relieving officer, Mr Pickard, had failed in his duty to provide Sarah with an order for relief and that she had died as a result.[13]

The keeper of the lodging house where Sarah Augur was staying had gone to ask Pickard for an order to admit Sarah to the workhouse. She was told to return at one o'clock, which she did, but Pickard did not return until two o'clock when he gave the lodging house keeper the admission order. By this time Sarah Augur was dead. In his defence, Pickard said that he had not realised Sarah Augur was in immediate danger and he 'did not have a book of orders with him.'[14] He was delayed in returning to his house because 'he had run out of silver coins.'[15]

The inquest was subsequently adjourned and a post-mortem ordered. The surgeon discovered 'a pregnancy of seven months gestation and that labour had commenced associated with a haemorrhage.' He said that 'death had occurred from the non-application of the proper means and exhaustion had followed from the want of stimulants.' There was 'a remote possibility that Augur might have been saved if medical aid had been called for earlier.' However, it was felt that she had been too ill to remove to the workhouse.

Despite this assertion, the jury recorded a verdict that 'death had occurred due to the neglect of Pickard and that he was in dereliction of his duty.' A criminal prosecution was ordered against Pickard who had previously been known for his 'kindness and humanity.' Fortunately for Pickard, his trial for manslaughter was stopped 'when it was clear that a case was not going to be made against him.'[16]

There were also cases where complaints were made directly from those involved. In many unions, literate paupers might write directly to the board of guardians to complain about the conduct of a relieving officer. A case in point was sixty-six-year-old Samuel Hall who, in 1878, wrote a letter of complaint to the guardians of the Dudley Union:

> This is a charge against Mr Fletcher the relieving officer for Sedgley lower side. I, Samuel Hall, was with him this morning for an order to go in the union but he told me he would not give me not till Wednesday. I am sixty-six years old and have lost my leg and my stump is very painful and I am very lame and I am destitute and I have lain this three nights on trespass his [sic] he right by causing me to break the law for he told me I may do as I liked he don't care as I must go somewhere else. I cant write very well for my eyes are very weak. (Sd. S. Hall)[17]

The outcome of this complaint is unknown.

Genuine cases of starvation through the neglect of a relieving officer were extremely rare. There were ninety-seven cases of starvation in London in 1872 and 'only one had refused the offer of admission to the workhouse: the rest had not applied for poor relief.'[18] In 1873, one Poor Law Inspector, Henry Longley, wrote that it should 'become a matter of wider notoriety that the duties of Relieving Officers are limited to the relief of destitute applicants, and that it is not incumbent upon them to protect the community generally...against the scandals of deaths by starvation, or to seek out applicants of relief.'[19]

INTO THE TWENTIETH CENTURY

Towards the end of the nineteenth century and the beginning of the twentieth, the work of Poor Law unions became increasingly complex. As a result, it became more and more common for relieving officers to combine other roles with their existing duties.

The Alton Union Workhouse. (Courtesy of Derek Jenkins.)

In November 1882, William Walton was appointed as relieving officer for the Tipton District of the Dudley Union.[20] By 1897, he also had to combine the posts of Inquiry Officer, Vaccination Officer and Collector of the Guardians for the Tipton District. That year he was promoted to the position of master of the Dudley Union Workhouse.[21]

NOTES

Introduction

1. Crowther, M.A., *The Workhouse System 1834-1929*, (1981), p3
2. *Ibid.*, p6
3. 1861 Census, Sedgley, RG 9/2046 E.D. 11
4. Crowther, *op. cit.*, p5

Chapter 1: The New Poor Law

1. Higginbotham, P., Abingdon Workhouse <http://www.workhouses.org.uk/Abingdon/> Oxford University web, Oxford, 2000
2. Murray, P., *Poverty and Welfare 1830-1914*, (1999), p26
3. *Ibid.*, p26
4. Englander, D., *Poverty and Poor Law Reform in 19th Century Britain, 1834-1914: From Chadwick to Booth*, (1998), p31
5. Digby, A., *The Poor Law in Nineteenth-Century England*, (1985), p11
6. Lewis, W.J., *A History of Lampeter*, (1997), p112
7. Murray, *op. cit.*, p35
8. Englander. *op. cit.*, p16
9. Murray, *op. cit.*, p35
10. GDU/1/4, 13 May 1859
11. See essay by R. Wildman in Longmate N., *The Workhouse*, (2003), p287
12. The British Almanac quoted by Wildman R. in *Ibid.*, p288
13. *Ibid.*, pp89-90

Chapter 2: The Workhouse System

1. Crowther, M.A., *The Workhouse System 1834-1929*, (1981), p3
2. Art. 88, Consolidated General Order, 1847
3. May, T., *The Victorian Workhouse*, (1997), p19
4. Art. 93, Consolidated General Order, 1847
5. Flett, J., *The Story of the Workhouse and the Hospital at Nether Edge*, (1985), p8
6. Forrest, D., *Warrington's Poor and the Workhouse 1725-1851*, (2001), p22
7. GDU/1/1, 30 December 1838
8. Digby, A., *Pauper Palaces*, (1978), p156
9. Charles Chaplin quoted in Land, N., *Victorian Workhouse: A Study of the Bromsgrove Union Workhouse 1836-1901*, (1990), p11

10. Horn, P., *Labouring Life in the Victorian Countryside*, (1987), p209
11. GDU/6/1/ 4, 20 October 1862
12. GDU/6/1/ 4, 29 November 1862
13. Longmate, N., *The Workhouse*, (2003), p92
14. Art. 104, Consolidated General Order, 1847
15. See Digby, *op. cit.*
16. GDU/1/5, 3 December 1861
17. Longmate, *op. cit.*, p92
18. Art. 111, Consolidated General Order, 1847
19. CBG Lampeter, 378, 26 January 1877
20. Longmate, *op. cit.*, p92
21. Englander, D., *Poverty and Poor Law Reform in 19th Century Britain, 1834-1914: From Chadwick to Booth*, (1998), p32
22. Longmate, *op. cit.*, pp93-94
23. G/DU 3/1/ 2, 20 July 1874
24. Crowther, *op. cit.*, p215
25. *Ibid.*, p215
26. Longmate, *op. cit.*, p94
27. Crowther, *op. cit.*, p215
28. G/DU 1/1/5, 21 December 1860
29. Art. 208, No. 6, Consolidated General Order, 1847
30. Art. 129, Consolidated General Order, 1847
31. Art. 130, Consolidated General Order, 1847
32. Castle E. and Wishart B., *Foleshill Union Workhouse Punishment Book 1864-1900*, (1999), p10
33. Longmate, op. cit., p21

Chapter 3: The Able-Bodied Men

1. Longmate, *The Workhouse*, (2003), p78
2. Watson, I., *The Westbourne Union: Life In and Out of the New Workhouse*, (1991), p13
3. *Ibid.*, p19
4. Land, N., *Victorian Workhouse: A Study of the Bromsgrove Union Workhouse 1836-1901*, (1990), p92
5. G/DU 1/3, 23 February 1855
6. Digby, A., *Pauper Palaces*, (1978), p109
7. G/DU 1/2, 20 December 1847
8. Crowther, M.A., *The Workhouse System 1834-1929*, (1981), p72
9. *Ibid.*
10. Horn, P., *Labouring Life in the Victorian Countryside*, (1987), p201
11. *Ibid.*, pp201-202
12. Longmate, *op. cit.*, p257
13. G/DU 3/1/3, 15 September 1877
14. Horn, *op. cit.*, p202
15. G/DU 1/13, 24 April 1879
16. Roberts, D., 'How Cruel was the Victorian Poor Law?', *Historical Journal VI*, (1963), p105
17. *Ibid.*
18. Englander, D., *Poverty and Poor Law Reform in 19th Century Britain, 1834-1914: From Chadwick to Booth*, (1998), pp98-99
19. With thanks to Ken Ripper for information about his ancestor William Ripper
20. Reid, A., *The Union Workhouse: A Study Guide for Teachers and Local Historians*, (1994), p49
21. Davies, P.P., *History of Medicine in Great Yarmouth Hospitals and Doctors*, (2003), p492
22. *Ibid.*
23. Newman, S., *The Christchurch and Bournemouth Union Workhouse*, (2000), p73
24. *Ibid.*, pp73-74

25. Longmate, *op. cit.*, p261
26. *Ibid.*
27. *Ibid.*, p259
28. *Ibid.*
29. G/DU 1 /4, 1 January 1858
30. G/DU 1/8, 15 May 1868
31. G/DU 1/14, 14 February 1879
32. Davies P.P., *op. cit.*, p494
33. *Ibid.*, p496
34. Newman, S., *op. cit.*, p74
35. Hardy, S., *The House on the Hill: The Samford House of Industry 1764-1930*, (2001), p48
36. Reid, A., op. cit., p52
37. Watson I., *op. cit.*, p21
38. G/DU 1/14, 14 November and 28 November 1879
39. Davies, P.P., *op. cit.*, p472
40. *Ibid.*
41. *Ibid.*
42. Englander, *op. cit.*, pp99-100
43. Crowther, *op. cit.*, p211
44. *Ibid.*, p100
45. Longmate, *op. cit.*, p258
46. *Ibid.*, p262

Chapter 4: The Able-Bodied Women

1. Longmate, N., *The Workhouse*, (2003), p156
2. G/DU 6/1/5, 12 October 1866
3. Emmeline Pankhurst quoted in Simkin, J. (ed.), *Voices from the Past: The Workhouse*, (1986), p16
4. Crowther, M.A., *The Workhouse System 1834-1929*, (1981), p42
5. Digby, A., *Pauper Palaces*, (1978), p154
6. Louisa Twining quoted in Hollis, P., *Women in Public 1850-1900: Documents of the Victorian Women's Movement*, (1979), document 8.6.2
7. With thanks to Colin Leathley for information about his great-great-grandmother Margaret Grundy and great-grandfather Christopher Grundy
8. With thanks to Yvonne Moore for information about her ancestor Emily Dolby
9. G/DU 1/13, 31 May 1878
10. Emmeline Pankhurst quoted in Simkin, *op. cit.*, p16
11. Longmate, *op. cit.*, p158
12. With thanks to Carl Higgs for information about his ancestor Jane Chetter
13. GDU 6/1/6, 9 June 1872
14. Land, N., *Victorian Workhouse: A Study of the Bromsgrove Union Workhouse 1836-1901*, (1990), p93
15. *Ibid.*
16. CBG Lampeter 434, 1888-1890
17. CBG Lampeter 436 1893-1895
18. U/Se 297 1875-1888
19. U/Se 31 1876-1878
20. Hatcher, D., *The Workhouse & The Weald*, (1988), pp12-13
21. Crowther, *op. cit.*, p195
22. *Ibid.*
23. Digby, A., *op. cit.*, p153
24. Reid, A., *The Union Workhouse: A Study Guide for Teachers and Local Historians*, (1994), p66
25. Watson, I., *The Westbourne Union: Life In and Out of the New Workhouse*, (1991), p23
26. Longmate, *op. cit.*, p156

27. G/DU 3/1/10, 6 November 1884
28. U/Se 123 1891-1894
29. U/Se 124 1894-1898
30. CBG Lampeter 428 1877-9
31. *Ibid.*
32. Watson, *op. cit.*, p53
33. *Ibid.*, pp53-54
34. G/DU 6/1/3, MFM 528
35. Longmate, *op. cit.*, p159
36. Reid, *op. cit.*, p21
37. G/DU 2/10/1, 7 February 1865
38. Castle, E. & Wishart, B., *Foleshill Union Workhouse Punishment Book 1864-1900*, (1999), p27
39. Longmate, *op. cit.*, p159
40. *Ibid.*
41. *Ibid.*
42. Digby, A., *op. cit.*, p154
43. U/Se 33, 1888-1890
44. Sheffield Union Special Report of the Classification Committee 1902
45. Newman, S., *The Christchurch and Bournemouth Union Workhouse*, (2000), p75
46. *Ibid.*
47. *Ibid.*

Chapter 5: The Children

1. Crowther M.A., *The Workhouse System 1834-1929*, (1981), p201
2. G/DU 3/1/24 , 5 October 1880
3. G/DU 1/20, 20 May 1887
4. Information kindly supplied by John Sayers
5. U/Se 34, 7 August 1891
6. U/Se 23, 1 September 1892
7. U/Se 35, 9 November 1893
8. U/Se 39, 30 October 1900
9. U/Se 39, 5 May 1902
10. U/Se 37, 26 April 1898
11. U/Se 38, 15 March 1900
12. With thanks to Roger Harpin and Fred's family in Australia for information about their ancestor Fred Dent
13. GDU 1/27, 20 November 1896
14. GDU 1/27, 11 December 1896
15. With thanks to Sandy Norman for information about his grandmother Mary Bates and his great-uncle John Bates
16. With thanks to Pat McGrath for information about her grandmother Mary Ann Mangan (Manggon)
17. Digby, A., *Pauper Palaces*, (1978), p157
18. Mary Carpenter, quoted in Simkin, J., *op. cit.*, p6
19. G/DU 2/10/1, 6 May 1862
20. Aston Union Punishment Book, 7 & 14 September 1869
21. See G/DU 1/1/6-18
22. G/DU 2/10/1 passim
23. Crowther, *op. cit.*, p204
24. *Ibid.*, p136
25. *Ibid.*, p203
26. *Ibid.*, p204

27. Digby, *op. cit.*, p159
28. Hackwood F. Wm., *A History of West Bromwich*, (1895, reprinted 2001), p255
29. Dickens, C., 'London Pauper Children', *Household Words*, 31 August 1850, p551
30. Dickens, C., 'A Day in a Pauper Palace', *Household Words*, 13 July 1850, pp361-364
31. CBG Lampeter 436, 1893-1895
32. Land, N., *Victorian Workhouse: A Study of the Bromsgrove Union Workhouse 1836-1901*, (1990), p68
33. Newman, S., *The Christchurch and Bournemouth Union Workhouse*, (2000), p77
34. *Ibid.*, p78
35. Howsam, L., (ed.), *Memories of the Workhouse & Old Hospital At Fir Vale*, (2002), p2
36. G/DU 3/1/23, 20 September 1876
37. G/DU 1/30, 5 October 1900
38. U/Cs 224 Chester-le-Street Children in Certified Schools & Institutions File
39. Quoted in Crompton, F., *Workhouse Children*, (1997), p37
40. G/DU 3/1/24, 15 August 1883
41. Crowther, M.A., *op. cit.*, p220
42. Longmate, N., *The Workhouse*, (2003), p189
43. With thanks to the late Maurice Cuerton for information about his ancestor Charles Cuerton, and to his widow Marie for granting permission to publish the information
44. Land, N., *op. cit.*, p63
45. Kohli, M., *The Golden Bridge: Young Immigrants to Canada 1833-1939*, (2003), p71
46. GDU 3/1/10, 3 November 1886
47. GDU 3/1/25, 16 August 1886
48. Information kindly supplied by Chris Sanham and John Sayers
49. With thanks to Maud Jarvis for information about her grandfather Stephen Geoghan (Gagan)
50. Crowther, M.A., *op. cit.*, p88

Chapter 6: The Elderly

1. Revd Hastings, F., 'Workhouse Worries', *The Quiver*, (July 1889), p646
2. Jefferies, Richard, Hodge and His Masters, II, p144-5, quoted in Horn, P., *Labouring Life in the Victorian Countryside*, (1987), p213
3. Thompson, F., *Lark Rise to Candleford*, (1945), p79
4. CBG Lampeter 436, 1893-1895, 8 May 1896
5. Revd Hastings, F., *op. cit.*, p644
6. Crowther, M.A., *The Workhouse System 1834-1929*, (1981), p196
7. Revd Hastings, F., *op. cit.*, p646
8. Crowther, M.A., *op. cit.*, p213
9. Rider-Haggard, H., *A Farmer's Year*, 1899
10. Dickens, C., 'A Walk in a Workhouse', *Household Words*, 25 May 1850, p206
11. CBG Lampeter 434, 1890-1891
12. Revd Hastings, F., *op. cit.*, p643
13. Longmate, N., *The Workhouse*, (2003), p143
14. Davies, P.P., *History of Medicine in Great Yarmouth Hospitals and Doctors*, (2003)
15. Murray, P., *Poverty and Welfare 1830-1914*, (1999), p52
16. Hackwood, F. Wm., *A History of West Bromwich*, (1895, reprinted 2001), p255
17. Crowther, M.A., *op. cit.*, p241
18. *Ibid.*, p31
19. *Ibid.*, p241
20. Harrison, J.F.C., *Late Victorian Britain 1875-1901*, (1990), p136
21. Brundage, A., *The English Poor Laws 1700-1930*, (2002), p81
22. G/DU 3/1/23, 15 October 1872
23. King's Norton Union House Committee Records, 27 November 1895

24. Dickens, C., *Ibid.*, p207
25. Horn, P., *op. cit.*, p210-211
26. G/DU 2/10/1, 6 March 1860
27. Longmate, N., *op. cit.*, p145
28. *Ibid.*
29. Horn, P., *op. cit.*, p213
30. Longmate, N., *op. cit.*, p145
31. *Ibid.*
32. Newman, S., *The Christchurch and Bournemouth Union Workhouse*, (2000), p85
33. Crowther, M.A., *op. cit.*, p201
34. Revd Hastings, F., *op. cit.*, p644
35. Crowther, M.A., *op.cit.*, p200
36. *Ibid.*, p70
37. Davies P.P., *op. cit.*, p507
38. Newman, S., *op. cit.*, p85
39. *Ibid.*
40. With thanks to Ken Ripper for information about his ancestor Alexander Ripper
41. CBG Lampeter, 433, 1888-1890, 6 September 1889
42. G/DU 1/26, 15 May 1896
43. Horn, P., *op. cit.*, p205
44. *The Household Narrative, Law and Crime*, (1850), p226
45. CBG Aberystwyth ACC 1099 - 78 (Letter File)
46. Horn, P., *op. cit.*, p206
47. *Ibid.*, pp205-206
48. Murray, P., *op. cit.*, p107
49. *Ibid.*, p108
50. Murray, P., *op. cit.*, p52
51. *Ibid.*
52. Longmate, N., *op. cit.*, p145
53. Sheffield Union Special Report of the Classification Committee 1902
54. Cuttle, *Rural Guardians*, p40-41 quoted in Horn, P., *op. cit.*, p213
55. Longmate, N., *op. cit.*, p147

Chapter 7: The Infirm

1. Mitton, L., *The Victorian Hospital*, (2001), p11
2. *Ibid.*, p20
3. Horn, P., *Labouring Life in the Victorian Countryside*, (1987), p185
4. *Ibid.*
5. G/DU 1/3, 13 July 1855
6. G/DU 1/3, 14 September 1855
7. With thanks to Benjamin Caine for information about his great-great-great-great grandmother Sarah Bradford
8. Longmate, N., *The Workhouse*, (2003), p198
9. G/DU 2/10/1, 4 November 1862
10. Crompton, F., *Workhouse Children*, (1997), p93
11. Cole, J., *Down Poorhouse Lane: The Diary of a Rochdale Workhouse*, (1994), pp40-41
12. Longmate, N., *op. cit.*, p198
13. *Jack's Reference Book for Home and Office*, (1923), p413
14. Longmate, N., *op. cit.*, p198
15. *Jack's Reference Book*, *op. cit.*, p413
16. Longmate, N., *op. cit.*, pp207-208
17. Murray, P., *Poverty and Welfare 1830-1914*, (1999), p53
18. Mitton, L., *op. cit.*, p20

19. Murray, Peter, *op. cit.*, p53
20. *Dudley Herald*, 1 February 1868
21. *Ibid.*
22. Cobbe, *Workhouse Sketches*, p456, quoted in Horn, P., *op. cit.*, p188
23. Supplement to the *Leeds Mercury*, 10 June 1848, www.learningcurve.gov.uk/victorianbritain/caring/source4
24. Quoted in Murray, *op. cit.*, pp53-54
25. Quoted in Mitton, L., *op. cit.*, p20
26. Crowther, M.A., *The Workhouse System 1834-1929*, (1981), p161
27. Twining, L., *Recollections of Life and Work*, (1893), p111
28. Digby, A., *Pauper Palaces*, (1978), p171
29. Lofthouse, F.H., *Keepers of the House: A Workhouse Saga*, (2001), p235
30. *Ibid.*, pp235-237
31. Crowther, M.A., *op. cit.*, p176
32. *Ibid.*, pp176-177
33. G/DU 3/1/ 4, 17 December 1879
34. G/DU 2/10/1, 5 February 1861
35. *Ibid.*
36. G/DU 2/10/1, 11 June 1867
37. G/DU 2/10/1, 21 December 1869
38. *Ibid.*
39. Flinn, M.W., 'Medical Services under the New Poor Law' in Fraser D. (ed.), *The New Poor Law in the Nineteenth Century*, (1976), p55
40. Digby, A., *op. cit.*, p170
41. Murray, P., *op. cit.*, p54
42. Brundage, A., *The English Poor Laws 1700-1930*, (2002), p122
43. Mitton, L., *op. cit.*, p22
44. *Ibid.*, p6
45. *Ibid.*, p22
46. With thanks to Sheila Kirk for information about her great-grandfather Thomas Preece.
47. With thanks to Benjamin Caine for information about his great-great-great-grandfather Thomas Edgington.
48. CBG Lampeter 438, 1899-1901.
49. U/Se 69, 23 January 1903.
50. G/DU 3/1/23, 10 January 1876.
51. G/DU 3/1/23, 18 March 1876.
52. G/DU 1/9, 7 July 1871.
53. G/DU 1/11, 22 January 1875.
54. CBG Cardigan Ladies' Committee Visiting Book.
55. Digby, A., *op. cit.*, p169
56. With thanks to Wilfred William Ellesmore for information about his great-grandmother Elizabeth Brant
57. Hackwood, F. Wm., *A History of West Bromwich*, (1895, reprinted 2001), p255
58. *Ibid.*

Chapter 8: The Lunatics

1. Digby, A., *Pauper Palaces*, (1978), p172
2. Newman, S., *The Christchurch and Bournemouth Union Workhouse*, (2000), p49
3. U/Da 713 Darlington Visiting Committee, 14 November 1890
4. Forrest, D., *Warrington's Poor and the Workhouse 1725-1851*, (2001), p15
5. CBG Lampeter 428 1877-9
6. Male Casebook No. 4 (1877-78): LMA Piece H11/HLL/B20/13

7.   Male Casebook No. 4 (1877–78): LMA Piece H11/HLL/B20/13
8.   With thanks to Christopher J. Hogger for information about his ancestor Alfred Woodhurst. Information reproduced by kind permission of Kevin Towers, Patient Services Manager, West London Mental Health NHS Trust
9.   Longmate, N., *The Workhouse*, (2003), p212.
10. Crowther, M.A., *The Workhouse System 1834-1929*, (1981), p164
11. Longmate, N., *op. cit.*, p212
12. Reid, A., *The Union Workhouse: A Study Guide for Teachers and Local Historians*, (1994), p67
13. G/DU 3/1/26, 20 April 1898
14. Dickens, C., 'A Walk in a Workhouse', *Household Words*, 25 May 1850, p205
15. Forrest, D., *Warrington's Poor and the Workhouse 1725-1851*, (2001), p15
16. G/DU 3/1/15, July 1891.
17. G/DU 3/1/26, 12 March 1900.
18. With thanks to Harry E. Clarke for information about his great-great-grandmother Esther Clarke
19. Crowther, M.A., *op. cit.*, p164
20. *Ibid.*
21. Crompton, F., *Workhouse Children*, (1997), pp82–83
22. CBG Aberystwyth Acc. 1099 – 78 Letter File
23. G/DU 1/7, 2 September 1864
24. G/DU 3/1/4, 9 November 1878
25. CBG Lampeter Visitors Book, 603 1899–1901
26. Hardy, S., *The House on the Hill: The Samford House of Industry 1764-1930*, (2001), p91
27. Longmate, N., *op. cit.*, p213
28. *Ibid.*
29. G/DU 3/1/5, 18 November 1880
30. *Ibid.*
31. G/DU 1/13, 19 November 1879
32. G/DU 3/1/12, 17 February 1888
33. G/DU 1/8, 19 November 1867
34. G/DU 1/13, 9 November 1878
35. Digby, A., *op. cit.*, p172
36. G/DU 3/1/14, 23 September 1890
37. G/DU 3/1/13, 29 March 1889
38. G/DU 3/1/20, 7 May 1896
39. G/DU 3/1/16, 28 September 1892
40. G/DU 1/9, 17 January 1873
41. G/DU 1/3, 17 March 1854
42. Best, G., *Mid-Victorian Britain 1851-75*, (1985), p162
43. With thanks to Sandy Norman for information about his ancestor Amelia Boyd.
44. G/DU 2/1/1, 30 August 1899
45. G/DU 3/1 /2 , 12 June 1874
46. Longmate, N., *op. cit.*, p219
47. *Ibid.*, p220
48. *Ibid.*, p219

Chapter 9: The Vagrants

1.   Digby, A., *Pauper Palaces*, (1978), p148
2.   Crowther, M.A., *The Workhouse System 1834-1929*, (1981), p249
3.   *Ibid.*, p248
4.   *Ibid.*
5.   *Justice of the Peace*, 'Casual Paupers', 31 March 1866, p193

6. King's Norton Admissions & Discharges for Casual Paupers, 29 March 1901

7. London, J., 'In Line At The Spike' in Peter Keating (ed.), *Into Unknown England 1866-1913: Selections from the Social Explorers*, (1976), p233

8. Digby, A., *op. cit.*, p148

9. G/DU 2/10/1, 16 November 1869

10. Fillmore, J., 'The female vagrant pauper', *The Local Historian*, Vol. 35, No. 3, August 2005, p149

11. Crowther, M.A., *op. cit.*, p247

12. Justice of the Peace, *op. cit.*, p193

13. *Ibid.*

14. CBG Lampeter 436 1893-1895

15. CBG Lampeter 438 1899-1901

16. Lofthouse, F.H., *Keepers of the House: A Workhouse Saga*, (2001), p230

17. CBG Lampeter 432 1886-1888

18. Newman, S., *The Christchurch and Bournemouth Union Workhouse*, (2000), p67

19. CBG Lampeter 429 1881-2

20. Longmate, N., *The Workhouse*, 2003, p237

21. CBG Lampeter 603, Visitors Book

22. Longmate, N., *op. cit.*, p234

23. *Ibid.*, pp237-8

24. G/DU 1/11, 9 January 1874

25. CBG Lampeter 604 Visitors Book

26. G/DU 1/9, 19 December 1871

27. Fillmore, J., *op. cit.*, p149

28. *Sheffield & Rotherham Independent*, 28 February 1878, with thanks to Lyn Howsam

29. Longmate, N., *op. cit.*, p233

30. Best, G., *Mid-Victorian Britain 1851-1875*, (1985), p162

31. Lofthouse, F.H., *op. cit.*, p195

32. G/DU 1/8, 19 December 1871

33. *Ibid.*

34. Longmate, N., *op. cit.*, p248

35. G/DU 1/8, 10 December 1869

36. Flett, J., *The Story of the Workhouse and the Hospital at Nether Edge*, (1985), p9

37. Fillmore, J., *op. cit.*, p157

38. Crowther M.A., *op. cit.*, p262

39. *Ibid.*

40. Newman, S., *op. cit.*, p67

41. U/Se 38, 5 May 1899

42. *Sheffield & Rotherham Independent*, *op. cit.*

43. G/DU 2/10/1, 1 May 1860

44. Fillmore, J., *op. cit.*, p157

45. King's Norton Admission Register of Casual Paupers

46. Fillmore J, op. cit., p149

47. Crowther, M.A., *op. cit.*, p255

48. Quoted in Brundage, A., *The English Poor Laws*, (2002), p119.

49. Fillmore, J., *op. cit.*, p149

50. Longmate, N., *op. cit.*, p239

51. *Ibid.*

52. U/Se 41, June 1905 Sedgefield

53. CBG Lampeter 434, 20 March 1891

54. Lofthouse, F.H., *op. cit.*, p145

55. *Sheffield & Rotherham Independent*, *op. cit.*

56. Justice of the Peace, *op. cit.*, p194

57. U/Se 35 Sedgefield, 10 August 1892

58. Longmate N, *op. cit.*, p250

59. *Ibid.*
60. *Ibid.*, pp248-249

Chapter 10: The Master And Matron

1.   Longmate, N., *The Workhouse*, (2003), p101
2.   Digby, A., *The Poor Law in Nineteenth-Century England*, (1982), p31
3.   CBG Lampeter 378, 23 February 1877
4.   CBG Aberystwyth ACC. 1099 – 78 – Letter File
5.   Crowther, M.A., *The Workhouse System 1834-1929*, (1981), p125
6.   *Ibid.*, p125
7.   CBG Lampeter 378, 9 March 1877
8.   Crowther, M.A., *op. cit.*, p124
9.   May, T., *The Victorian Workhouse*, (1997), p15
10. *Ibid.*
11. Crowther, M.A., *op. cit.*, p116
12. Reid, A., *The Union Workhouse: A Study Guide for Teachers and Local Historians*, (1994), p57
13. U/Da 785, 10 April 1893
14. Piggott, R., 'Workhouse Connections' in *Midland Ancestor*, June 2002, p140
15. *Ibid.*, p141
16. Frederick Wm. Hackwood, *A History of West Bromwich*, (1895, reprinted 2001), p255
17. With thanks to Ruth Piggott for information about her grandparents William James and Emma Gilpin
18. Art. 208, No. 2 and Art. 210, No. 2 , Consolidated General Order, 1847
19. Art. 208, No. 7 and Art. 210, No. 6, Consolidated General Order, 1847
20. Art. 210, No. 3 and No. 4 and Art. 208 No. 6, Consolidated General Order, 1847
21. Art. 210, No. 8, Consolidated General Order, 1847.
22. Art. 210, Nos 7, 9 and 12, Consolidated General Order, 1847.
23. Art. 208, Nos 8, 9, 11, 13 and 17, Consolidated General Order, 1847.
24. Art. 208, Nos 15 and 16, Consolidated General Order, 1847.
25. Art. 208, No. 14, Consolidated General Order, 1847.
26. Crowther M.A., op. cit., p118
27. Art. 208, Nos 19, 21 and 28, Consolidated General Order, 1847
28. Art. 208 No. 4, Consolidated General Order, 1847
29. Reid, A., *op. cit.*, pp44-5
30. U/Se 33, 5 October 1888
31. U/Se 33, 14 June 1889
32. Crowther, M.A., *op. cit.*, p124
33. G/DU 1/1 /4, 25 February 1859
34. Crowther, M.A., *op. cit.*, p124
35. *Ibid.*
36. G/DU 3/2/14, 19 May 1882
37. *Dudley Herald*, 10 September 1881
38. With thanks to Norma Robinson and Lynn Nugent for information about their ancestors, the Ditchburns
39. CBG Lampeter 603 Visitor's Book, 14 March 1901
40. With thanks to Phil Bristow for information about his ancestor Harry James Bristow
41. G/DU 1/1 /4, 25 February 1859 and G/DU 3/1/23, 30 April 1873
42. G/DU 1/1 /4, 11 March 1859
43. G/DU 1/1/11, 9 May 1873
44. G/DU 3/1/23, 6 November 1875
45. G/DU 3/1/23, 6 November 1875
46. G/DU 3/1/3, 20 November 1875

47. U/Se 34, 13 November 1891
48. U/Se 89, 27 January 1899
49. U/Se 41, 27 April 1906
50. U/Se 40, 5 September 1902
51. Land, N., *Victorian Workhouse: A Study of the Bromsgrove Union Workhouse 1836-1901*, (1990), p34
52. CBG Cardigan Ladies' Committee Visiting Book
53. With thanks to Edwin Pickett for information about his great-grandparents Daniel and Eleanor Pickett
54. Crowther, M.A., *op. cit.*, p118
55. Roberts, D., 'How Cruel was the Victorian Poor Law?', *Historical Journal VI*, 1963, p102
56. *Ibid.*, p98
57. Crowther, M.A., *op. cit.*, p122
58. Stevens, J., *Faversham Union Workhouse: The Early Years 1838-1850*, (2002), p28
59. *Dudley Herald*, 25 February 1882
60. *Ibid.*
61. Crowther, M.A., *op. cit.*, p143
62. *Ibid.*

Chapter 11: The Schoolteachers

]1. Art. 114, Consolidated General Order, 1847
2. Art. 212, No. 2, Consolidated General Order, 1847
3. Art. 212, No. 3, Consolidated General Order, 1847
4. Art. 212, No. 4, Consolidated General Order, 1847
5. Art. 212, No. 5, Consolidated General Order, 1847
6. Quoted in Newman, S., *The Christchurch and Bournemouth Union Workhouse*, (2000), p47
7. G/DU 1/9, 3 November 1871
8. Longmate, N., *The Workhouse*, (2003), p106
9. *Ibid.*
10. Brundage, A., *The English Poor Laws 1700-1930*, (2002), p94
11. Crompton, F., *Workhouse Children*, (1997), p114
12. *Ibid.*, Illustration 10, 25 April 1865
13. G/DU 1/11, 27 November 1874
14. G/DU 3/1/23, 27 June 1876
15. G/DU 3/1/5, 28 August 1880
16. G/DU 3/1/24, 8 March 1884
17. G/DU 3/1/8, 11 September 1885
18. Newman, S., *op. cit.*, pp45–46
19. Crompton, F., *op. cit.*, p108
20. *Ibid.*, p113
21. *Ibid.*
22. G/DU 1/4, 11 March 1859
23. Crompton, F., *op. cit.*, pp123-124
24. Crowther, M.A., *The Workhouse System 1834-1929*, (1981), p131
25. Digby, A., *Pauper Palaces*, (1978), p187
26. Crompton, F., *op. cit.*, p118
27. Crowther, M.A., *op. cit.*, p132
28. Stevens, J., *Faversham Union Workhouse: The Early Years 1838-1850*, (2002), pp24-25
29. *Ibid.*
30. *Ibid.*, p25
31. Digby, A., *op. cit.*, p187
32. *Ibid.*
33. Crompton, F., *op. cit.*, p155

34. *Ibid.*
35. *Ibid.*, p116
36. Crowther, M.A., *op. cit.*, p205
37. Longmate, N., *op. cit.*, p168
38. Crompton, F., *op. cit.*, p141
39. Crowther, M.A., *op. cit.*, pp131–132
40. Sir Henry Morton Stanley, *The Autobiography of Sir Henry Morton Stanley: The Making of a 19th Century Explorer*, Narrative Press, (2001)
41. Moore I.S., *Oldchurch: The Workhouse Story*, (1999), p105
42. G/DU 1/5, 4 May 1860
43. G/DU 1/6, 26 December 1862
44. G/DU 2/10/1, 1 July 1862
45. G/DU 2/10/1, 2 February 1864
46. G/DU 1/6, 5 February 1864
47. G/DU 1/7, 9 March 1866
48. Quoted in Frank Crompton, *op. cit.*, p122
49. U/Da 785, 23 February 1892
50. U/Da 785, 29 August 1899
51. Crowther, M.A., *op. cit.*, p151
52. *Ibid.*, p206

Chapter 12: The Medical Officer

1. Englander, D., *Poverty and Poor Law Reform in 19th Century Britain, 1834-1914*, (1998), p36.
2. May, T., *The Victorian Workhouse*, (1997), p16
3. Letter to *Yarmouth Independent*, 1879, quoted in Davies, P.P., *History of Medicine in Great Yarmouth Hospitals and Doctors*, (2003), p489
4. Art. 168, Consolidated General Order, 1847
5. Digby, A., *Pauper Palaces*, (1978) p167
6. Art. 207, No. 2, Consolidated General Order, 1847
7. Art. 92, Consolidated General Order, 1847
8. Art. 207, No. 4, Consolidated General Order, 1847
9. Art. 207, No. 5, Consolidated General Order, 1847
10. Art. 207, No. 4, Consolidated General Order, 1847
11. Art. 207, No. 6, Consolidated General Order, 1847
12. Digby, A., *op. cit.*, p171
13. *Ibid.*
14. Art 207, No. 7, Consolidated General Order, 1847
15. Longmate, N., *The Workhouse*, (2003), p201
16. *Ibid.*
17. Art. 207, Nos 8 and 9, Consolidated General Order, 1847
18. Art. 206, No. 1, Consolidated General Order, 1847
19. *Ibid.*
20. Art. 206, Nos 3 and 4, Consolidated General Order, 1847
21. Horn, P., *Labouring Life in the Victorian Countryside*, (1987), p190
22. Brundage, A., *The English Poor Laws 1700-1930*, (2002), p97
23. G/DU 1/4, 12 June 1857
24. G/DU 1/4, 21 January 1859
25. Higginbotham, P., 'Workhouse Administration and Staff' <http://www.workhouses.org.uk/admin/> Oxford University web, Oxford, 2000
26. Hardy, S., *The House on the Hill: The Samford House of Industry 1764-1930*, (2001), p69
27. G/DU 1/1/4, 11 March 1859
28. G/DU 2/10/1, 16 November 1869

29. U/Da 766 – Service Register of Officers
30. G/DU 3/1/25, 24 May 1890
31. G/DU 3/1/26, 7 August 1900
32. G/DU 1/31, 15 May 1903
33. G/DU 3/2/14, 31 March 1882
34. Letter to *Yarmouth Independent*, 1879, quoted in Davies, P.P., *op. cit.*, p489
35. Crowther, M.A., *op. cit.*, p159
36. *Ibid.*, p160
37. G/DU 3/1/23, 10 January 1876
38. Horn, P., *op. cit.*, p191
39. G/DU 1/1, 19 June 1839
40. Crowther, M.A., *The Workhouse System 1834-1929*, (1981), p159
41. Horn, P., *op. cit.*, p191
42. Lofthouse, F.H., *Keepers of the House: A Workhouse Saga*, (2001), p267
43. *Ibid.*, p247
44. G/DU 3/1/26, 21 September 1900
45. Longmate, N., *op. cit.*, p102
46. G/DU 3/1/23, 26 April 1877
47. G/DU 3/1/23, 21 July 1877
48. G/DU 1/25, 27 April 1894
49. Hardy, S., *op. cit.*, p138
50. Crowther, M.A., *op. cit.*, p157
51. *Ibid.*

Chapter 13: The Nursing Staff

1. Hardy, S., *The House on the Hill: The Samford House of Industry 1764-1930*, (2001), p80
2. Art. 213, No. 2, Consolidated General Order, 1847
3. Crowther, M.A., *The Workhouse System 1834-1929*, (1981), p165
4. G/DU 3/1/26, 30 September 1901
5. G/DU 2/1/1, 21 February 1902
6. G/DU 1/31, 30 January 1903
7. G/DU 1 /4, 11 March 1859
8. G/DU 1/5, 4 May 1860
9. Reid, A., *The Union Workhouse: A Study Guide for Teachers and Local Historians*, (1994), p61
10. U/Da 785, 21 March 1894
11. Crowther, M.A., *op. cit.*, pp165-166
12. *Ibid.*, p165
13. Newman, S., *The Christchurch and Bournemouth Union Workhouse*, (2000), p89
14. Mrs Brewer 'Workhouse Life in Town and Country' in *Sunday at Home*, August 1890, quoted in Horn, P., *Labouring Life in the Victorian Countryside*, (1987), p254
15. Crowther, M.A., *op. cit.*, p165
16. B. Abel-Smith quoted in Crowther, *op. cit.*, p166
17. Reid, A., *op. cit.*, p61
18. G/DU 3/1/25, 5 August 1896
19. G/DU 3/1/20, 27 July 1896
20. *Ibid.*
21. With thanks to Janette Woodhead for information about her great-grandmother Sarah Grace Hannam
22. With thanks to Judith Holmes for information about her great-great-grandmother Charlotte Evans
23. G/DU 1/7, 6 April 1866
24. G/DU 1/12, 17 March and 24 March 1876

25. Digby, A., *Pauper Palaces*, (1978), p172
26. Quoted in Crowther, M.A., *op. cit.*, p165
27. Reid, A., *op. cit.*, p47
28. G/DU 3/1/18, 2 April 1894
29. Digby, A., *op. cit.*, p172
30. G/DU 3/1/3, 4 February 1877
31. With thanks to Alan Tweedale for information about his grandparents Walter and Hannah (Maria) Tweedale
32. Quoted in Brundage, A., *The English Poor Laws 1700-1930*, (2002), p97.
33. Anstie, F.E., 'Workhouse infirmary reform', *Macmillan Magazine xiii*, 1865-6, p480 quoted in Crowther, M.A., *op. cit.*, p167
34. *Ibid.*, p175
35. *Ibid.*, p176
36. U/Da 785, 16 August 1899
37. Twining, L., *Workhouses and Pauperism*, p202 quoted in Crowther M.A., *op. cit.*, p177.
38. *Ibid.*, p180
39. *Ibid.*, p177
40. Digby, A., *op. cit.*, p172
41. Crowther, M.A., *op. cit.*, p180
42. *Ibid.*, p178
43. U/Da 785, 11 June 1901
44. Crowther, M.A., *op. cit.*, p178
45. Davies, P.P., *History of Medicine in Great Yarmouth Hospitals and Doctors*, (2003), p506
46. Quoted in Crowther M.A., *op. cit.*, p179
47. Quoted in *Ibid.*, p181

Chapter 14: The Porter

1. Longmate, N., *The Workhouse*, (2003), p105
2. Crowther, M.A., *The Workhouse System 1834-1929*, (1981), p132
3. *Ibid.*, p127
4. Art. 214 No. 2, Consolidated General Order 1847
5. G/DU 3/1/6, 22 February 1882
6. *Dudley Herald*, 5 November 1881
7. *Ibid.*
8. G/DU 1/15, 2 September & 16 September 1881
9. Art. 214, No. 5, Consolidated General Order, 1847
10. Art. 214, No. 4 and 6, Consolidated General Order, 1847
11. Art. 214, No. 7, Consolidated General Order, 1847
12. Art. 214, No. 9, Consolidated General Order, 1847
13. Hardy, S., *The House on the Hill: The Samford House of Industry 1764-1930*, (2001), p201
14. CBG Aberystwyth ACC 1099 – 78
15. Moore, I.S., *Oldchurch: The Workhouse Story*, (1999), p78
16. Crowther, M.A., *op. cit.*, p127
17. G/DU 3/1/11, 17 October 1890
18. G/DU 1/4, 1 April 1859
19. G/DU 3/1/21, 17 March 1897
20. G/DU 3/1/26, 30 December 1899
21. G/DU 1/7, 12 February 1864
22. G/DU 1/3, 17 February 1854
23. G/DU 1/1, 27 July 1846
24. With thanks to Mari Ambrose for information about her ancestor Alfred Lyons
25. G/DU 4/4/1, 1896-1902

26. G/DU 2/10/2, 11 October 1904
27. G/DU 2/10/2, 4 April 1905
28. G/DU 1/32, 23 June 1905
29. Reid, A., *The Union Workhouse: A Study Guide for Teachers and Local Historians*, (1994), p59
30. *Ibid.*
31. Hailsham Union Workhouse Minute Book G51a/5 page 132
32. National Archives Kew: MH12/12938
33. Hailsham Union Workhouse Minute Book G5/1a/7 page 203L
34. Hailsham Union Workhouse Letter Book G5/8/1 page 14. With thanks to Bruce Isted for information about his ancestor William Isted
35. Land, N., *Victorian Workhouse: A Study of the Bromsgrove Union Workhouse 1836-1901*, (1990), p25
36. G/DU 1/5, 18 October 1861
37. Sheila Hardy, *op. cit.*, p202
38. With thanks to Sandy Norman for information about his ancestor Henry Boyd
39. U/Da 785, 5 March 1894

Chapter 15: The Chaplain

1. Crompton, F., *Workhouse Children*, (1997), p109.
2. Crowther, M.A., *The Workhouse System 1834-1929*, (1981), p128.
3. *Ibid.*, p129.
4. *Ibid.*
5. Digby, A., *Pauper Palaces*, (1978), p27.
6. Crowther, M.A., *op. cit.*, p129.
7. *Ibid.*, p128.
8. Englander, D., *Poverty and Poor Law Reform in 19th Century Britain, 1834-1914*, (1998), p36.
9. Longmate, N., *The Workhouse*, (2003), p100.
10. *Ibid.*
11. Art. 211, Nos 1 and 2, Consolidated General Order, 1847.
12. G/DU 2/10/1, 14 May 1867.
13. Art. 211, No. 3, Consolidated General Order, 1847.
14. Crowther, M.A., *op. cit.*, p128.
15. *Ibid.*, p127.
16. G/DU 1/1/ 4, 11 March 1859.
17. Crowther, M.A., *op. cit.*, p128.
18. Longmate, N., *op. cit.*, p101.
19. Crowther, M.A., *op. cit.*, p128.
20. G/DU 1/8, 29 May 1868.
21. G/DU 1/8, 12 June 1868.
22. GDU 1/12, 26 November 1875.
23. Reid, A., *The Union Workhouse: A Study Guide for Teachers and Local Historians*, (1994), p61
24. Digby, A., *op. cit.* p184
25. Davies, P.P., *History of Medicine in Great Yarmouth Hospitals and Doctors*, (2003), p484.
26. *Ibid.*
27. Longmate, N., *op. cit.*, p101.
28. *Ibid.*
29. Davies, P.P., *op. cit.*, p476.
30. Longmate, N., *op. cit.*, p156.
31. G/DU 1/9, 18 March 1870.
32. G/DU 1/10, 24 May 1872.
33. G/DU 1/10, 26 July 1872.
34. G/DU 3/1/23, 18 Jan 1876.
35. Art. 211, No. 3, Consolidated General Order, 1847.

Chapter 16: The Guardians

1. Higginbotham, P., Guardians <http://www.workhouses.org.uk/administration/> Oxford University web, Oxford, 2000
2. Longmate, N., *The Workhouse*, (2003), p69
3. *Clarke's Curiosities of Dudley & the Black Country*
4. Powell, J., *The Hayfield Union Workhouse: A History*, (1999), p17
5. Digby, A., *Pauper Palaces*, (1978), p109
6. Higginbotham P., Guardians <http://www.workhouses.org.uk/guardians/ > Oxford University web, Oxford, 2000
7. Crowther, M.A., *The Workhouse System 1834-1929*, (1981), p75.
8. Longmate, N., *op. cit.*, p65
9. Digby, A., *op. cit.*, p78
10. *Ibid.*
11. *Ibid.*
12. Crowther, M.A., *op. cit.*, p75
13. Englander, D., *Poverty and Poor Law Reform in 19th Century Britain, 1834-1914*, (1998), p15
14. G/DU 1/ 2, 22 December 1845
15. G/DU 1 /2, 13 April 1846
16. G/DU 1/ 2, 11 May 1846
17. Quoted in Digby, A., *op. cit.*, pp137-138
18. *Ibid.*, p80
19. Quoted in Digby, *The Poor Law in Nineteenth-Century England*, (1985) p30
20. Longmate, N., *op. cit.*, p268
21. *Ibid.*, p269
22. Simkin, J. (ed.), *Voices from the Past*, (1986), p4
23. Longmate, N., *op. cit.*, p269
24. *Ibid.*, p267
25. Pankhurst, E., *My Own Story*, (1914)

Chapter 17: The Clerk

1. Longmate, N., *The Workhouse*, (2003), p98
2. Crowther, M.A., *The Workhouse System 1834-1929*, (1981), p142
3. Watson, I., *The Westbourne Union Life In and Out of the New Workhouse*, (1991), p7
4. With thanks to Derek Jenkins, Barbara Towle, Richard Robinson and Joy Bedson for information about their ancestors Matthew Heath Moss and Matthew Hale Moss
5. Longmate, N., *op. cit.*, p98
6. Art. 184, Consolidated General Order, 1847
7. Art. 202. No. 2
8. Art. 202, No. 3
9. Art. 202, Nos 4 and 11
10. Art. 202, Nos 6, 7, 8 and 9
11. The Justice of the Peace, 31 March 1866
12. Art. 202, Nos. 10 and 12
13. Lofthouse, F.H., *Keepers of the House: A Workhouse Saga*, (2001), p281
14. G/DU 1/1, 15 October 1836
15. G/DU 1/7, 21 July 1865
16. G/DU 4/4/1
17. G/DU 1/31, 22 August 1902
18. With thanks to Jill Barrett for information about her ancestors, the Barretts. Research by Angela Tuddenham
19. Hailsham Union Workhouse Minute Book G5/1a/1 page 29L

20. Hailsham Union Workhouse Minute Book G5/1a/2 page 14L
21. Hailsham Union Workhouse Minute Book G5/1a/8 page 20L
22. National Archives Kew: MH12/12938 #150535
23. Hailsham Union Workhouse Minute Book G5/1a/8 page 98R. With thanks to Bruce Isted for information about his 3x great-grandfather Henry Isted
24. Crowther, M.A., *op. cit.*, p136
25. Land, N., *Victorian Workhouse: A Study of the Bromsgrove Union Workhouse 1836-1901*, (1990), p46

Chapter 18: The Relieving Officer

1. Art. 164, Consolidated General Order, 1847
2. Testimonials of Robert May, 1879, Dudley Archives
3. Art. 215, No. 2, Consolidated General Order, 1847
4. Art. 215, Nos 3, 4 and 5, Consolidated General Order, 1847
5. Art. 215 No. 6, Consolidated General Order, 1847
6. Art. 215, Nos 10 and 11, Consolidated General Order, 1847
7. Art. 215, No. 12, Consolidated General Order, 1847
8. Arts. 60, 61 and 62, Consolidated General Order, 1847
9. Longmate, N., *The Workhouse*, (2003), p99
10. G/DU 1/3, 11 February 1853
11. G/DU 3/1/22, 6 July 1863
12. Longmate, N., *op. cit.*, p99
13. Davies, P.P., *History of Medicine in Great Yarmouth Hospitals and Doctors*, (2003), p471
14. *Ibid.*
15. *Ibid.*
16. *Ibid.*
17. G/DU 1/13, 2 September 1878
18. Crowther, M.A., *The Workhouse System 1834-1929*, (1981), p222
19. *Ibid.*
20. GDU 4/4/1
21. G/DU 1/27, 5 November 1897

BIBLIOGRAPHY

Primary Sources

Aston Union Punishment Book
Cardigan Union Ladies' Visiting Committee Book
Chester-le-Street Union Children in Certified Schools & Institutions File (U/CS 224)
Darlington Union Workhouse records (U/Da series)
Dudley Union Workhouse records (G/DU series)
King's Norton Union Admission and Discharges of Casual Paupers
Lampeter Union Workhouse records (CBG Lampeter series)
Sedgefield Union Workhouse records (U/Se series)
Sheffield Union Special Report of the Classification Committee, 1902

Contemporary Printed Sources

Charles Dickens, 'A Walk in a Workhouse', *Household Words*, 1850
Charles Dickens, 'London Pauper Children', *Household Words*, 1850
Charles Dickens, 'A Day in a Pauper Palace', *Household Words*, 1850
Clarke's Curiosities of Dudley & the Black Country
Frederick Wm. Hackwood, *A History of West Bromwich*, Brewin Books, 1895, reprinted 2001
H. Rider-Haggard, *A Farmer's Year*, Ebury Press, 1899, reprinted 1987
Revd Frederick Hastings, 'Workhouse Worries', *The Quiver*, July 1889
Jack's Reference Book for Home and Office, T.C. & E.C. Jack Ltd, 1923
Emmeline Pankhurst, *My Own Story*, Greenwood Press, 1914, reprinted 1985
Sir Henry Morton Stanley, *The Autobiography of Sir Henry Morton Stanley: The Making of a 19th Century Explorer*, Narrative Press, 2001
Louisa Twining, *Recollections of Life and Work*, 1893
Justice of the Peace, 31 March 1866
Dudley Herald, 1882
Sheffield & Rotherham Independent, 28 February 1878

Secondary Sources

Best, G., *Mid-Victorian Britain 1851-75*, Fontana Press, 1985
Brundage, A., *The English Poor Laws 1700-1930*, Palgrave, 2002
Castle, E. & Wishart, B., *Foleshill Union Workhouse Punishment Book 1864-1900*, Coventry Family History Society, 1999
Cole, J., *Down Poorhouse Lane: The Diary of a Rochdale Workhouse*, George Kelsall Publishing, 1994
Crompton, F., *Workhouse Children*, Sutton Publishing, 1997

Crowther, M.A., *The Workhouse System 1834-1929*, The University of Georgia Press, 1981

Davies, P.P., *History of Medicine in Great Yarmouth Hospitals and Doctors*, Paul P. Davies, 2003

Digby, A., *The Poor Law in Nineteenth-Century England*, The Historical Association, 1982

Digby, A., *Pauper Palaces*, Routledge and Kegan Paul, 1978

Englander, D., *Poverty and Poor Law Reform in 19th Century Britain, 1834-1914*, Longman, 1998

Fillmore, J., 'The female vagrant pauper', *The Local Historian*, Vol. 35, No. 3, August 2005, pp148-158

Flett, J., *The Story of the Workhouse and the Hospital at Nether Edge*, ALD Design & Print, 1985

Flinn, M.W., 'Medical Services under the New Poor Law' in Derek Fraser (ed.), *The New Poor Law in the Nineteenth Century*, Macmillan, 1976

Forrest, D., *Warrington's Poor and the Workhouse 1725-1851*, David Forrest, 2001

Fraser, D. (ed.), *The New Poor Law in the Nineteenth Century*, Macmillan, 1976

Hatcher, D., *The Workhouse & The Weald*, Meresborough Books, 1988

Hardy, S., *The House on the Hill: The Samford House of Industry 1764-1930*, Sheila Hardy, 2001

Harrison, J.F.C., *Late Victorian Britain 1875-1901*, Fontana Press, 1990

Higginbotham, P., <http://www.workhouses.org.uk>, 2000

Hollis, P., *Women in Public 1850-1900: Documents of the Victorian Women's Movement*, George Allen & Unwin (Publishers) Ltd, 1979

Horn, P., *Labouring Life in the Victorian Countryside*, Alan Sutton Publishing, 1987

Howsam, L., (ed.), *Memories of the Workhouse & Old Hospital At Fir Vale*, ALD Design & Print, 2002

Keating, P. (ed.), *Into Unknown England 1866-1913: Selections from the Social Explorers*, Fontana, 1976

Kohli, M., *The Golden Bridge: Young Immigrants to Canada 1833-1939*, Natural Heritage, 2003

Land, N., *Victorian Workhouse: A Study of the Bromsgrove Union Workhouse 1836-1901*, Brewin Books, 1990

Lewis, W.J., *A History of Lampeter*, Ceredigion County Council, 1997

Lofthouse, F.H., *Keepers of the House: A Workhouse Saga*, Hudson History, 2001

Longmate, N., *The Workhouse*, Pimlico, 2003

May, T., *The Victorian Workhouse*, Shire Publications, 1997

Mitton, L., *The Victorian Hospital*, Shire Publications, 2001

Moore, I.S., *Oldchurch: The Workhouse Story*, Workhorse Productions, 1999

Murray, P., *Poverty and Welfare 1830-1914*, Hodder and Stoughton, 1999

Newman, S., *The Christchurch and Bournemouth Union Workhouse*, Sue Newman, 2000

Noyes, A., *Sheer Poverty: From Parish Workhouse to Union Workhouse*, Twiga Books, 1996

Piggott, R., 'Workhouse Connections', *Midland Ancestor*, June 2002, pp140-142

Powell, J., *The Hayfield Union Workhouse: A History*, New Mills Local History Society, 1999

Reid, A., *The Union Workhouse: A Study Guide for Teachers and Local Historians*, Phillimore, 1994

Roberts, D., 'How Cruel was the Victorian Poor Law?', *Historical Journal VI*, 1963, pp97-107

Rose, M.E., 'The Crisis of Poor Relief in England, 1860-1890' in Wolfgang. J. Mommsen (ed.), *The Emergence of the Welfare State in Britain and Germany*, Croom Helm, 1981

Rose, M., *The Relief of Poverty 1834-1914*, Palgrave Macmillan, 1986

Royston-Pike, E., *Human Documents of the Age of the Forsytes*, George Allen and Unwin, 1969

Royston-Pike, E., *Human Documents of the Victorian Golden Age*, George Allen and Unwin, 1967

Simkin, J. (ed.), *Voices from the Past: The Workhouse*, Spartacus Educational, 1986

Smith, S., *The Workhouse Southwell*, National Trust, 2002

Stevens, J., *Faversham Union Workhouse: The Early Years 1838-1850*, The Faversham Society, 2002.

Thompson, F., *Lark Rise to Candleford*, 1945.

Tuddenham, A., *Dear Mother: The Story of a Letter*, Angela Tuddenham and the Slough Museum, 1995.

Watson, I., *The Westbourne Union Life In and Out of the New Workhouse*, Westbourne Local History Group, 1991

Wildman, R., 'Workhouse Architecture' in Longmate, N., *The Workhouse*, Pimlico, 2003

INDEX

If you are interested in purchasing other books published by The History Press,
or in case you have difficulty finding any of our books in your local bookshop,
you can also place orders directly through our website

www.thehistorypress.co.uk